Beckett, Literature, and the Ethics of Alterity

Shane Weller

School of European Culture and Languages
University of Kent, Canterbury

palgrave
macmillan

© Shane Weller 2006

All rights reserved. No reproduction, copy or transmission of this publication may be made without written permission.

No paragraph of this publication may be reproduced, copied or transmitted save with written permission or in accordance with the provisions of the Copyright, Designs and Patents Act 1988, or under the terms of any licence permitting limited copying issued by the Copyright Licensing Agency, 90 Tottenham Court Road, London W1T 4LP.

Any person who does any unauthorized act in relation to this publication may be liable to criminal prosecution and civil claims for damages.

The author has asserted his right to be identified as the author of this work in accordance with the Copyright, Designs and Patents Act 1988.

First published in 2006 by
PALGRAVE MACMILLAN
Houndmills, Basingstoke, Hampshire RG21 6XS and
175 Fifth Avenue, New York, N.Y. 10010
Companies and representatives throughout the world.

PALGRAVE MACMILLAN is the global academic imprint of the Palgrave Macmillan division of St. Martin's Press, LLC and of Palgrave Macmillan Ltd. Macmillan® is a registered trademark in the United States, United Kingdom and other countries. Palgrave is a registered trademark in the European Union and other countries.

ISBN-13: 978–1–4039–9581–0 hardback
ISBN-10: 1–4039–9581–8 hardback

This book is printed on paper suitable for recycling and made from fully managed and sustained forest sources.

A catalogue record for this book is available from the British Library.

Library of Congress Cataloging-in-Publication Data

Weller, Shane.
    Beckett, literature, and the ethics of alterity / Shane Weller.
      p. cm.
    Includes bibliographical references and index.
    ISBN 1–4039–9581–8
     1. Beckett, Samuel, 1906—Criticism and interpretation. 2. Other (Philosophy) in literature. 3. Criticism–20th century. I. Title.
PQ2603.E378Z96 2006
848'.91409—dc22   2005056412

10 9 8 7 6 5 4 3 2 1
15 14 13 12 11 10 09 08 07 06

Printed and bound in Great Britain by
Antony Rowe Ltd, Chippenham and Eastbourne

Beckett, Literature, and the Ethics of Alterity

Other related titles

PALGRAVE ADVANCES IN SAMUEL BECKETT STUDIES – ed. Lois Oppenheim (2004)

BECKETT AND PHILOSOPHY – ed. Richard Lane (2002)

BECKETT'S EIGHTEENTH CENTURY – Frederik N. Smith (2001)

BECKETT AND EROS – Paul Davies (2000)

For L.

Contents

Preface   viii

Introduction: Literature and Alterity   1

Part I   In Other Words: On the Ethics of Translation

1   Translation and Difference: Dispatching Benjamin   33

2   Translation and Negation: Beckett and the Bilingual Œuvre   57

Part II   The Laugh of the Other: On the Ethics of Comedy

3   Pratfalls into Alterity: Laughter from Baudelaire to Freud and Beyond   83

4   Last Laughs: Beckett and the *'risus purus'*   111

Part III   The Difference a Woman Makes: On the Ethics of Gender

5   Feminine Alterities: From Psychoanalysis to Gender Studies   137

6   'As If the Sex Mattered': Beckett's Degenderations   164

Conclusion: Beckett and the Anethical   192

Notes   196

Bibliography   203

Index   212

Preface

A long and highly influential critical tradition, grounded in the notion that a certain kind of literary practice constitutes a genuine resistance to nihilism, finds one of its major points of origin in the work of Theodor Adorno, for whom Beckett's *œuvre* possesses exemplary value. As I sought to demonstrate in *A Taste for the Negative: Beckett and Nihilism*, since Adorno's championing of Beckett in the early 1960s the latter's works have repeatedly been deployed to the same end by some of the most important philosophers and literary theorists of the postwar era, including Blanchot, Derrida, Deleuze, Cixous, Cavell, and, most recently, Alain Badiou, who, ironically, sees himself as countering the latter-day sophists (including Blanchot and Derrida) with whom he none the less joins ranks in his conception of Beckett's resistance to nihilism. If, in each case, the nihilism against which Beckett's works are taken to stand is defined differently, there remains the shared sense that not only literature but also thought itself is to be conceived and evaluated in terms of a struggle against that which, since Nietzsche, has gone by the name of 'nihilism'.

In this book, my principal aim has been to explore the works of Beckett and others in a manner that is less polarized by the nihilist/anti-nihilist model, but that does not assume either the possibility of an analysis of literature that would be clearly distinguishable from the ethical, or the possibility of a literary practice that would have, as Blanchot argues in his 1963 preface to *Lautréamont and Sade* (1949), a power of affirmation wholly liberated from the notion of value.[1] That towards which I have sought to direct the reader's attention here, in my analyses of the ethics of translation, comedy, and gender in Beckett and others, is what I have termed the *anethical*. This is to be distinguished from, although not necessarily to be thought as either prior or posterior to, the 'ethics of alterity' or 'ethics of difference' that has come to dominate what is generally termed 'postmodern' thought, but which, for reasons that should become clearer in the course of this study, might more accurately be described as post-Holocaust thought. If I have chosen to explore the anethical here in relation to the three, interrelated topics of translation, comedy, and gender, this is not because I consider these topics to exhaust either the field of the anethical or indeed Beckett's own treatment of alterity. Far from it. Indeed, among the many other topics that might be explored in a broadly similar manner, one of the more obvious would be unreason or madness – or what Beckett in his last work, 'What is the Word' (his own translation of the poem 'Comment dire'), terms 'folly' (*folie*).

If, at times, the analyses undertaken in this book appear to exhibit an aggressivity at odds with the life or the spirit of both literature and literary criticism, this should not be taken as a sign that the various works to which I am responding here are, in my eyes, either insignificant or simply misguided contributions to their various fields. Indeed, with regard to works of Beckett criticism in particular, I have for the most part restricted my reflections to readings that have shaped the contemporary understanding of Beckett. That said, my attempt to take issue with a prevailing sense of the ethical – and, in particular, the ethicality of a certain kind of literary practice – has made it difficult to avoid what will on occasion no doubt appear to be acts of critical violence. Were I to attempt to justify this violence, then this justification would open with the counter-claim that no reading, no interpretation, no response to any work, literary or otherwise, is ever free from such violence. If I do not seek to justify the critical violence in this work in terms of a given reading's factual or interpretative value, then this has everything to do with the experience of the anethical that I have sought to adumbrate in the pages that follow.

Justifiable or not, this violence is of course, among other things, a sign of my own debts, the most easily identifiable of which are recorded in the bibliography, which includes all those works from which I have quoted. For permission to include Walter Benjamin's German translation of Baudelaire's 'Les Aveugles', I express my gratitude to Suhrkamp Verlag, Frankfurt am Main. Chapters 1 and 4 originally appeared in slightly different forms in *Angelaki* and the *Journal of Beckett Studies* respectively, and I wish to thank the editors of those journals for permission to reproduce the material here. Lastly, I would like to express my gratitude to Matthew Feldman for his generosity in making his own research on Beckett available to me prior to its publication in book form.

Introduction
Literature and Alterity

Alterity in the Holocaust's wake: Adorno

For all their diversity, the various strains of postmodern thought, and in particular postmodern theories of literature, share a concern for difference that is never simply analytic or descriptive. And, in their affirmation beyond the limits of any thematization of forms of alterity so radical that they resist dialectical mastery and indeed all thinking governed by a principle of identity, they arguably mark their adherence to a particular historical moment. That this is the case is suggested by one of the most forceful advocates of modernism, Theodor Adorno, who in *Negative Dialectics* (1966) argues not simply that Western philosophy has hitherto predominantly taken the form of identity-thinking, but that the philosopheme underlying this procedure finds its confirmation (*Bestätigung*) only in Auschwitz, that synecdoche for the Holocaust which challenges the universalizing ambitions of philosophical discourse: 'Auschwitz confirmed [*bestätigt*] the philosopheme of pure identity as death' (Adorno 1973, 362). If one accepts Adorno's contention, then however radically one might tamper with the commonsense notion of history as a more or less coherent diachronic sequence, and even if one defines the postmodern, as Lyotard does, as that which both precedes and makes possible the modern,[1] the postmodern remains a strictly post-Holocaust phenomenon, since only in the Holocaust's wake does it become possible to confirm the thesis that identity-thinking constitutes the greatest threat to human – and not just human – life and its value.

That nihilism which Nietzsche so momentously declares to be the 'uncanniest of all guests' (*unheimlichste aller Gäste*) in a fragment from 1887 later included in *The Will to Power* (1901), and which he is the first to identify as the essence of philosophy at least since Plato, would confirm itself at Auschwitz to be not merely (as Nietzsche claims) a devaluation of the highest values, nor even (as Heidegger claims) the forgetting of Being (*Seinsvergessenheit*), the thinking of Being (*Sein*) as a being (*Seiendes*), but the radical nihilation (*Nihilisierung*) of the other, the attempted reduction to nothing of an alterity that in Europe in the first half of the twentieth century is figured (for reasons that go beyond the purely philosophical) predominantly, although not exclusively, as 'the Jew'. The Holocaust, then, becomes both the confirmation and the consummation of European nihilism, its *telos* if not necessarily its end, as recent history so obviously testifies. And if one accepts the deliberately crooked logic of Derrida's deconstruction of what he terms 'Western metaphysics', nihilism is the attempted reduction to nothing of an alterity that is both the condition of possibility and the condition of impossibility of identity. Remaining within the aporetic logic of Derrida's thought, one could press still further, and argue that nihilism may be defined as the nihilation of an alterity that can be shown to be irreducible, not just beyond all possible negation but beyond the very dialectical opposition of affirmation and negation, beyond the power of what in *Glas* (1974) Derrida terms the 'all-burning' (*brûle-tout*) (Derrida 1986, 238).

Given this perceived relation between the nihilistic appropriation of alterity within metaphysical thought and the historical reality of genocide, it is scarcely surprising that most attempts to think the post-metaphysical or the postmodern, and in particular most attempts to think the possibility of a post-metaphysical or postmodern ethics, have been orientated by an (albeit highly paradoxical) effort to identify an irreducible alterity, or (less often) alterities, not only within the discourse of philosophy itself but also in, or as, art or literature. In a paradox the significance of which is still far from easy to calculate, that privileging of the aesthetic so characteristic of the modern also characterizes the discourses of the postmodern, with the aesthetic now becoming that realm in which it remains possible to encounter what Thomas Docherty terms 'substantial *alterity*' (Docherty 1996, vii). So it is that in the postmodern the aesthetic, for all its reinscription, remains no less tied to the ethical than it does in Kant's *Critique of Judgement* (1790), in which the gulf between the realms of necessity and freedom is to be negotiated by the aesthetic.

Put bluntly, the history of post-Holocaust thought is the history of the attempt to think a saving alterity. Anticipating in important respects Derrida's conception of *différance*, Adorno thinks this saving alterity not as anything substantial but rather as a slightest difference (*kleinste*

Differenz) within the negative, a difference that Adorno finds disclosed above all in the works of Samuel Beckett, who, for Adorno as for many more recent commentators, is never simply one example among others. Adorno identifies this difference as a no man's land (*Niemandsland*) situated 'between the border posts of being and nothingness', an interval that is not to be confused with Heidegger's ontological difference, since it is a difference within the same, a difference between nothingness (*das Nichts*) and having come to rest (*zur Ruhe Gelangten*) (Adorno 1973, 381). For Adorno, this scarcely discernible difference is the post-Holocaust world's sole haven of hope (*Zuflucht der Hoffnung*), anticipating in a negative form an as yet unrealized, and perhaps even historically unrealizable, reconciliation (*Versöhnung*), an overcoming of antagonisms that is neither integrative nor totalizing, is not governed by a principle of identity, does not negate alterity, but saves difference in its multiplicity rather than in its conflictual binarity. The reconciliation of which he dreams 'would release the nonidentical, would rid it of coercion, including spiritualized coercion; it would open the road to the multiplicity of different things and strip dialectics of its power over them. Reconcilement [*Versöhnung*] would be the thought of the many as no longer inimical [*feindseligen*], a thought that is anathema to subjective reason' (Adorno 1973, 6). Adorno, then, remains important beyond any debate as to the relative values of various kinds of aesthetic practice because he is among the first in the post-Holocaust age to think the possibility – or at least the reasons, not simply historical, political, or economic, for the present impossibility – of a non-integrative reconciliation, a multiplicity in which alterity survives within a non-violent economy. And crucially, for Adorno as for so many others after him, it is art – and above all the works of Samuel Beckett, strange as this might seem – that can grant the post-Holocaust world the negative image, the only possible image, of this utopian reconciliation in what Adorno characterizes as the nihilistically positivistic present.

From one to the absolutely other: Levinas

If Adorno's influence on the various strains of post-Holocaust thought has been considerable, despite his championing of the modernist over both the realist and the postmodernist in the arts, it is Emmanuel Levinas who has proven to be arguably the most influential thinker of alterity, and indeed of the relation between literature and ethics, in post-Holocaust Europe. Levinas's attempt to conceive an alterity beyond the principle of identity received what he later termed its 'birth and first formulation' in *Time and the Other* (1948), originally delivered as a series of lectures at the Collège Philosophique in Paris in 1946–47, and developing the analysis of time and alterity in the final chapter of *Existence and Existents* (1947). This first formulation of an ethical philosophy of the Other receives its two most significant reformulations in *Totality and Infinity* (1961) and *Otherwise Than Being or Beyond Essence* (1974). If Levinas shares with Adorno a concern for both difference and reconciliation, his distance from Adorno lies most obviously in his characterization of the absolute alterity of the Other (*autrui*) in terms of inequality, transcendence, infinity, and responsibility.[2] The 'main thesis' of *Time and the Other* consists 'in thinking time not as a degradation of eternity, but as the relationship to *that* which – of itself unassimilable, absolutely other [*absolument autre*] – would not allow itself to be assimilated by experience; or to that which – of itself infinite – would not allow itself to be com-prehended [*com-prendre*]' (Levinas 1987, 32–3). Only if the other is thought as *absolutely other* can an ethics as first philosophy counter the history of philosophy as that project to achieve a totality or 'universal synthesis' which reaches its culmination in Hegel (Levinas 1985, 75), the absolute mastery of thought as knowledge or Reason (*Vernunft*), the political equivalent of which would be totalitarianism.

Although the term 'nihilism' does not appear in *Time and the Other*, and although he tries assiduously to keep his distance from Nietzsche's critique of metaphysics, it is clear that for Levinas the history of philosophy (as the history of the attempt to accomplish the reduction to nothing of alterity) is in fact the history of nihilism defined as unethical thought. The accomplishing of a universal synthesis at Auschwitz is, then, not just the confirmation but also the consummation of nihilism. Whereas for Heidegger, from whose fundamental ontology Levinas strives to distance his own philosophy as ethics, nihilism consists in the reduction to nothing of Being (*Seinsvergessenheit*), for Levinas nihilism consists in the reduction to nothing of the absolutely other. No less than Heidegger's fundamental ontology, then, Levinas's ethics as first philosophy is the attempt to resist that nihilism which he locates at the very heart of metaphysics.

According to Levinas, there have been scarcely any protestations against this nihilism, the work of Franz Rosenzweig being one of the very few. Here, it might seem justifiable to object that the existentialism originating in Kierkegaard and Nietzsche and passing (arguably, in a series of misreadings) by way of Heidegger to Sartre, is patently nothing other than the philosophical attempt to think in a manner that is non-systematic, non-totalizing, and thus non-totalitarian; in short, an attempt to resist Hegel. For Levinas, however, existentialism remains the other face of the Hegelian project, since it locks us within a kind of microcosmic totality: the individual in its essential solitude. For this reason, the alterity that Levinas thematizes in *Time and the Other* is the key to a philosophy that is at odds not only with metaphysics from Parmenides to Hegel, but also with Heidegger's ontology and the Sartrean existentialism that derives from it. That Sartrean existentialism might be grounded in a very basic misunderstanding of Heidegger, as Heidegger himself argues in his *Letter on Humanism* (1947), would be of no real significance here, since Levinas sets out to define his first philosophy in contradistinction to both Hegel and Heidegger, both of whom remain tied, as he sees it, to the principle of identity, the Parmenidean thought of the One, and both of whom fail to think the other in its absolute alterity. Furthermore, Levinas's insistence that first philosophy is an ethics is an unambiguous rejection of Heidegger's declaration in the *Letter on Humanism* that fundamental ontology precedes ethics.[3] That said, Levinas remains perilously close to Heidegger in some of his key formulations, and never more so than in his thought of the 'there is' (*il y a*), which both translates and marks a departure from Heidegger's thinking of Being as *es gibt*.

In both *Existence and Existents* and *Time and the Other*, Levinas argues that in *Being and Time* (1927) Heidegger's conception of Dasein's being towards death, and of death as 'the possibility of the absolute impossibility of Dasein' (Heidegger 1962, 294), fails to take account of death's radical impossibility, which is to say the impossibility of nothingness (*néant*). In short, Heidegger fails to think existence without existents, and may therefore be accused (although Levinas himself does not make this accusation) of having collapsed the very ontological difference between Being and beings that *Being and Time* is supposed to reopen. Once one thinks the possibility of existence without existents, it becomes clear that beyond any possible negation there will always remain an irreducible 'there is' (*il y a*), even if nothingness is precisely all that *there is*. As death's impossibility, this *il y a* is the 'fatality of irremissible being' (Levinas 2001, 57). It differs from Heidegger's thinking of Being (*Sein*) in that it is the scene of being (*la scène de l'être*) rather than an event of being (*un événement d'être*) (Levinas 1985, 48–9). Essentially impersonal or anonymous, the *il y a* can be described only in a language of paradox in keeping with its 'fundamental absurdity' (Levinas 1987, 51): 'The absence of everything returns as a presence, as the place where the bottom has dropped out of everything, an atmospheric density, a plenitude of the void, or the murmur of silence' (Levinas 1987, 46).

It is precisely the irremissibility of the *il y a* that distinguishes it from the Other as absolutely other, since one can always kill the Other: 'the ethical exigency is not an ontological necessity' (Levinas 1985, 87). That said, although the *il y a* is irremissible, it can be escaped. Indeed, Levinas's entire philosophy will be the attempt to think this departure from the absurd horror of the *il y a* by way of an ethical relation with the Other, a taking responsibility for the Other, and ultimately a taking responsibility for the death of the Other. It is precisely this escape from the *il y a* by taking responsibility for the death of the Other that makes the fundamental philosophical question not the ontological question posed by Leibniz, 'Why are there beings at all instead of nothing?', with which Heidegger opens his *Introduction to Metaphysics* (1953), but rather the ethical question: 'Do I not kill by being?' (Levinas 1985, 120). Although Levinas himself does not remark upon this fact, the thought of being as killing – or, more precisely, of both being and non-being as dependent upon the killing of the other – is, as we shall see, one that lies at the heart of Beckett's *œuvre*, as does the sense that suicide, as what Levinas terms 'the final mastery one can have over being' (Levinas 1987, 50), is in fact not an effective means of escape from that fatality of irremissible being which both Levinas and Beckett figure as the voice – more precisely, the murmur – of silence.

To enter into relation with the Other is, then, not just to escape from that solitude of being which is a founding tenet of existentialism and has such an important role to play in Beckett's *œuvre*, but more essentially to escape from an *il y a* that is neither an event of being nor nothing. It is to escape from the absurd fatality of irremissible being into the ethical, from an ontological questioning of the *il y a* into an ethical questioning of being in relation to the absolutely other. That this notion of a leap into the ethical generates formidable complications is apparent as soon as it is borne in mind that escape is itself a form of negation. If the *il y a* can be escaped or left behind, then it is not simply irreducible or irremissible. Furthermore, given that the relation to the *il y a* is not an ethical relation, is not strictly speaking an exigency, and is not a relation of knowledge, or ecstasis, or even (as the relation with the Other will be) an erotic or a paternal relation, but rather a relation of horror, one might argue that the *il y a* itself is in Levinas an unthought other that is in fact far more radically alterior than the Other (as *autrui*) with which one enters into ethical relation. Put slightly differently, the *il y a* might be said to be that other from which Levinas's own ethics of alterity will be in constant flight.

Before looking more closely at the place and status of the *il y a* in Levinas's reflections upon the relation between literature and alterity, it is worth sticking for a little longer with Levinas's argumentation concerning the escape from the *il y a* by way of the ethical relation with the Other. As we have seen, paradoxically it is the very experience (as horror) of the impossibility of nothingness, and thus of the irreducibility of the *il y a*, that is the first step in the escape from the *il y a*, the muffling of its murmurous silence. Were it not for that initial sense of the *il y a*, there would be no possibility of transcendence, since it is the very impossibility of nothingness that makes of death itself the first form of absolute alterity: 'Death is the impossibility of having a project. This approach to death indicates that we are in relation with something that is absolutely other [*absolument autre*]' (Levinas 1987, 74). This relation with the absolutely other in the form of death becomes a first step in the escape from the *il y a*. As Levinas puts it in *Totality and Infinity*, albeit with the significant, if problematical, reservation of an *as though* and a limitation of death as but one modality among others, it is 'as though the approach of death remained one of the modalities of the relation with the Other' (Levinas 1969, 234).

As for the Other as absolutely other, it is 'something bearing alterity [*l'altérité*] not as a provisional determination we can assimilate through enjoyment, but as something whose very existence is made of alterity' (Levinas 1987, 74). Our relation to this absolute alterity is itself highly paradoxical, and unlike any other; it is what Blanchot will term a 'relation without relation', a relation with that over which we can exercise no cognitive mastery: 'If one could possess, grasp, and know the other [*l'autre*], it would not be the other. Possessing, knowing, and grasping are synonyms of power' (Levinas 1987, 90). Inexhaustibly resistant to comprehension, appropriation, or integration, the alterity that Levinas is attempting to think here is also alien to any mystical ecstasis, since in ecstasis 'the subject is absorbed in the object and recovers itself in its unity' (Levinas 1987, 41). In both cognition and ecstasis, the Other disappears as other, and with it disappears the possibility of an ethical relation. And yet, such is the paradoxicality of our relation with the Other that, while we cannot master it, and while our relation to it is radically asymmetrical and unequal, we are none the less responsible for it.

If the Other as absolutely other can become the object of neither a knowledge nor an ecstasis, is neither an alter ego nor anything with which one can enter into a reciprocal or equal relationship, then what form might it take, beyond that of death? In short, how is this absolute alterity to be figured? It is in responding to this question that Levinas articulates a process with an unambiguous trajectory, leading from the *il y a* in all its horror to God – in other words, from the depths to the heights, from fundamental absurdity to infinite transcendence. Aside from death, the two forms that absolute alterity will take in *Time and the Other* are the feminine and the son (*fils*), with the corresponding ethical relations being the erotic and the paternal. If alterity begins with death, it 'is accomplished [*s'accomplit*] in the feminine' (Levinas 1987, 88). Why in the feminine? As Simone de Beauvoir was among the first to observe, Levinas's argument here appears to be determined by his unanalysed inheritance of an entire tradition's conception of woman as other: 'Hiding is the way of existing of the feminine, and this fact of hiding is precisely modesty' (Levinas 1987, 87).[4] That said, the feminine here is not to be mistaken for an existent; rather, it is an event of alterity (*événement de l'altérité*) (Levinas 1987, 87). And the relation with this event is not visual but tactile: it takes the form of the caress (*caresse*). To caress is not to touch, in that it is a seeking governed by unknowing and directed openly not towards contact but towards that which remains for ever to come (*à venir*), alien to any possible present:

> The seeking [*recherche*] of the caress constitutes its essence by the fact that the caress does not know what it seeks. This 'not knowing' ['*ne pas savoir*'], this fundamental disorder, is the essential. It is like a game with something slipping away [*comme un jeu avec quelque chose qui se dérobe*], a game absolutely without project or plan, not with what can become ours or us, but with something other, always other, always inaccessible, and always still to come [*à venir*].
> (Levinas 1987, 89)

Levinas is at pains here to distinguish his conception of the feminine from Plato's. Not only is the feminine not to be thought as passivity or matter, but the erotic relation to the feminine is non-reciprocal, non-fusional, non-communal, and not even a mode of 'being with' – it is not covered by Heidegger's *Miteinandersein*. In the face-to-face (*face-à-face*) with the Other, there is neither identification nor communication, but rather, and solely, responsibility. In other words, the feminine as absolutely other is never responsible for itself. Responsibility is always responsibility for the feminine.

Just as the relation with the Other constitutes an escape from the *il y a*, so the passage from death to the feminine is a transcending negation, a victory over death (*victoire sur la mort*). In paternity, the relation with the Other reaches a still higher stage. It lies beyond that relation achieved with the feminine because now the ego itself becomes other than itself, becomes its own unmasterable other, which is never the case in the erotic relation, given that the one who caresses is never feminine. The relation with the Other as son in paternity is, then, considerably more paradoxical than the erotic relation, since here alterity is located both inside and outside the ego that is the subject of the ethical relation:

> Paternity is the relationship with a stranger [*étranger*] who, entirely while being Other [*autrui*], is myself, the relationship of the ego [*moi*] with a myself [*moi-même*] who is nonetheless a stranger to me. The son [*fils*], in effect, is not simply my work, like a poem or an artifact, neither is he my property. Neither the categories of power nor those of having can indicate the relationship with the child [*enfant*]. Neither the notion of cause not the notion of ownership permit one to grasp the fact of fecundity. I do not have my child; I am in some way my child. (Levinas 1987, 91)

We shall have cause to revisit the connection that Levinas makes here between alterity and the feminine, and between alterity and filiation, when we come to consider the ethics of gender in Part III of the present study.

To summarize, then: the trajectory towards the ethical relation passes from the *il y a* to death, from death to the feminine, from the feminine to the son, and ultimately from the son to God. Each stage in this trajectory involves a transcending negation the ethicality of which remains in question. And yet, despite this apparent teleology, and despite the possibility that the ethical is being grounded here in the unethical, Levinas, like Adorno, is clearly attempting to think beyond Hegel, beyond the mastering concept (*Begriff*), beyond Reason (*Vernunft*), beyond the principle of identity, beyond totality and universal synthesis, beyond teleology, but without falling for the lure of existentialism, which for both Levinas and Adorno remains another form of identity-thinking. Like Adorno, too, Levinas thinks alterity in the shadow of Auschwitz: 'My critique of the totality has come in fact after a political experience that we have not yet forgotten' (Levinas 1985, 78–9). And, for all their differences, not least that between the alterior negativity of Adorno's negative dialectics – as the 'consistent sense of nonidentity' (Adorno 1973, 5) – and the Other as transcendent absolutely other in Levinas's first philosophy as ethics, Levinas, like Adorno, thinks alterity in relation to literature, even if, unlike Adorno, he does not wish to privilege literature or the aesthetic, but rather to use it as a source of examples. Indeed, Levinas expresses his disappointment at Heidegger's reliance upon *Dichtung*, and in particular upon Hölderlin, in the works of the 1930s and 1940s (Levinas 1985, 42). That said, it is in his reflections on literature, and on Blanchot in particular, that Levinas returns to the question of what might be termed the *other* other haunting his thinking of the ethical, namely the *il y a*.

Literature and the alterity of the neutral: Blanchot

Although he does not explicitly privilege the aesthetic in general or literature in particular, Levinas none the less conceives of the authentic relationship (*relation authentique*) with the Other as discursive. Indeed, in conversation with Philippe Nemo in 1981, he emphasizes the connection between responsibility (the ethical) and response (speech): 'I have just refused the notion of vision to describe the authentic relationship with the Other; it is discourse [*discours*] and, more exactly, response or responsibility which is this authentic relationship' (Levinas 1985, 87–8). Like literature, this discourse is defined not by its content, by its said (*dit*) – it can be about anything at all – but rather by its saying (*dire*): 'the *saying* [dire] is the fact that before the face [of the Other] I do not simply remain there contemplating it, I respond to it. The saying is a way of greeting the Other [*saluer autrui*], but to greet the Other is already to answer for him [*répondre de lui*]. It is difficult to be silent in someone's silence; this difficulty has its ultimate foundation in this signification proper to the saying, whatever is the said' (Levinas 1985, 88).

In *Maurice Blanchot* (1975), Levinas clarifies this distinction between saying and said in the following manner: 'The mode of revelation of what remains *other* [*ce qui demeure* autre], despite its revelation, is not the thought, but the language [*langage*] of the poem' (Levinas 1996, 130). What specific forms might this saying take? That retaining the distinction between saying and said is far from easy, even when one is seeking this revelation of the Other in literature, is evident from the approach Levinas takes in his short essay on 'The Other in Proust', included in *Proper Names* (1976). Here, he identifies the Other in *À la recherche du temps perdu* in a straightforwardly thematic manner, as a said rather than a saying, in the figure of Albertine. Her reality (*réalité*) he describes as a nothingness (*néant*), which in turn 'uncovers her total alterity' (*découvre son altérité totale*) (Levinas 1996, 103). If the Other here takes the form of the feminine – at least in the novel, if not necessarily in the major biographical source for Albertine – it is an irreducible feminine alterity that, as Levinas argues in *Time and the Other*, is characterized by its mystery, its evanescence, its paradoxical presence as that which withdraws from the present: 'Proust's most profound teaching [*enseignement*] – if indeed poetry teaches – consists in situating the real in a relation with what for ever remains other [*ce qui à jamais demeure autre*] – with the other [*autrui*] as absence and mystery' (Levinas 1996, 105). Continuing this decidedly thematic analysis, Levinas argues that the value of Proust's novel lies above all in its revelation of the nature of the ethical relation with this figure of feminine alterity: 'Marcel did not love Albertine, if love is a fusion with the other [*autrui*], the ecstasy of one being [*un être*] before the perfections of the other [*l'autre*], or the peace of possession. [...] The story of Marcel's love is laced with confessions apparently designed to put in question the very consistency of that love. But that non-love is in fact love; that struggle with the ungraspable, possession; that absence of Albertine, her presence' (Levinas 1996, 104).

For an analysis that comes closer to the saying (*dire*) of the Other, one has to turn to Levinas's essay on Paul Celan, in the same collection. Here, relying on Celan's statement in a letter of 18 May 1960 to Hans Bender that he 'cannot see any basic difference between a handshake and a poem' (Celan 1986, 26), Levinas argues that a saying of the Other that does not master or appropriate it through its thematization would take the form of a poem that greets, responds to, and accepts responsibility for the Other in advance. Poetry as a greeting of the Other interrupts the aesthetic, the language of poetry being 'the first of the languages, response preceding the question, responsibility for the neighbor, by its *for the other* [*son* pour l'autre], the whole marvel of giving' (Levinas 1996, 41). This saying is a response that, in *Otherwise than Being*, is thought as a testifying or bearing witness to the Other: 'No theme, no present, has a capacity for the Infinite. The subject in which the other is in the same [*le sujet où l'autre est dans le même*], inasmuch as the same is for the other, bears witness [*témoigne*] to it' (Levinas 1998, 146). Thus Celan's poems – all of them – may be said to testify to the Other, rather than to thematize it in the manner that it is thematized or figured in Proust's Albertine. The ethicality of Celan's poetry does not lie in its being about the Other, and if it cannot help being about the Other, if it cannot help thematizing or figuring the Other, this thematization and this figuration are not in themselves the ethical relation with the Other that Levinas thematizes in his own philosophical works.

If, in his essays on Proust and Celan, Levinas attempts to think literature in terms of the ethical relation to the Other, in his essays on Blanchot he thinks it in terms of the experience of the *il y a*, from the horror of which the ethical relation with the Other is, as we have seen, an escape. In *Ethics and Infinity*, Levinas claims that the *il y a* is 'probably the real subject of [Blanchot's] novels and stories' (Levinas 1985, 50), and, in the small collection of texts on Blanchot published in 1975, he locates the *il y a* in Blanchot's notion of the second or '*other* night' in *The Space of Literature* (1955). This '*other* night' is a highly paradoxical presence of absence, a constant murmuring that belongs neither to being nor to nothingness, a *ressassement éternel* (Blanchot 1982, 163–70). In Blanchot's later works – and, in particular, in the chapter on the narrative voice in *The Infinite Conversation* (1969) – this murmuring becomes the neutral (*le neutre*), of which Levinas observes that it is 'neither affirmation nor pure negation of being', although it 'bears an exclusively negative quality' (Levinas 1996, 152). If Levinas hears the impersonal or anonymous voice of the *il y a* in Blanchot's works, Blanchot in his turn hears it in Beckett's: in *The Unnamable* (1953), for instance, where the reader encounters what Blanchot describes as 'experience lived under the threat of the impersonal, the approach of a neutral speech [*une parole neutre*] that speaks itself alone, that goes through the one who hears it, that is without intimacy, excludes any intimacy, one that cannot be silenced, for it is the incessant, the interminable' (Blanchot 2003, 213).

For Blanchot, as for Levinas, the *il y a* is quite simply irremissible and interminable. But whereas Levinas's thought of the ethical relation to the Other is the escape from this irreducible *il y a*, Blanchot thinks literature itself in terms of this voice, and, far from attempting to silence it, he attempts to identify it, disclose it – in Kafka and Beckett, among others. For Blanchot, literature is the voice of an alterity that is to be sharply distinguished from the Other as *autrui* in Levinas:

> The narrative 'he' ['*il*'], whether absent or present, whether it affirms itself or hides itself, and whether or not it alters the conventions of writing – linearity, continuity, readability – thus marks the intrusion of the other – understood as neutral – in its irreducible strangeness and in its wily perversity. The other speaks. But when the other is speaking, no one speaks because the other, which we must refrain from honoring with a capital letter that would determine it by way of a majestic substantive, as though it had some substantial or even unique presence, is precisely never simply the other. (Blanchot 1993, 385)

As for Blanchot's identification of this voice of the other in Beckett, the murmur of the *il y a* does indeed seem to be present in *The Unnamable* and the *Texts for Nothing* (1958), which ends with an 'it murmurs', a 'voice murmuring a trace' (Beckett 1995a, 152). In Beckett, though, there is no acceptance of the *il y a*, no living with it, but rather, as in Levinas, an unremitting attempt to escape it. Whether such an escape is possible, whether the *il y a* is in fact disclosed as irreducible, and whether its negation is in any sense ethical, or even the unethical precondition for the ethical, are questions that in Beckett will be articulated in, and constitute the very form of, what in the novella *First Love* (written in 1946) is termed the 'hell of unknowing' (Beckett 1995a, 43).

For Levinas, the neutral voice of the *il y a* is profoundly ambiguous, indeed reversible, and this ambiguity and reversibility is essential for Levinas's thought of the escape from it into the ethical. Just as Nietzsche thinks nihilism as that which must be consummated in order to be overcome, so Levinas thinks the experience of the horror and fundamental absurdity of the *il y a* as the precondition for its overcoming. Were it not for the experience of this horror and absurdity, there could be no ethical relation, precisely because the latter is defined first and foremost as the experience of death's impossibility. Ultimately, for Levinas, it is not literary texts, not even Celan's, but the Bible – 'the book par excellence', the 'Book of Books, which all the Letters of the world awaited or upon which they comment' (Levinas 1985, 22, 117) – that is the privileged site for an experience of the saying of the Other. The Bible possesses an 'incomparable prophetic excellence' in that it constitutes ethical testimony (*témoignage éthique*) to the Other in its purest form (Levinas 1985, 115). It seems, then, that for an experience of the ethical relation with the Other, one has simply to turn to the Bible, while for the non-ethical experience of the *il y a*, which is the precondition for the flight into the ethical, one has to rely upon literature, and in particular upon Blanchot.

Things are slightly more complicated than this, however. If the Bible is the book *par excellence* on account of its testifying to the Other, it is literature that grants us that experience of the *il y a* without which the ethical relation would remain simply impossible. The escape into the ethical is, then, a movement from literature to the Bible, from scripture to Scripture. This movement is achievable only because the *il y a* as presented in literature, or at least in Blanchot, is fundamentally ambiguous, at once ethical and non-ethical, nihilist and non-nihilist, scriptural and Scriptural. In other words, the distinction between literature (as experience of the *il y a*) and Scripture (as testimony to the Other) is internal to Blanchot's work. On the one hand, that work is

> the announcement of a loss of meaning [*sens*], a scattering of discourse, as if one were at the extreme pinnacle of nihilism [*l'extrême pointe du nihilisme*] – as if nothingness [*le néant*] itself could no longer

be thought peacefully, and had become equivocal to the ear listening to it. Meaning, bound to language, in becoming literature, in which it should be fulfilled and exalted, brings us back to meaningless repetition [*ressassement insignifiant*] – more devoid of meaning than the wandering structures or piecemeal elements that might make it up. We are delivered up to the inhuman, to the frightfulness of the Neuter [*Neutre*]. That is one direction. (Levinas 1996, 154)

On the other hand, this threat of meaning's loss reveals that identity-thinking, totalization, the drive to cognitive mastery, cannot master the *il y a*, which lies beyond the limits of metaphysics and beyond Heidegger's fundamental ontology. The *il y a* is an other the experience of which renders possible a movement beyond, by disclosing the limits of, identity-thinking, and which therefore renders possible the very thought of the Other. The announcement of meaning's loss is, then, nihilism as the precondition of the ethical relation. For this reason, the *il y a* as neutral or anonymous murmur can be said, on the one hand, to constitute the horror of meaning's loss, and, on the other hand, to contain 'more transcendence than any world-behind-the-worlds [*arrière-monde*] ever gave a glimpse of' (Levinas 1996, 155). Therein, for Levinas, lies the privilege of literature: it is at once nihilist and non-nihilist, an experience of meaning's loss and the transcendence of that loss, the bridge between the non-ethical and the ethical. Were it not for literature, the murmuring silence of the *il y a* would remain unheard, and thus the transcending negation of the *il y a* could not take place. Were it not for literature, the ethical relation to the Other would remain impossible.

Literature and the alterity of the trace: Derrida

Literature as both nihilism and the transcendence of nihilism: this thesis returns in Derrida's brief remarks on Beckett, in whose works he finds both the 'nihilist' and the 'not nihilist'. And these two sides to Beckett are also closely akin to the two sides of poetic discourse that Levinas terms the 'saying' and the 'said'; for, according to Derrida, the non-nihilist Beckett is to be found precisely in the manner rather than the matter of his works, in that 'remainder which remains when the thematics is exhausted', an irreducible affirmation, beyond all possible negation, and thus beyond nihilism, to be sought not in those works' themes, content, or subject, but in 'the composition, the rhetoric, the construction and rhythm' (Derrida 1992c, 61). This notion of a in that 'ever so little'. Now, in place of literature or the literary as such, we find the 'literary event': 'the existence of something like a *literary reality in itself* will always remain problematic. The literary event is perhaps more of an event (because less natural) than any other, but by the same token it becomes very improbable, hard to verify' (Derrida 1992c, 73). Thus, if literature lacks any essence, if it hardly exists, if it 'voids itself in its limitlessness' (Derrida 1992c, 73), this does not mean that it lacks all specificity. And not only does literature not simply disappear as a category under the pressure of its deconstruction, but it retains a certain privilege – as an event that is 'perhaps more of an event (because less natural) than any other'. Paradoxically, the specificity or singularity of literature as event lies precisely in its not having an essence, in its exceeding itself or being other than itself, in its resistance to the metaphysical question *par excellence*: 'What is ... ?' In his questioning of the 'presumed authority under which one submits anything whatever, *and particularly literature*, to the form of [this question's] inquisition' (Derrida 1981a, 177; emphasis added), Derrida affirms the particularity of literature by way of its singular resistance to the question of essence or identity.

Less warily than Derrida, Paul de Man will come to privilege the literary on account of its disclosure of the rhetoricity of language, the unreliability of linguistic utterance, an 'autonomous potential of language', a 'considerable freedom from referential restraint', that may be common to all language but can become the object of a 'negative knowledge' only through literature (de Man 1986b, 10). If this knowledge about the alterity of word to world is only ever negative, then this is because it can authorize no reliable metalanguage free of, or in a position to master, the very rhetoricity that is disclosed in literature. Although he does not fully endorse de Man's position, Derrida too insists upon a certain irreducibility of the literary: 'there is here, certainly, something irreducible in poetic or literary experience' (Derrida 1992c, 50). This irreducibility lies precisely in literature's singular capacity to suspend, rather than simply annul or free itself from, both meaning and reference. Owing to this suspension – which, Derrida argues, occurs differently in every text – literature 'perhaps stands on the edge of everything, almost beyond everything, including itself' (Derrida 1992c, 47).

Alterity is related to literature, then, not as theme or content, not as literature's said (*dit*), but through literature's being always already other than, always already at odds with, itself: 'In its suspended condition, literature can only exceed itself' (Derrida 1992c, 48). By way of example, in his reading of Kafka's 'Before the Law' (1919), which forms part of *The Trial* but was published as a separate work during Kafka's lifetime, Derrida returns to this strange being-other-than-itself of literature:

> [Kafka's] text also points obliquely to literature, speaking of itself as a literary effect – and thereby exceeding the literature of which it speaks.
>
> But is it not necessary for all literature to exceed literature? What would be a literature that would be only what it is, literature? It would no longer be itself if it were itself. (Derrida 1992a, 215)

Perhaps surprisingly for those who would accuse him of a radically dehistoricizing approach to both literature and philosophy, Derrida ties this conception of literature as alterior to itself to a history, not just of literature but also of the experience of alterity itself. Literature, he argues, may become the privileged form of this experience of alterity at a particular historical moment. Indeed, the specificity of the modern lies, at least in part, in this privileging of literature. That said, Derrida's gesture towards the historicization of literature as the experience of alterity occurs in the interests of the radically ahistorical truth of what he terms 'writing in general':

> it is quite possible that literary writing in the modern period is more than one example among others, rather a privileged guiding thread for access to the general structure of textuality [...]. What literature 'does' with language holds a revealing power which is certainly not unique, which it can share up to a point with law, for example with judicial language, but which in a given historical situation (precisely our own, and this is one more reason for feeling concerned, provoked, summoned by 'the question of literature') teaches us more, and even the 'essential', about writing in general, about the philosophical or scientific (for example linguistic) limits of the interpretation of writing. (Derrida 1992c, 71–2)

In a paradox that is characteristic of deconstruction, while on the one hand insisting that there is no essence to literature, and that literature in suspending meaning and reference tends towards without ever achieving pure self-referentiality, and may therefore be described as the 'nothing-ing of nothing' (Derrida 1992c, 47), on the other hand Derrida makes of this very lack of essence, and of literature's being always beyond or alterior to itself, the very definition of the literary event.

double or divided Beckett is already present in Ihab Hassan's *The Dismemberment of Orpheus* (1971), in what Hassan identifies as the 'two accents of silence' in Beckett's *œuvre*: on the one hand, a silence that is 'autodestructive, demonic, nihilist'; on the other hand, a silence that is 'self-transcendent, sacramental, plenary' (Hassan 1971, 248). As we have seen, for Levinas the nihilist moment is the necessary precursor to the flight into the ethical. For Derrida, however, the logic governing the relation between the nihilist and the non-nihilist in Beckett is to be thought aporetically. It is not a matter of passing from one to the other by way of a negation, and thereby escaping into the ethical, but rather a matter of experiencing the aporia. This experience of the aporia *is* deconstruction. When seeking to justify deconstruction itself, however, Derrida does come to rely upon an ethics of alterity, an affirmation of the absolute value of the other, closely akin to Levinas's.

The relation between Levinas and Derrida is complicated, to say the least, and these complications are apparent in Derrida's own deconstructive readings of Levinas, and in particular his patient questioning of Levinas's attempts to establish a clear distinction between his own ethics as first philosophy and Heidegger's fundamental ontology, and of the determination of that ethics by what remains a phallogocentric model of sexual difference.[5] However, Levinas's presence is apparent at key moments in Derrida's own deconstructive enterprise, not least in his earliest formulations of the alterity of the trace and his later work towards an ethics of hospitality. As early as *Of Grammatology* (1967), Derrida states: 'I relate this concept of *trace* to what is at the center of the latest work of Emmanuel Levinas and his critique of ontology: relationship to the illeity as to the alterity of a past that never was and can never be lived in the originary or modified form of presence' (Derrida 1976, 70). In 'Différance' (1968), he again relies on Levinas when clarifying the nature of that 'certain alterity' characterizing *différance*, an alterity to which Freud 'gives the metaphysical name of the Unconscious' (Derrida 1982, 20). Again, the alterity of the trace is conceived as a past that is absolutely alien to any present and any possible presentation: the trace is 'definitively exempt from every process of presentation by means of which we would call upon it to show itself in person' (Derrida 1982, 20). Derrida continues:

> One cannot think the trace – and therefore *différance* – on the basis of the present, or of the presence of the present.
>
> A past that has never been present: this formula is the one that Emmanuel Levinas uses, although certainly in a non-psychoanalytic

way, to qualify the trace and enigma of absolute alterity: the Other. (Derrida 1982, 21)

From these remarks it is clear that the alterity of the trace lies in its very unpresentability. For all its elusiveness, the trace can be known definitively as that which will remain for ever alien to presence. Although Derrida will go on to argue that, in accordance with the aporetic logic of deconstruction, the trace is at once the condition of possibility and the condition of impossibility of both presence and identity, such aporetic doubleness does not characterize the alterity of the trace itself, which cannot be said to be both presentable and unpresentable. In its alterity, the trace is to be known only by way of differing-deferring.

The trace is thought by Derrida in terms of an alterity that, while not identical to that characterizing the transcendent Other in Levinas, is common to a philosophical approach that is post-Heideggerian, which is to say that it breaks with the thought of Being as presence or presencing. And this commonality survives Derrida's persuasive challenging of Levinas's claim to have passed beyond Heidegger in his thought of ethics (rather than ontology) as first philosophy. Both Derrida and Levinas think an alterity that is irreducible (in that it precedes all possible negation), that is alien to all possible presence and all possible presentation, and that is located in a past that has never been present and a future that will never be present, a future (*avenir*) that remains for ever to come (*à venir*).

In his later work on the ethics of hospitality, Derrida again follows Levinas in his deployment of the 'other', if again marking his distance from Levinas through his insistence upon the aporetic logic that will govern a deconstructive ethics, and in particular the aporia of necessity and impossibility that has to be taken into account in any attempt to theorize the ethical, an aporia that makes of hospitality a 'hostipitality' in which openness to the other cannot exclude a certain hostility to the other. However, despite the many precautions taken in his thinking of the ethical in both its necessity and its impossibility, in response to the question 'Why deconstruct?' – in other words, why practice deconstruction rather than, for instance, fundamental ontology or phenomenology, or anything or nothing? – Derrida unsurprisingly finds it necessary to resort to an unambiguously ethical justification, a justification for deconstruction in terms of value and, more precisely, in terms of the 'value of the other or of alterity' (Derrida 2001, 83).

Deconstruction is undertaken in the interests of the future, in accordance with the fundamental ethical principle that 'it's better that there be a future, rather than nothing' (Derrida 2001, 83). Deconstruction is itself the keeping open of this future, from which the other arrives, although only ever in the form of that which remains for ever to come (*à venir*), definitively exempt, as we have seen, from any present:

> For something to come there has to be a future, and thus *if there is* a categorical imperative, it consists in doing everything for the future to remain open. I am strongly tempted to say this, but then – in the name of what would the future be worth more than the past? More than repetition? Why would the event be preferable to the non-event? Here I might find something that resembles an ethical dimension, because the future is the opening in which the other happens [*arrive*], and it is the value of the other or of alterity that, ultimately, would be the justification. (Derrida 2001, 83)

If this discourse on the value of the other only 'resembles' the ethical, it is because that categorical imperative to keep the future open for the other which lies at the origin of deconstruction is not simply an obligation but also a necessity that is quite simply unavoidable. In a paradox that Derrida himself does not address here, and whose force turns back upon deconstruction, although we are ethically obliged to keep the future open (if, that is, we accept the value of the other), we cannot help but keep that future open, even if we do not accept the value of the other, even if we dream of nothing but the absolute reduction to nothing of that other. Similarly, although it may have taken Derrida to reveal this to us, deconstruction was always already taking place, whether we like it or not, given that, according to Derrida, the other which is only ever to come is also always already there, within the very 'I' whose status as ethical subject is always already compromised by the other within: 'There is no "I" that ethically makes room for the other, but rather an "I" that is structured by the alterity within it, an "I" that is itself in a state of self-deconstruction, of dislocation' (Derrida 2001, 84).

If the other is both always already there in the 'I' and for ever to come, if it is both the condition of possibility and the condition of impossibility of all identity, then any unreserved insistence upon an obligation or an imperative to keep the future open for the other, and any reliance upon an ethical discourse, becomes highly problematic. That Derrida continues to deploy an ethical rhetoric is beyond doubt, if not beyond question: in his 1997 seminar on 'Hostipitality', for instance, he defines deconstruction as 'hospitality to the other' (Derrida 2002d, 364), and the conversation 'I Have a Taste for the Secret' ends with the assertion that the violence which 'does not leave room for the other' is 'bad violence, impoverishing, repetitive, mechanical' (Derrida 2001, 92).

By insisting on the value of the other, by deploying an ethical rhetoric to describe the other, by referring in *Force of Law* (1994) to a justice that is ultimately indeconstructible, a justice that *is* deconstruction, Derrida may seem to be operating in accordance with an aporetic logic. And yet the question 'Why deconstruct?' demands, as we have seen, an ethical response, if one is not simply to see deconstruction as requiring no justification at all, as being one method among others for analysing literary or philosophical texts. And Derrida's response is indeed ethical, making of deconstruction itself ultimately an ethical practice on the side of that which is not nihilist, even if it can never wholly free itself from nihilism. That Derrida refers to the justice of deconstruction as indeconstructible indicates that, as soon as it becomes ethical, as soon as it has to justify itself in terms of the value of the other, the difference between deconstruction and metaphysics disintegrates, as does the difference between Derrida and Levinas. It is unsurprising, then, that Derrida should evoke Levinas at this very moment: 'I recalled [in *Force of Law*] that powerful statement of Levinas, "the relation to the other [*autrui*], i.e. justice", which says something analogous in so few words' (Derrida 2001, 56). Were he not to resort to the thought of an indeconstructible, Derrida would be unable to defend deconstruction against the force of the question 'Why deconstruct?', other than to claim that one cannot help doing so – scarcely an ethical position – or to admit that, if it is indeed a matter of ethical choice, this is not a choice that can ultimately be justified by an appeal to the indeconstructible.

From the outset, one of Derrida's central concerns is the deconstruction of the opposition between philosophy and literature. In order to achieve this, he has to demonstrate that there is in fact no essence to literature, nothing that can be identified and demarcated as the strictly literary. This demonstration is undertaken perhaps most forcefully in the reading of Mallarmé entitled 'The Double Session', in *Dissemination* (1972), which includes the following statement: 'If this handbook of literature [Mallarmé's *Mimique*] meant to *say* something, which we now have some reason to doubt, it would proclaim first of all that there is no – or hardly any, ever so little [*à peine, si peu de*] – literature; that in any event there is no essence of literature, no truth of literature, no literary-being or being-literary of literature' (Derrida 1981a, 223). This take on literature and the literary is still in place almost two decades later, in the interview 'This Strange Institution Called Literature' (1989), although here Derrida elaborates on the residual possibility for literature retained

For Derrida, then, alterity is written into the heart of the literary event, as it is into the trace. Were not literature other than itself, there would be no literary event at all. And it is precisely in its being other than itself that literature, in the present 'historical situation', has what Derrida terms a 'revealing power' that is greater than that of other forms of writing, a power whose object of revelation is precisely the alterity of the trace as that which is both always already (*toujours déjà*) and for ever to come (*à venir*). That all value will lie, if anywhere, only in this other beyond all presentation, makes of deconstruction itself perhaps the most paradoxical form yet taken by the ethics of alterity.

From modern to postmodern alterity

To summarize the various theoretical positions taken on the relationship between literature and alterity analysed above: Adorno finds in Beckett a negative image of that utopian reconciliation (*Versöhnung*) in which a multiplicity would coexist in non-antagonistic, non-dialectical, relation with each other. The alterity of this future is to be glimpsed in the present, in literature, only in the least palpable of forms: as a slightest difference (*kleinste Differenz*) within the negative. For Levinas, the ethical relation to the Other (*autrui*) is conceived as essentially discursive, at once a response to, and a responsibility for, the Other as absolutely other. In literature, and more precisely in the works of Blanchot, Levinas hears the horrifying murmur of the *il y a*, that nihilistic absurdity which takes the form of the neutral (*le neutre*), but also finds the possibility for a transcendence of the absurd, the leap from scripture to Scripture. The metaphysical concept of alterity is subjected to deconstruction by Derrida, but remains crucial to his thinking of the trace, of *différance*, and of literature in their irreducibility and their foreignness to all presentation, essentiality, and identity; beyond that, alterity remains at the very heart of his attempt to think an ethics of hospitality, grounded as that ethics is in the value of the other.

The relationship between literature and an ethics of alterity is also at the centre of recent commentaries on the postmodern. Indeed, one might even go so far as to argue that hospitality to an irreducible other is the defining characteristic of the postmodern. This can mean either that a certain kind of literature is defined as postmodern, on account of its comportment towards alterity, or that a postmodern theory of literature is used to define the literary as such in terms of a certain comportment towards, or experience of, alterity. For a modern, or at least pre-postmodern, theory of the relationship between literature and alterity, one might turn to the reflections on art and its power to disclose the other in Proust's *Le Temps retrouvé* (1927), the final part of *À la recherche du temps perdu* (1913–27):

> Through art alone are we able to emerge from ourselves, to know what another person sees of a universe which is not the same as our own and of which, without art, the landscapes would remain as unknown to us as those that may exist in the moon. Thanks to art, instead of seeing one world only, our own, we see that world multiply itself [*se multiplier*] and we have at our disposal [*à notre disposition*] as many worlds as there are original artists, worlds more different one from the other than those which revolve in infinite space, worlds which, centuries after the extinction of the fire from which their light first emanated, whether it is called Rembrandt or Vermeer, send us still each one its special radiance. (Proust 1982, iii. 932)

Proust's narrator expresses a quintessentially modern view of art and its absolute privilege – which is to say, the singularity of the aesthetic in its power to produce singularities, as evident in Joyce and Woolf as it is here in Proust. That privilege is justified by art's power to disclose alterity in the form of other worlds – more precisely, others' worlds – that are placed at the reader's disposal (*disposition*). The postmodern turn of this screw takes the form of a radical questioning, not of the privileging of the aesthetic as such, and certainly not of the intimate relation between art and alterity, but rather of the author or the reader having the other at his or her disposal, of our being in any position to experience the other as simply another version of the same.

From a postmodern point of view, the other world to which we are granted access is what J. Hillis Miller, borrowing the term from Blanchot, describes as the 'imaginary'. Literature has the power to produce the imaginary because it 'derails or suspends or redirects the normal referentiality of language' (Hillis Miller 2002, 20). The imaginary world that literature produces is neither real nor unreal but virtual, 'a new, supplementary world, a metaworld, a hyper-reality' (Hillis Miller 2002, 18). Literature's 'other world' is doubly alterior, being neither the world in which the acts of writing and reading take place, nor an entirely unreal or non-existent world. Following both Derrida's and de Man's definitions of the literary in terms of a suspension of reference, although taking far fewer precautions, Hillis Miller offers not a definition of postmodern as distinct from modern literature, but rather a postmodern definition of literature as such. He does not address the question of how one might begin to distinguish between modern and postmodern literature – assuming this were possible – and the extent to which such a distinction would rely upon the notion of alterity, and of literature's comportment towards it.

Hillis Miller's evasion of this question is understandable, for the definition of the postmodern in literature has remained a subject of unremitting contention. One of the earliest theorizations of a specifically postmodern literature – Hassan's *The Dismemberment of Orpheus* – now appears in many respects distinctly modernist, not least in some of the examples it supplies of postmodern works, including Beckett. In surveying more recent theories of the postmodern it is possible to distinguish not only between those that champion and those that deplore the postmodern, but also between modern and postmodern conceptions of the postmodern. For all the confusion, however, Beckett has repeatedly been seen as exemplary of – and even as originating – postmodern literature.[6] Thomas Docherty, for instance, is not alone in arguing that Beckett's mode of characterization in *The Unnamable* is postmodern in that, abandoning the modernist aesthetic model of appearance and reality, surface and depth, Beckett presents the self in terms of pure surface, endless spectrality. Having quoted a passage from *The Unnamable* that includes the narrator's self-identification 'I'm neither one side nor the other, I'm in the middle, I'm the partition, I've two surfaces and no thickness, perhaps that's what I feel, myself vibrating, I'm the tympanum, on the one hand the mind, on the other the world, I don't belong to either' (Beckett 1959, 352), Docherty concludes: 'This *ghostly* "medium" is [...] the typical postmodern figure. The spatial metaphor of surface and depth is replaced, after the influence of cinema, by temporal sequence and development: a figure in one scene or "shot" can be thoroughly transfigured by the next, thus countering the notion of a transcendent self lying "behind" the surface "apparitions" and "disappearances" ' (Docherty 1996, 54–5).

The Unnamable certainly appears to be structured as a sequence of shots, each one of which is transfigured by another. There are, however, at least two other aspects to the novel that do not fit quite so neatly with Dochery's conception of the postmodern. First, the passage quoted by Docherty, in which the 'I' is identified as a pure surface, is but one in a sequence of attempted self-identifications. In other words, postmodern depthlessness remains a hypothesis here rather than the text's governing principle. Furthermore, this sequence of self-identifications is not simply without trajectory, thereby excluding the possibility of transcendence, the accomplishing of a self-identification that is not affected by an unintegrated and unmastered alterity. Indeed, the very failure to negate all possibility of a trajectory, and thus the failure to negate all possibility of transcendence, might be seen as responsible for the sequence of self-identifications. Were the notion of a 'transcendent self' to be countered or even left behind as a myth, a fiction, or a piece of modernist naïvety, there is every reason to believe that the process of self-identification that constitutes as it deconstitutes *The Unnamable* would reach an unambiguously consummating end. Were Beckett's 'I' or even the text as a whole to have achieved and be governed by the knowledge of the impossibility of transcendence, were it to have achieved and be governed by the knowledge that there is nothing but pure immanence, an a-teleological sequence of transfigurations across a surface behind which lurks no depth and no secret, then that 'I' and that text would constitute the overcoming of the very experience that is enacted in *The Unnamable* and again, if more disintegratively, in the *Texts for Nothing*, in which the figure of the pure surface is displaced by another, namely that of the 'voice murmuring a trace' (Beckett 1995a, 152).

The other in Beckett: from alter ego to *il y a*

At first glance, it might seem more than a little strange that Beckett's *œuvre* should have become such a privileged site for the valorization of an alterity that does not simply resist appropriation but itself makes possible (as it disrupts) all identity. For while, again and again, Beckett's works undoubtedly thematize the experience of seemingly unmasterable alterity in the most explicit fashion, that experience is situated within an unremitting struggle to reduce the other to nothing, to achieve a labour of negation (or *Nihilisierung*) that would put an end to being as such, and with it the being (or otherwise) of all alterity.

On the thematic level, alterity in Beckett is experienced principally as a threat to the freedom of the subject, a threat that is to be nullified not through the shoring up of that subject but through its happy dissolution into an indifference associated with what in Beckett's first novel, *Dream of Fair to Middling Women* (written in 1931–32), is termed the 'wombtomb'. This indifference beyond the antagonism of self and other finds perhaps its most explicit thematic inscription in chapter 6 of *Murphy* (1938), where it bears a close resemblance to Schopenhauerian *Gleichgültigkeit*, a condition of being that can be achieved only through the withdrawal from all contact with the 'outer reality', in accordance with the Belgian Occasionalist Arnold Geulincx's ethical imperative, *Ubi nihil vales, ibi nihil velis* (where you are worth nothing, there you should want nothing),[7] and that complete negation (*Verneinung*) of the will advocated by Schopenhauer. This indifference is to be distinguished, not least in the mood of its presentation, from the intolerable decomposition of the subject enacted in the postwar trilogy.

In the early phase of Beckett's career, alterity is repeatedly figured as the feminine, securely alterior to the male protagonist, whose attitude to the feminine other is none the less radically ambiguous, dividing the male subject from himself. Murphy, for instance, cannot help himself both loving and hating Celia Kelly. However, when the other is not so securely alterior – when it bears an uncanny resemblance to the self – the ambiguities of love and hate are resolved into murderous violence. In part II of *Molloy* (1951), for instance, Moran recounts the murder of a stranger whose face, he believes, 'vaguely resembled my own, less the refinement of course, same little abortive moustache, same little ferrety eyes, same paraphimosis of the nose, and a thin red mouth that looked as if it was raw from trying to shit its tongue' (Beckett 1959, 151). If, in the wake of the violence that renders this uncannily familiar face a 'pulp', Moran concludes that the not-quite-other is now securely a dead other – 'He no longer resembled me' (Beckett 1959, 152) – the reaction of Moran's son to his father's state after the murder suggests that, ironically, such violence against the other has only increased its troubling resemblance to the self, that the negation of the other is the machinery of what might be termed a process of *saming*.

That such attempted reductions to nothing of a threatening alterity will become not just a theme but the very object or aim of the textual event is suggested by a series of laborious returns to what, in his 1931 monograph on Proust, Beckett terms the 'irremediable solitude to which every human being is condemned' (Beckett 1987, 63). In both *How It Is* (1961) and *Company* (1980), the reader is carried slowly towards an apocalyptic affirmation of identity for which there is simply no other. *How It Is* ends with the affirmation of a being 'alone in the mud' (Beckett 1964, 160), while *Company* closes with the promise of an absolute solitude, the reduction to nothing of any possible other, and indeed the affirmation of both the truth and the value of this reduction:

> Till finally you hear how words are coming to an end. With every inane word a little nearer to the last. And how the fable too. The fable of one with you in the dark. The fable of one fabling with you in the dark. And how better in the end labour lost and silence. And you as you always were.
> Alone. (Beckett 1980, 88–9)

For all these affirmations of an essential solitude, however, there is also considerable evidence to support the counter-argument – that Beckett's *œuvre* discloses an alterity that is quite simply irreducible, though not necessarily a value and thus not proof that the work is governed by an ethics of alterity. The experience of the self as fundamentally self-alienated, or 'schizophrenic' (Deleuze 1995, 23), appears to reach an extreme in *The Unnamable*. Like many of the plays, the trilogy is populated by a host of what in *The Unnamable* are termed 'pseudocouple[s]'; in other words, couples that resemble egos and alter egos, belonging neither together nor apart, trapped within a paralysing economy that resists both dissolution and sublimation. These pseudocouples include Watt and Knott, Mercier and Camier, Molloy and Moran, Malone and Macmann, Vladimir and Estragon, Pozzo and Lucky, Hamm and Clov, Nagg and Nell, Winnie and Willie, and, much later, Reader and Listener.

With a few notable exceptions, analyses of alterity in Beckett have tended to focus on these self–other or subject–object relations, which is to say on the decomposition or disintegration of the Cartesian subject that is enacted so explicitly in the postwar trilogy and that appears to reach a limit with the *Texts for Nothing*, which were completed in 1952. In conversation with Israel Shenker in 1956, however, Beckett makes it clear that by the time of *The Unnamable* this disintegration has spread beyond the self–other relation to the very language in which that disintegration of identity is expressed:

> In the last book – *L'Innommable* – there's complete disintegration. No 'I', no 'have', no 'being'. No nominative, no accusative, no verb. There's no way to go on.
> The very last thing I wrote – *Textes pour rien* – was an attempt to get out of the attitude of disintegration, but it failed. (Beckett in Shenker 1979, 148)

On the one hand, Beckett's response to the failure to escape the 'attitude of disintegration' so prevalent in *The Unnamable* and *Texts for Nothing* was to seek in the theatre what he terms a 'habitable space' beyond the 'wasteland of prose' (Beckett in Brater 1989, 55). On the other hand, it was to take a new approach to the relation of form and content. While this relation is still mimetic in the trilogy, such that the disintegration of self and world is accompanied by a disintegration of the work's form, it becomes increasingly antithetical in the later works. Although the experience of disintegration continues to be thematized, in both the prose fiction and the plays, Beckett's works are no longer entirely governed by that 'principle of disintegration' to which he refers in his 1934 review of Sean O'Casey's *Windfalls* (Beckett 1983a, 82). Indeed, by 1961 Beckett is conceiving of the writer's task as the search for a form that will 'accommodate' rather than simply reflect the 'mess' of the real. Form and content will henceforth 'remain separate', with the form being a 'preoccupation, because it exists as a problem separate from the material it accommodates' (Beckett in Driver 1979, 219). By 1973, Beckett is prepared to go even further, claiming that the work's formal coherence is not simply an accommodation but a saving affirmation in its own right: 'Paradoxically, it's through the form that the artist can find a kind of solution [*une sorte d'issue*] – by giving form to what has none [*l'informe*]. It is perhaps only at that level that there may be an underlying affirmation [*une affirmation sous-jacente*]' (Beckett in Juliet 1995, 149).

Since the late 1980s, commentators of a poststructuralist persuasion have seen Beckett's radical decomposition of the subject as part of a more general deconstructive approach to all binary oppositions, including presence and absence, fact and fiction, inside and outside, narrator and narrated. The result is an *œuvre* characterized ever more clearly by aporias and undecidabilities of the kind at which the narrator of *Texts for Nothing* arrives when he declares: 'it's true and it's not true, there is silence and there is not silence, there is no one and there is someone' (Beckett 1995a, 154). In the major deconstructive readings of Beckett – by Connor (1988), Hill (1990b), Locatelli (1990), Tresize (1990), and Begam (1996) – the aim is not to deconstruct Beckett, not to expose his logocentric underbelly, but rather to demonstrate that his textual practice is itself thoroughly deconstructive. In each case, Beckett is seen to submit all metaphysical oppositions to a differing-deferring that anticipates the *différance* first theorized by Derrida in the 1960s. The deconstructive take on Beckett, and its ethical insistence upon the value of the other as it is disclosed in Beckett's works, is expressed perhaps most clearly and succinctly by Leslie Hill in his Beckett obituary. According to Hill, what an attentive reading of Beckett discovers is 'the power of Beckett's commitment to an ethics of writing, his respect for the trace of otherness, the alterity and difference at the heart of assumed identity that, for Beckett, was what was at stake in literature' (Hill 1990a). Similarly, for Begam, with *The Unnamable* Beckett opens literature to a 'pantextuality' that is indistinguishable from what Derrida later thinks as *écriture*. In their openness or undecidability, Beckett's self-deconstructing works become sites of resistance. In short, they become the most ethical form of textual production, ethical precisely through their inexhaustible resistance to what are taken to be the totalitarian threats of meaning, stability, fixity, and identity, each of which is predicated on a negation of alterity. These deconstructive readings of Beckett are no less concerned with the ethicality of Beckett's enterprise than are those earlier thematizing readings from which the deconstructive commentators wish to take their critical distance. As David Pattie observes: 'As earlier, humanist critics of Beckett discovered something positive in the stoic resignation of the Beckettian character, so the new generation of Beckett critics found something useful in his denial of textual determinism' (Pattie 2004, 242).

One of the more obvious risks of the deconstructive approach to Beckett is that any sense of historical contextuality can simply disappear. To give just one example of this: in the course of Begam's Beckett-anticipating-Derrida argument, no mention is made of Blanchot. And yet, in the early 1940s, not only was Blanchot conceiving of the writer's predicament in a manner not easy to distinguish from Beckett's,[8] but he also went on to exert a scarcely calculable influence on Derrida. To leave Blanchot out of account, however, is not merely to distort the history of both the practice and the theorization of literature in France since the 1940s; it is to encourage the notion that Beckett simply stands alone, as some kind of scarcely conceivable originator and anticipator of deconstruction. Furthermore, by arresting his own hermeneutic narrative at *The Unnamable*, without mentioning the *Texts for Nothing*, Begam avoids having to consider what other commentators – most recently, Alain Badiou – see as a radical new departure dividing Beckett's *œuvre* into two quite distinct phases, a second, reconstructive phase following the disintegrative *impasse* that Beckett claimed to have reached with the writing of the *Texts for Nothing*.

Beyond all the differences separating the deconstructive take on Beckett from both Badiou's and that of Beckett's 'humanist' critics, however, all of these schools agree on the ethicality of his works. Where the deconstructive Beckett would maintain an ethical openness to alterity on both the thematic level (as the self's radical splitting) and the textual level (openness as indeterminacy), Badiou's Beckett moves in the direction of an openness for which perhaps the best, if also most surprising, term is 'love'. This openness to the other is to be found not simply in the thematics, but also in the constitution of the works as events: 'Beckett's evolution goes from a programme of the One – obstinate trajectory or interminable soliloquy – to the pregnant theme of the Two, which opens out onto infinity' (Badiou 2003, 17). From an initial fidelity to that 'irremediable solitude' to which the Beckett of the 1931 monograph on Proust declares that 'every human being is condemned', to the absolute disintegration of the subject – in other words, its absolute alterification – in the postwar trilogy and *Texts for Nothing*, to an openness to, and affirmation of, alterity in later works such as 'Enough' (1966) and *Ill Seen Ill Said* (1981) – this would be the essentially linear, soteriological trajectory of Beckett's *œuvre*. Despite Andrew Gibson's claim that Badiou's 'ethical' Beckett marks a radical break with the deconstructive approach so dominant in the late 1980s and early 1990s,[9] it is precisely the notion that Beckett's textual practice is ethical that constitutes their common ground, for textual openness is always treated, if not as the defining characteristic of the literary, as a value. Given, however, that the narrator of *First Love* describes the experience of unknowing as 'hell' (Beckett 1995a, 43), the legitimacy of such an ethicalization of textual openness is surely no less questionable than Badiou's claim that Beckett undertakes an ethical journey from the One to the Two.

In addition to the pseudocouples, the One and the Two, and the experience of the aporia, there is also another kind of alterity to be considered, namely the *il y a* of which Levinas writes in *Existence and Existents*. To what extent does Beckett's *œuvre* disclose an alterity with which no ethical relation can be maintained? This other alterity would not be that of a second self, the alter ego that prevents the ego from being at one with itself, the kind of disruption familiar to readers of Gogol's Petersburg tales (1835–36) or Dostoevsky's *The Double* (1846). Rather, it would be the *il y a* as defined by Levinas in its horror and fundamental absurdity: 'Neither nothing nor being. I sometimes use the expression: the excluded middle. One cannot say of this "there is" which persists that it is an event of being. One can neither say that it is nothingness, even though there is nothing' (Levinas 1985, 48–9).

While, for Levinas, it is precisely the ethical relation with the Other that constitutes an escape from the horror of the *il y a*, in Beckett the *il y a* certainly appears to be irreducible and inescapable in a way that it is not for Levinas, blocking the path to the ethical. In the *Texts for Nothing*, for instance, this persistence that is not an event of being is figured as a 'voice murmuring a trace' which appears to resist all efforts to silence it with 'no's knife' (Beckett 1995a, 154). The Beckettian *il y a* appears, then, to be the most radical form of unmasterable alterity. Certainly, Blanchot, in his seminal essay on Beckett's trilogy in *The Book to Come* (1959), sees Beckett disclosing an irreducible alterity in the form of an *il y a* figured as a 'neutral speech' that 'cannot be silenced, for it is the incessant, the interminable' (Blanchot 2003, 213). More recently, Simon Critchley has heard in Beckett, as in Blanchot, the irreducible 'tinnitus of existence', a 'void that speaks as one vast, continuous buzzing, a dull roar in the skull like falls, an unqualifiable murmur, an impersonal whining, the vibration of the tympanum'. Indeed, Critchley is prepared, like Hillis Miller, to generalize this argument beyond Beckett's *œuvre* to literature as a whole, and to argue that this murmur of being is also figured in an 'irreducible logic of spectrality at work in literature' which operates 'in the name of justice', even if only (and aporetically) to deny its readers 'the sleep of the just' (Critchley 1997, 174–5).

But, one might ask, is this murmur of the *il y a* in fact disclosed as an irreducible alterity in Beckett, and to what extent can the experience of it found a post-metaphysical ethics? Is it the limit to the power of the negative, and indeed the limit to the power of a nihilism whose end and aim would be the reduction to nothing, not of being, but precisely of that alterity which neither is nor is not, but takes the form of a 'voice murmuring a trace' in the *Texts for Nothing* and of the spectral in Beckett's later works, particularly the later plays for television? In other words, does literature, and Beckett in particular, have what Derrida terms the 'revealing power' to disclose an irreducible alterity that would be not just the origin of all value but a value in and of itself, even if it is also that which prevents the construction of a systematic or institutionalized ethics, even if it validates an ethics of alterity that is only ever at the disposal of the other, and can only ever be seen as the other's ethics?

In order to begin to formulate a response to these questions, my focus in this book will be not on the subject–object relation, but rather on three interrelated topics through which alterity has been thought in postwar philosophy and literary theory, namely translation, the comic, and the feminine. Through a series of readings of works by Beckett and others, my aim will be to suggest that the attempt to establish an ethics of alterity, even an ethics of alterity thought, as it is by Derrida, aporetically, in its 'im-possibility',[10] in relation to these three elements cannot necessarily depend upon Beckett – or at least upon all of Beckett – for support. More generally, I hope to reopen the question of the relation between literature and ethics, a question that, despite the considerable attention paid to it in recent years, has in fact remained closed, which is to say already decided in literature's favour. What that decision in literature's favour obscures, at least in Beckett, is the experience of what here will go by the name of the *anethical*.

Part I
In Other Words:
On the Ethics of Translation

And the whole earth was of one language, and of one speech.

And it came to pass, as they journeyed from the east, that they found a plain in the land of Shinar; and they dwelt there.

And they said one to another, Go to, let us make brick, and burn them thoroughly. And they had brick for stone, and slime had they for mortar.

And they said, Go to, let us build us a city, and a tower, whose top may reach unto heaven; and let us make us a name, lest we be scattered abroad upon the face of the whole earth.

And the Lord came down to see the city and the tower, which the children of men builded.

And the Lord said, Behold, the people is one, and they have all one language; and this they begin to do: and now nothing will be restrained from them, which they have imagined to do.

Go to, let us go down, and there confound their language, that they may not understand one another's speech.

So the Lord scattered them abroad from thence upon the face of all the earth: and they left off to build the city.

Therefore is the name of it called Babel; because the Lord did there confound the language of all the earth: and from thence did the Lord scatter them abroad upon the face of all the earth.

(Genesis 11: 1–9)

1
Translation and Difference
Dispatching Benjamin

'Translation proper': the interlingual and its others

Is it ever ethical to translate? In other words –

But already, as though it refused to await any decision concerning its relation to the ethical, translation of a kind is taking place here. For one definition of translation – one translation of the word 'translation' – is precisely: *in other words*. According to Roman Jakobson, however, in his seminal 1959 essay 'On Linguistic Aspects of Translation', such a dispatching of words into other words is merely an instance of intralingual translation ('an interpretation of verbal signs by means of other signs of the same language'), and, as another way of saying the same thing in the same language, intralingual translation is, like intersemiotic translation ('an interpretation of verbal signs by means of signs of nonverbal sign systems'), to be distinguished from interlingual translation, or 'translation proper': 'an interpretation of verbal signs by means of other verbal signs' (Jakobson 1987, 429). For Jakobson, then, translation proper takes place across a clearly measured difference, greater than that within any historically existent language, but less than that between the linguistic and the non-linguistic.

It is precisely the very possibility of any such rigorous organization of kinds of translation that Derrida aims to place in question in 'Des Tours de Babel', his 1980 essay on Walter Benjamin's 'The Task of the Translator' (1923). Derrida's deconstruction of Jakobson's distinction between the intralingual, interlingual, and intersemiotic depends upon his successfully demonstrating that the integrity of any given language, of any intralingual space, is always already compromised. But even if one does not accept Derrida's argument on the impossibility of linguistic self-identity, even if one remains unconvinced by his examples of undecidability (the word 'Babel' itself, or 'he war' in *Finnegans Wake*), it

33

seems evident that translation of some form (proper or not, ethical or not) is taking place not just between one language and another, not just between one sign system and another, but within any given language, not least one's own, every time the principle 'in other words' governs what is being written or spoken. Paraphrase would be a subcategory of translation in this more general sense, as would commentary and, indeed, interpretation itself. The word 'translation' would in fact be a translation of 'interpretation', and hermeneutics a theory of translation.

Returning, then, to the question of whether it is ever ethical to translate, but this time dispatching it in other words: If to comport oneself ethically is, as Derrida argues in *A Taste for the Secret*, to show 'respect for the other' – which it to say, not just to acknowledge the other as other, but to recognize the other in its value, and to locate that value precisely in the other's alterity (see Derrida 2001, 63) – can we ever know if we are translating ethically or not, if we are respecting the alterity of the original or not?

It is generally assumed that a translation only becomes a translation by making a given text readable (which is to say, accessible, intelligible, appropriable, or integratable) in another language or sign system. Translation is grounded in a principle of relative if not absolute equivalence or transferability between languages. Now, ethical translation would have to avoid overstepping the limits of this relative equivalence and transferability. This respect for the limits of equivalence would have to go beyond that respect for the original upon which Umberto Eco insists when he declares that 'In translation proper there is an implicit law, that is, the ethical obligation to respect what the author has written' (Eco 2003, 3). However, in order to avoid any negation of difference in translation, one would first have to achieve a reliable identification of the *particular* alterity of the original. And then, wherever this alterity is seen, the translator would have not simply to avoid reducing it, not simply to mark it by some form of translationese, but to communicate the imperative: *here translation must not take place*.

To be ethical or unethical, then, translation would have to be securely grounded in an identification of the particular alterity in the original that the translation would then either respect or disrespect. In the following analyses – first of Benjamin's essay on 'The Task of the Translator', then of three influential readings of it (by Blanchot, de Man, and Derrida), and finally of its relation to Benjamin's own practice as a translator of Baudelaire – my aim will be to demonstrate the following:

(1) Benjamin's essay, in which he proposes a practice of literal translation, is not only a theory of ethical translation, but one in which nihilism has a hitherto unrecognized, and yet none the less decisive, role to play.

(2) Beyond their quite explicit interest in the question of the possibility or impossibility of translation, Blanchot, de Man, and Derrida are, like Benjamin before them, all concerned principally with the ethics of translation. Indeed, their theories of translation are grounded in an ethics of alterity, even if the question of value might appear to have been bracketed from the outset. They all characterize what Benjamin terms bad (*schlecht*) translation as an attempt to efface the differences between languages, to reduce and even to abolish the otherness of the other tongue. For each of them, this negation of difference is precisely what the translator *ought* to avoid, even if it proves impossible to do so. And even if both de Man and Derrida argue that purely ethical translation is strictly speaking impossible, this does not mean that they themselves are not intent upon translating Benjamin's theory of translation ethically.

(3) Their own practice of translation (or what I shall have reason to term their *dispatching* of Benjamin) is not necessarily as respectful of the other as their own theories might lead one to expect. However, this is not because they have reached the limits of the possible in translation, but rather because they continue to think translation in ethical terms, and indeed by way of an ethics of alterity, even (and especially) when they invoke a certain nihilism in translation. It is as though the very defence of alterity in its value were one more way, not necessarily more or less naïve than any other, of attempting to dispatch the other (in this case, Benjamin) for good.

(4) Although they do not take any account of Benjamin's own practice of translation, to which his essay on 'The Task of the Translator' constitutes a foreword, his translation of Baudelaire's 'Tableaux parisiens' from the 1868 edition of *Les Fleurs du mal* – or at least his translation of the sonnet 'Les Aveugles' – radically qualifies his own theory of literal translation, calling into question not just the identifiability of both the literal and the alterior in the original, but also the very distinguishability of the ethical and the unethical in translation. Out of the strange conjunction of Benjamin's essay on literal translation and his translations of Baudelaire, there emerges the thought of what I term *anethical* translation. It is towards this thought of translation as an anethical practice that this chapter will be directed.

The threat and the promise of good translation: Walter Benjamin

Any reflection upon recent theories of translation is almost obliged to pass by way of Benjamin's foreword to his translations of Baudelaire. The theory of translation that he elaborates in this foreword relates not to the translation and translatability of just any text, but specifically to the translation and translatability of poetic or literary texts (*Dichtung*). The significance of this generic limitation can scarcely be exaggerated, since Benjamin concerns himself with the strange relation between poetic or literary texts and the sacred (*heilig*) text, and thus with the relation between literature and religion, art and ethics.

In 'The Task of the Translator', Benjamin distinguishes between two basic kinds of translation of literary works:

(1) On the one hand, there is what he quickly dismisses as bad translation. This is the kind of translation that concerns itself with the preservation (*Erhaltung*) and transmission of the meaning (*Sinn*) of the original. Its aim is to produce a translation that corresponds to the original in accordance with a principle of resemblance (*Ähnlichkeit*) – which is to say, likeness of meaning. The bad translator sets out to find in the target language a linguistic arrangement or formulation through which simply to reproduce or redispatch (*wiedergeben*) the meaning of the original.

(2) On the other hand, there is a practice of translation that simply ignores the meaning of the original. This second kind of translation, and the one advocated by Benjamin, obeys a principle of pure literality (*Wörtlichkeit*). It takes the word as its primary element (*Urelement*), and aims to give a 'literal rendering' of the syntax of the original. Unlike bad translation, literal translation 'casts the reproduction of meaning [*Sinneswiedergabe*] to the winds and threatens [*droht*] to lead directly to incomprehensibility' (Benjamin 1996, 260). A literal rendering of the original simply ignores the historical fact that the syntax of one language may differ radically from that of another.

For a sense of the kind of translation that such a theory would justify, one might consider two translations (one by Michael Brodsky, the other by Barbara Wright) of a question asked by Mme Piouk in Samuel Beckett's first completed play, *Eleutheria*, a work written in French in 1947 but published in the language of its original composition only posthumously, in 1995, once Brodsky's English-language translation was already scheduled for publication. At first sight, Mme Piouk's question regarding the location of the play's protagonist, Victor Krap – 'Il est toujours impasse de l'Enfant-Jésus?' – seems simple enough to translate, and the translator's task would scarcely appear to be complicated by the fact that, this question going unanswered, as questions so often do in Beckett, it is repeated in exactly the same form: 'Il est toujours impasse de l'Enfant-Jésus?' (Beckett 1995b, 28). Brodsky certainly respects both the syntax of the original and its repetition, translating the question in both instances as: 'He's still at the Impasse de l'Enfant-Jésus?' (Beckett 1995c, 15, 16). Wright, however, opts for two translations, in both of which the original syntax is altered to suit the more usual phrasing of questions in English. On its first appearance, she translates Mme Piouk's question as: 'Is he still living in that cul-de-sac – l'Impasse de l'Enfant-Jésus?' When repeated, it becomes: 'Is he still living in the Impasse de l'Enfant-Jésus?' (Beckett 1996, 18). Now, if one accepts Benjamin's argument in favour of absolute literality in translation, then, however strange it might seem, Brodsky's translation (which appears to be blind to the syntactical difference in the phrasing of questions in English and French, and which might well be taken as a sign that he is far from proficient in French, as is suggested by many others peculiarities in his translation of Beckett's play) would in fact be a better translation than Wright's.

Beyond the issue of literal fidelity to the syntax of the original, these two translations of a question in Beckett also reveal some of the difficulties faced by any theory of translation that would distinguish between interlingual and intralingual, and indeed between the literal and the figurative. Not only does Wright translate the French 'est' as 'living' – an equivalence that does not always go without saying in Beckett – but, when Mme Piouk's question is first asked in Wright's translation, it also includes, within the interlingual translation of French into English, a kind of intralingual translation of 'impasse' as 'cul-de-sac'. Why include both words? Whereas Brodsky simply reproduces the word 'impasse', Wright presumably considers it too foreign to be simply reproduced when it first appears, but not foreign enough, or perhaps too close to a proper noun, to exclude, whereas she considers the status of 'cul-de-sac' within the English language to be more assured. But, then, is 'cul-de-sac' an intralingual or an interlingual translation of 'Impasse'? What we find is that in their very different ways Brodsky and Wright cast doubt on the limits of translation, on where to start and where to stop translating Beckett. These problems are compounded by the fact that the word 'impasse' is not just any word in Beckett. Indeed, Hugh Kenner identifies it as nothing less than the keyword in Beckett's *œuvre* when he gives the title 'Comedian of the Impasse' to his chapter on Beckett in *The Stoic Comedians* (1962). In *Eleutheria* itself the impasse in which Victor Krap (and the Son of God before him) finds himself appears to be more than a literal one, the play exploring various forms of paralysis. Furthermore, the notion of not having been properly born – which Beckett first heard referred to in the third of Carl Jung's Tavistock Lectures in October 1935[1] – is included in the 'Addenda' to the novel *Watt* (written during the Second World War, but not published until 1953), and recurs in his first radio play, *All That Fall* (1957), and again in the late stage play *Footfalls* (1976). In Beckett, then, the word 'impasse' is located not only somewhere between French and English, and between proper and common noun, but also somewhere between the literal and the figurative. The problem of whether or not – and if so, how – to translate 'impasse' arises, of course, only because *Eleutheria* is one of the few of his own works that Beckett did not translate. However, in his French translation of *Murphy*, published in 1947, Beckett translates Murphy's address ('a mew in West Brompton') as 'l'impasse de l'Enfant-Jésus, West Brompton, Londres' (Beckett 1938, 1; 1965, 7). So, Beckett's own translation of a Parisian 'impasse' is a London 'mew', a word that also works between the literal and figurative.

Returning to Benjamin: his theory of good translation as literality, or *verbum pro verbo*, not only goes against the principle of translation recommended by Cicero in his *Libellus de optimo genere oratorum* but is antithetical to translation as defined by Jakobson, for whom it is to be understood in accordance with a principle of equivalence on the semantic level of the message: 'most frequently [...] translation from one language to another substitutes messages in one language not for code units but for entire messages in some other language. Such a translation is a reported speech: the translator recodes and transmits a message received from another source. Thus translation involves two equivalent messages in two different codes' (Jakobson 1987, 430). Benjamin's metaphor (in other words, his translation) for literal translation is an arcade (*Arkade*), as opposed to the wall (*Mauer*) of bad translation. To understand this metaphor, one has first to consider how he justifies his privileging of absolute literality in translation. Benjamin characterizes literality as a mode of translation that indicates or (as translated by Harry Zohn) 'points the way' towards – Benjamin's word is *hindeuten* – the suprahistorical kinship (*überhistorische Verwandtschaft*) of historically existent languages, their belonging together within, and deriving from, one suprahistorical pure language (*reine Sprache*): 'In translation the original rises to a higher and purer linguistic air, as it were. It cannot live there permanently, to be sure; neither can it reach that level in every aspect of the work. Yet in a singularly impressive manner, it at least points the way [*hindeutet*] to this region: the predestined, hitherto inaccessible realm of reconciliation and fulfillment of languages' (Benjamin 1996, 257). While all historically existent languages differ from each other in their way of meaning (*Art des Meinens*), what each of them as a whole means is 'one and the same thing' (*eines und zwar dasselbe*), namely the pure language itself. And this pure language 'no longer means or expresses anything [*nichts mehr meint und nichts mehr ausdrückt*] but is, as expressionless and creative Word, that which is meant by all languages' (Benjamin 1996, 261). Put simply, good translation points towards (*hindeutet*) the overcoming of the differences in the way of meaning between historically existent languages. Good translation is, however, only ever a 'temporary and provisional solution' (*zeitliche und vorläufige Lösung*) to this problem of difference. In its literality, good translation is not the accomplishing but rather the promise of a permanent reconciliation. What good translation promises, then, is the overcoming of foreignness (*Fremdheit*) and the realization of kinship (*Verwandtschaft*). Good translation is a kind of proleptic negation. It anticipates the permanent or final negation of foreignness and historical differences.

As an arcade rather than a wall, literality in translation leaves holes through which the relation between the pure language and the language of the original is disclosed. As the choice of the term 'arcade' itself indicates, Benjamin's theory of translation (which precedes his translations of Baudelaire) opens onto the entire Arcades project (*Passagenwerk*) of the 1930s. It is only appropriate, then, that Baudelaire's 'Rêve parisien' should be among the poems that Benjamin translates, given that in this poem Babel and the arcades are named together: 'Babel d'escaliers et d'arcades'. However, it is hardly coincidental that in translating this line as 'Gestuftes Babel von Arkaden' (Benjamin 1991, 57) Benjamin ignores his own principle of literality, tampering with the syntactical equivalence of staircases and arcades in Baudelaire's poem in order to privilege the latter by preserving its status as noun or name.

The pure language itself is situated beyond all the antagonisms of historical difference: it is the 'realm of reconciliation and fulfillment of languages' (*Versöhnungs- und Erfüllungsbereich der Sprachen*). Benjamin's celebrated figure for this pure language, a figure that has generated much commentary in recent decades, is a vessel (*Gefäß*) that has been broken into fragments (*Scherben*). Breakage, destruction – a certain negativity – is for Benjamin the very process of history itself. Much later, after destructions of a kind even Benjamin would have been hard-pressed to imagine, Adorno will write of a reconciliation in which difference is preserved as a kind of non-antagonistic indifference: 'Reconcilement [*Versöhnung*] would release the nonidentical, would rid it of coercion, including spiritualized coercion; it would open the road to the multiplicity of different things and strip dialectics of its power over them. Reconcilement would be the thought of the many as no longer inimical, a thought that is anathema to subjective reason' (Adorno 1973, 6). In 'The Task of the Translator', Benjamin undoubtedly anticipates Adorno's thought of a reconciliation beyond both history and dialectics. However, unlike Adorno's view of reconciliation as a kind of indifference, Benjamin's Messianic thought of linguistic reconciliation in the reconstructed vessel of the pure language by way of translation certainly seems to be governed by a principle of totalization.

This fundamental difference between Benjamin's position and Adorno's appears only to be increased when one analyses a little more closely Benjamin's characterization of literality in translation. Good translation's task (*Aufgabe*) is 'to release in [the translator's] own language that pure language which is exiled among alien tongues' (*Jene reine Sprache, die in fremde gebannt ist, in der eigenen zu erlösen*). Literal translation saves the pure language from its historico-linguistic diaspora. Such literality is thought by Benjamin in terms of relieving (*entbinden*), regaining (*zurückgewinnen*), releasing (*erlösen*), and liberating (*befreien*). This saving return of language to itself is good translation's 'tremendous and only capacity [*Vermögen*]': it alone can deliver the pure language from its exile in a multiplicity of foreign languages, return it to its proper place, beyond the exile of history. Even here, though, complications accrue. For instance, those historically existent languages in which the pure language is exiled themselves belong to the pure language. As we have seen, they are the unrecognized fragments of the pure language, which it is translation's task to make recognizable in their original belonging. What Benjamin refers to as the exile of the pure language is, then, something other than exile pure and simple. It is rather the passage into the unrecognized (because fragmented) same.

Now, nothing hitherto in this commentary on Benjamin's theory of translation appears to suggest that difference, alterity, or foreignness has any kind of value in it. Indeed, is Benjamin not simply the naïve (at once nostalgic and utopian) thinker of totalization and transcendence, dreaming of the broken vessel's reconstruction, the pre-Holocaust theorist whose notion of reconciliation through the negation of difference will be subjected to severe revision by an Adorno who has witnessed the horrific consequences of identity-thinking and the unchecked rhetoric of the pure? In fact, things are far from being so simple. However, in order to grasp the crucial role of foreignness and difference in Benjamin's theory of translation, one has to turn to his remarks upon a case of what he considers to be exemplary translation: Hölderlin as a translator of Sophocles. According to Benjamin, Hölderlin is the most literal of translators. Indeed, his translations of *Oedipus Tyrannus* and

Antigone were, Benjamin observes, considered 'monstrous examples of such literalness' (*monströse Beispiele solcher Wörtlichkeit*) by nineteenth-century commentators. We have seen that literal translation involves a complete disregard for the meaning (*Sinn*) of the original, and, according to Benjamin at least (though the truth of this assertion has perhaps been rather too readily accepted rather than examined in some of the commentaries on Benjamin's foreword), so little does Hölderlin respect the meaning of Sophocles' texts that his translations tend towards the madness of meaning's loss: 'in them meaning plunges [*stürtz der Sinn*] from abyss to abyss until it threatens [*droht*] to become lost in the bottomless depths of language' (Benjamin 1996, 262). Literal translations of the kind produced by Hölderlin would be characterized, then, by a linguistic alterity that is doubly foreign: foreign to both the language of the original (in this instance, Greek) and the target language (in this instance, German). The language of literal translation would resemble no historical language, would be a kind of synthetic language, akin to the languages in which, according to Beckett, Dante's *Divine Comedy* and Joyce's *Finnegans Wake* are written, languages spoken by 'no creature in heaven or earth' (Beckett 1983a, 30). In its very alterity, the language of literal translation threatens incomprehensibility, foreignness, madness. In short, it threatens a word folly.

Now, one translation for what Benjamin refers to as the 'enormous [and original] danger' (*ungeheure und ursprüngliche Gefahr*)[2] of such a loss of meaning would be *nihilism*, characterized by Nietzsche as the 'uncanniest of all guests' (*unheimlichste aller Gäste*) (Nietzsche 1968, 7). If, as Freud suggests, there is always a connection between the foreign and the familiar in the uncanny, then it should perhaps not be all that surprising that Benjamin's inclusion of the threat of nihilism in his theory of literal translation heralds a highly paradoxical turn towards an economy of tragicomic sacrifice. Twice in his essay, Benjamin refers to the threat of literal translation (see Benjamin 1996, 260, 262). Literality of the Hölderlinian kind loosens the attachment of meaning to language to such an extent that it threatens unintelligibility, alterity, madness, meaning's disappearance. It is clear, then, that literal translation threatens nihilism, thought by Hölderlin in his ode 'Bread and Wine' (1802), to which Benjamin alludes, as the meantime (*indessen*) of a mean time (*dürftige Zeit*). But, crucially, if literality threatens (*droht*) nihilism, it also points towards or promises (*hindeutet*) that which lies beyond nihilism, beyond history, beyond both the history of nihilism and the nihilism of history. Nihilism, then, as meaning's loss, is itself both a threat and a promise here. The tragicomic economy of literal translation involves both *drohen* and *hindeuten*, both the threat of nihilism's consummation (meaning's loss) and the promise of nihilism's overcoming (the return to itself of the suprahistorical pure language).

If nihilism is the risk of literal translation, this risk is not to be underestimated. Indeed, Benjamin emphasizes that the threat of meaning's loss can lead to silence, to the death of the work: 'Hölderlin's translations from Sophocles were his last work' (Benjamin 1996, 262). That said, the promise is no less great, since meaning's plunge can be interrupted, the leap from consummation to overcoming achieved, the production of the sacred realized: 'There is, however, a stop [*Halten*]. It is vouchsafed in Holy Writ alone, in which meaning has ceased to be the watershed for the flow of language and the flow of revelation' (Benjamin 1996, 262). This interruption of meaning's plunge, this leap from meaning to revelation, is the interruption of history itself. It is an interruption that can happen at any time, if one accepts that the present (as *Jetztzeit*) is, as Benjamin puts it almost 20 years later, in 'On the Concept of History' (1940), 'shot through with splinters of messianic time', such that every second is 'the small gateway in time through which the Messiah might enter' (Benjamin 2003, 397). In a highly paradoxical fashion, then, the stop (*Halten*) to which Benjamin refers is at once the interruption of translation and the fulfilment of its promise. The sacred text differs from the poetic or literary text in that its literality is united with its truth (*Wahrheit*) or doctrine (*Lehre*), 'without any mediating sense' (*ohne vermittelnden Sinn*) (Benjamin 1996, 262). So it is that the interlinear version of the sacred text produces truth immediately, without any detour by way of meaning. If this interlinear version is the 'prototype or ideal of all translation' (*Urbild oder Ideal aller Übersetzung*) (Benjamin 1996, 263), it is precisely because it marks both nihilism's consummation (the abandonment of meaning) and its overcoming (the immediate production of truth in the letter of the text): manner and matter, body and spirit, reconciled, the immediacy of madness having, in the *Jetztzeit*, beyond any dialectic, become the immediacy of sacred revelation. For Benjamin, then, the task (*Aufgabe*) of translation is a highly paradoxical dispatching (*aufgeben*), at once a threatening and a promising, a sending and a rendering. In literal translation, it is nihilism itself that is dispatched. By *dispatching* here is to be understood the tragicomic economy of threat and promise. The threatening madness of purely literal translation is also the promise of that which lies beyond the literal madness of history.

What might become of such a theory of translation when it is, in its turn, dispatched into foreign languages – into French or English, for instance? If Benjamin theorizes good translation as a *dispatching of nihilism*, when we turn to the commentaries on Benjamin's essay by Blanchot, de Man, and Derrida we find another kind of dispatching taking place, namely the recurrent attempt to subordinate Benjamin the thinker of the Messianic (that is, Benjamin the thinker of reconciliation, harmony, utopia, the end of history, the negation of all antagonistic difference, the overcoming of nihilism) to Benjamin the thinker of difference, alterity, and foreignness, as though the two did not have to be thought together. For what tends to be obscured as a result of this dispatching of Benjamin is precisely the strange economy of translation as that which both threatens nihilism and promises its overcoming. And yet, in an irony the significance of which is far from easy to calculate, the attempts made by Blanchot, de Man, and Derrida to save the Benjamin who thinks translation as difference and alterity from the Benjamin who thinks Messianic reconciliation and fulfilment are themselves part of a more general programme that is in fact Benjamin's own, namely the argument for literature (or, in Derrida's case, for a certain writing) as a form of resistance to nihilism. And this, as we shall see, is the case even when nihilism is explicitly invoked (as it is by de Man) as a necessary moment within translation.

Translation and originary difference: Blanchot reading Benjamin

Maurice Blanchot concludes his essay 'The Time of Encyclopedias' (in the 1971 collection *Friendship*) with the laconic phrase: 'Translating, the bringing into "work" of difference' (*Traduire, mise en 'œuvre' de la différence*) (Blanchot 1997a, 56), and in the following essay ('Translating') he proceeds unequivocally to privilege the Benjamin who theorizes translation in terms of difference over the Benjamin who theorizes it within the Messianic horizon of reconciliation, harmony, and fulfilment. For Blanchot, this second Benjamin is present simply as the naïve dreamer of a naïve past, enraptured and mystified by the utopian thought of that past's return: 'In the past, one believed it possible thus to return to some originary language [*langage originaire*], the supreme language that needed only to speak in order to speak truly. Benjamin retains something of this dream' (Blanchot 1997b, 58). The other Benjamin, however, Benjamin the thinker of difference and alterity, is the figure with whom Blanchot would have us dwell. Indeed, so privileged is this Benjamin that the strange logic of translation (whereby it depends upon that very difference of languages which it is also its aim to reduce if not to abolish) is itself threatened by Blanchot when he insists that translation only *appears* to aim at the negation of difference: 'every translation is founded upon this difference [of languages] even while pursuing, or so it appears [*apparemment*], the perverse design of suppressing it' (Blanchot 1997b, 58). Paradoxically, then, Blanchot aims to save Benjamin from the thought of salvation. However, in order to achieve this, he has to resort very quickly to an absolute hyperbole, to the nihilation of all degree, passing beyond the hesitation of *apparemment* to the certainty of *nullement*, the unambiguous truth of an absolute negation: 'In fact [*À la vérité*] translation is not at all [*nullement*] intended to make the difference [between original and translation] disappear – it is, on the contrary, the play of this difference [...] translation is the very life of this difference' (Blanchot 1997b, 58). Here, the word *nullement* is Blanchot's own nihilating translation of Benjamin as the thinker of both the threat and the promise of translation. Benjamin is dispatched to us by way of that *nullement*, anticipated as it is by an *apparemment*. And this dispatching occurs without any time being given to Benjamin's own practice of translation.

Once the naïve thought of the Messianic return of the naïve has been dispatched by the thought of difference, once the sacred has been dispatched by the poetic (*Dichtung*), once Benjamin has been saved from himself, he can become the thinker not just of difference as the effect of a fall – the moment of Babel, and the linguistic diaspora that it represents, as the beginning of history itself – but the thinker of difference as originary or, more precisely, as *always already*. The translator becomes 'the secret master of the difference of languages, not in order to abolish the difference but in order to use it to awaken in his own language, through the violent or subtle changes he brings to it, a presence of what is different, originally, in the original [*une présence de ce qu'il y a de différent, originellement, dans l'original*]' (Blanchot 1997b, 59). The very difference between the native and the foreign cannot withstand the force of translation as it is theorized through Blanchot's dispatching of Benjamin.

Hölderlin's translations now disclose the truth that difference, as 'pure scission', is always 'prior' (Blanchot 1997b, 61), always already present in language. In other words, for Blanchot's non-naïve Benjamin, in the beginning was not the Word, but *in other words*. The original is always already foreign to itself. The pure or selfsame language is always already divided from itself. However, it takes the madness of good translation to disclose this always-already. And, for Blanchot, good translation is quite simply literature. Through Blanchot's hyperbolizing dispatching of

Benjamin, then, literature has become that scripture which saves us from Scripture, a desacralizing translation forever at odds with any *reine Sprache*.

Translation as literature: de Man reading Benjamin

Like Blanchot before him, in his late essay on Benjamin's 'Task of the Translator' Paul de Man attempts to save the Benjamin who thinks translation in terms of absolute difference from the Benjamin who thinks it in terms of the Messianic and the pure language as the place of reconciliation and harmony. Like Blanchot before him, de Man aims to save Benjamin from a theory of salvation, and to save literature from the sacred (*heilig*). Unlike Blanchot, however, de Man remains tellingly indecisive when it comes to identifying the origin of this theory of translation as salvation. On the one hand, he argues, like Blanchot before him, that it comes from Benjamin's own text, even if Benjamin is actually trying to save himself from it: the Messianic is there, de Man states, 'as a desire in Benjamin'. On the other hand, he argues that the Messianic comes very much from beyond Benjamin, in the form of an 'unhappy misinterpretation' of his work, principally by Gershom Scholem, who, de Man says in the discussion following his paper, 'deliberately tried to make Benjamin say the opposite of what he said for ends of his own' (de Man 1986a, 103).

The Benjamin that de Man would dispatch to us is the thinker of translation as disarticulation, decanonization, and desacralization. Translation becomes that activity which grants us a 'negative knowledge' of the relation between poetic and sacred language (de Man 1986a, 92). In another late essay, 'The Resistance to Theory', de Man identifies this negative knowledge as specific to the literary (de Man 1986b, 10), and it is clear that translation (*Über-setzung*), metaphor (*meta-phorein*), and literature are thought together by de Man in terms of this negative knowledge. Translation as literature is de Man's *in other words*, and, at the heart of this particular *in other words* is the claim that translation as literature is demystifying (it demystifies us regarding the rhetoricity of language) but not liberating, since the knowledge it grants us is negative in the sense that no new system or order of knowledge can be built upon it. Rather, it leaves us only to repeat the experience of negative knowing – which is not to be mistaken for unknowing – through the reading of literature. In his essay on Benjamin, de Man provocatively names this negative knowledge 'nihilism' (de Man 1986a, 92, 103–4). If translation (as metaphor) is itself a metaphor for literature, then literature in its turn is a metaphor for nihilism. For de Man, then, literature is nihilism, but, crucially, a nihilism that saves us from that real nihilism which lies in canonization, sacralization, Messianism, soteriology – in short, the nihilism of any final solution, of any final and absolute integration, of that identity-thinking which would abolish all difference and is, according to Adorno, radically evil.

However, in order to dispatch to us a Benjamin who thinks translation as a kind of nihilism that would save us from real nihilism, de Man has himself to translate him. And, as always when it comes to translation, de Man's choice of other words is far from being simply unmotivated. Indeed, one might argue that it is no less motivated than Scholem's, whose reading of Benjamin he is so quick to dismiss. This motivation is evident from the outset in de Man's insistence that the word *Aufgabe* (translated by Harry Zohn as 'task') can, and indeed should, also be taken to mean 'giving up', and that this immediately alerts us to the impossibility of translation. Now, while this particular *in other words* of *Aufgabe* may not be wrong, it is a selection that would none the less blind us to some of the other semantic possibilities borne by the German word. For, in addition to both 'task' and 'giving up', *Aufgabe* can also mean 'sending', 'handing-in', 'rendering', and 'dispatch', and is thus also and already a translation of translation (*Übersetzung*), since translation itself can, of course, take the form of a dispatching into other words of the other's words. One could therefore translate Benjamin's title 'Die Aufgabe des Übersetzers' as 'The Translation of Translation', but with translation signifying not just disarticulation and failure ('giving up') but also sending in the sense of the Messianic: translation as *dispatching*, then. It is precisely this play of the two translations of translation that de Man chooses to think ethically when he writes of Benjamin's 'extraordinarily refined and deliberate strategy' (de Man 1986a, 103) to save us from the Messianic and the sacred – in other words, his reduction to nothing of the Messianic.

That de Man chooses to call this salvation from the very idea of salvation 'nihilism' should not be all that surprising, given that nihilism is thought as countering nihilism even by Nietzsche, as de Man himself observes in the discussion following the delivery of his paper: 'In the same way that in Nietzsche nihilism is a necessary stage, and is accounted for in those terms. Understand by nihilism a certain kind of critical awareness which will not allow you to make certain affirmative statements when those affirmative statements go against the way things are' (de Man 1986a, 103–4). That everything in this attempt to save Benjamin the thinker of difference, error, and negative knowledge from

Benjamin the thinker of the Messianic, utopia, harmony, and reconciliation, depends upon translation, upon an *in other words* that recuperates the thought of nihilism, is evident not just from de Man's countering translation of the word *Aufgabe*, but also from his reflections upon what, following the lead of Carol Jacobs,³ he sees as the failings of Harry Zohn's translation of the passage in Benjamin's essay where the translation and the original are compared to the fragments (*Scherben*) of a broken vessel. Again, de Man insists upon absolute difference between the translation and the original on the one hand, and the pure language on the other; which is to say, again he insists upon the absolute difference between literature and Scripture: 'any work is totally fragmented in relation to this *reine Sprache*, with which it has nothing in common' (de Man 1986a, 91).

'Nothing in common': like Blanchot before him, de Man hyperbolizes Benjamin, insisting upon absolute difference. That this hyperbolization requires a certain blindness is evident when we consider de Man's reading of Benjamin on what happens in literal translation. According to de Man, Benjamin conceives of literal translation as accomplishing the absolute disappearance of meaning, with language being disclosed as essentially 'inhuman'. Leaving out of account Benjamin's own translations of Baudelaire, de Man focuses instead on Hölderlin's translations of Sophocles, which, he claims, are 'totally unintelligible', 'completely incomprehensible'; the meaning simply 'disappears'; 'all control over meaning is lost' (de Man 1986a, 88). As we have seen, however, even if one believes this to be true of Hölderlin's translations (something that does not go without saying), one might argue that this is precisely what Benjamin does not say. According to Benjamin, it is the sacred text that does not mean anything, since it operates without the mediation of meaning (*Sinn*). Of Hölderlin's translations, however, Benjamin states that they loosen meaning to such an extent that it 'plunges from abyss to abyss until it threatens [*droht*] to become lost in the bottomless depths of language' (Benjamin 1996, 262). Not the absolute loss of meaning, then, as de Man suggests, but the *threat* of its absolute loss.

It is as though, mimicking Sophocles' Oedipus, de Man blinds himself to the word *drohen* in Benjamin's foreword, and to the threat it poses to his own argument. Furthermore, when he states that for Benjamin sacred language (Scripture) has 'nothing in common' with 'poetic language' (scripture) (de Man 1986a, 91), he is seeing a pure scission where Benjamin thinks a stop (*Halten*) that is also a strange reversal. For what poetic and sacred language have in common is precisely that they belong together within the thought of translation as both threat and promise, plunging and indicating. If de Man is counter-translating Benjamin here, insisting that *Halten* be translated not as 'stop' but as 'holding on' (de Man 1986a, 104), a 'holding on' to the thought of meaning's plunge, he is also nihilating something in Benjamin's text, blinding both himself and his reader to something in that text, in order to save Benjamin as the thinker of translation as desacralization, decanonization, and disarticulation, and of literature as that which can save us from the dream of salvation. In other words, de Man is blinding himself to, or perhaps being blinded by, the uncanniness of the very nihilism he would deploy in his theory of literature as negative knowledge.

The aporia of translation: Derrida reading Benjamin

The question of translation is broached early in Derrida's work. In an interview with Julia Kristeva in 1968, he argues that 'In the limits to which it is possible, or at least *appears* possible, translation practices the difference between signified and signifier. But if this difference is never pure, no more so is translation, and for the notion of translation we would have to substitute a notion of *transformation*' (Derrida 1981b, 20). At first glance, the kind of literal translation theorized by Benjamin might appear to be an exception to this law. However, even such a practice of absolutely literal translation would have to be grounded in a clear distinction between signifier and signified, letter and meaning, if only so that it can proceed to disregard the latter.

Whereas de Man insists upon the absolute difference between poetic language and sacred language, Derrida insists upon the aporia of translation, its being at once necessary and impossible. This aporia is what Derrida terms the 'Babelian situation' (Derrida 1988, 125). The story of the Tower of Babel, he states early in 'Des Tours de Babel' (1980), 'recounts, among other things, the origin of the confusion of tongues, the irreducible multiplicity of idioms [*la multiplicité des idiomes*], the necessary and impossible task of translation, its necessity *as* impossibility' (Derrida 2002b, 109). If translation is at once necessary and impossible, then this is owing to a difference that is irreducible. If, as is in fact the case, the word 'irreducible' (*irréductible*) does not appear *literally* in the original French of the above-quoted passage, the translator having introduced it there, it does appear earlier in Derrida's essay: 'The "tower of Babel" does not merely figure the irreducible multiplicity [*multiplicité irréductible*] of tongues; it exhibits an incompletion, the impossibility of finishing, of totalizing, of saturating, of completing something on the order of edification, architectural construction, system and architectonics' (Derrida 2002b, 104). By 'irreducible multiplicity', Derrida means not that there exists a plurality of distinct languages, each possessing an essential idiomaticity or uniqueness, but rather that no language is ever simply one language, intact and self-identical. Like both Blanchot and de Man, he sees Benjamin conceiving of the original as always already open to an unmasterable alterity that comes not from without but from within: 'if the original calls for a complement, it is because at the origin it was not there without fault, full, complete, total, identical with itself. From the origin of the original to be translated there is fall and exile' (Derrida 2002b, 121).

However, to Derrida's reading of 'Babel' as the figure for antitotalization, for the irreducibility of a difference – more precisely, a *différance* – that is always already at work in any language, one might respond that one of the 'other things' the story of Babel recounts is precisely the nihilation of alterity, since it involves God's denial of limitless power to the other (in this instance, 'the children of men'):

> And the Lord came down to see the city and the tower, which the children of men builded.
> And the Lord said, Behold, the people is one, and they have all one language; and this they begin to do: and now *nothing will be restrained from them, which they have imagined to do*.
> Go to, let us go down, and there confound their language, that they may not understand one another's speech. (Genesis 11: 5–7; emphasis added)

Furthermore, if we accept Derrida's notion of the aporia of translation, its being both necessary and impossible, then one might ask what the difference is, if there is one, between necessity and obligation here, given that Derrida also sees this necessity as a 'command' (Derrida 2002b, 133).

If there is a fundamental difference between Derrida's position on translation and those taken by Blanchot and de Man, it lies in an undecidability that characterizes the difference within the original. This undecidability emerges briefly when Derrida supplies examples to show difference already at work: the phrase 'he war' in *Finnegans Wake* (1939)[4] and the word 'Babel' itself. If these examples are rather disappointing, it is because they are hardly instances of the ostensibly monolingual. That said, Derrida's introduction of undecidability at least leaves open the possibility that the original might be intact, despite all his insistence on its being always already multiple: 'at the very moment when pronouncing "Babel" we sense the impossibility of deciding [*l'impossibilité de décider*] whether this name belongs, properly and simply, to *one* tongue' (Derrida 2002b, 111). Even here, though, the emphasis falls squarely upon impossibility and necessity: at once the impossibility and the necessity of decision.

Now, we have seen that in Benjamin's theory of translation a place remains open for integrity and the reconciliation of all antagonisms (of all 'he war'), and the name of this place is the sacred text, which he describes as 'unconditionally translatable' (*übersetzbar schlechthin*), translatability itself, the interlinear version of the sacred text being 'the prototype or ideal of all translations' (Benjamin 1996, 262–3), that end to which translation points. It is precisely this promise of reconciliation that Derrida, like Blanchot and de Man, aims to challenge, through dispatching Benjamin in such a way as to grant an absolute privilege to a difference that is both always already there and irreducible. So it is that Derrida concludes aporetically by insisting that the sacred depends upon translation, although translation is also that which renders the sacred impossible. For both de Man and Derrida, then, we can at least know both the impossibility of translation and the irreducibility of difference.

The ethical and the unethical in translation

In each of the three readings of Benjamin's essay analysed above, translation is presented as a practice or an event in which an irreducible difference is disclosed, a difference that precedes all identity and survives all labours of identification. Alterity is always already there in the original, even if it takes translation to reveal it. An ethical practice of translation would aim to respect this alterity. An unethical practice of translation would denegate it. This would also be the case for any theory of translation. As we have seen, however, the very insistence upon an irreducible difference, in each of the three readings of Benjamin's essay analysed above, itself involves a denegation of the interplay between threat and promise that characterizes the role of nihilism (meaning's disappearance) in Benjamin's theory of translation. Paradoxically, then, the ethical insistence upon irreducible alterity appears to be the unethical moment in Blanchot's, de Man's, and Derrida's readings of Benjamin.

Not only do they all ground their readings of Benjamin's essay in the identification of irreducible difference, but none of them considers Benjamin's foreword on translation in relation to his own practice of translation. By avoiding any consideration of this relation between his theory and his practice of translation, they miss Benjamin's own problematization of literal translation. The kind of translation advocated by Benjamin is, of course, possible only if the translator is in a position to see the literal in the original. That such a seeing of the literal – and indeed a seeing of the difference between the ethical and the unethical in translation – is not necessarily as straightforward a matter as one might imagine is precisely what is suggested by Benjamin's own translation of Baudelaire's sonnet 'Les Aveugles'.

Blindness and desacralization:
Benjamin translating Baudelaire

As its title suggests, 'Les Aveugles' is a poem that would thematize seeing and not seeing in the most explicit – the most visible – manner. More precisely, it is a poem that asks what, if anything, remains to be seen in that sky once populated by the gods; in other words, what, if anything, remains to be seen in the time of nihilism, the Hölderlinian *indessen* of the gods' absence. In the context of its translation by Benjamin, then, the poem refers us back to Hölderlin's translations of Sophocles, and in particular to his translation of *Oedipus Tyrannus*, in which, of course, blindness and the translation of signs will have a not insignificant role to play, in conjunction with a radical desacralization in the form of a killing of the father, king, origin, and original (*arche*). Indeed, Benjamin's practice of translation suggests that Sophocles' play might itself be about nothing other than translation and the ethics of translation, treating the question of whether it is ever ethical to dispatch the *arche* or *logos*, whether self-blinding is a kind of self-translation, a translation of self-translation, disclosing a nihilism at the very heart of translation.

At first glance, Benjamin's translation of Baudelaire's poem appears to effect a very literal, perhaps even an all too crudely literal, desacralization of the original, through a sequence of omissions, additions, and modifications:

Les Aveugles

Contemple-les, mon âme; ils sont vraiment affreux!
Pareils aux mannequins; vaguement ridicules;
Terribles, singuliers comme les somnambules;
Dardant on ne sait où leurs globes ténébreux.

Leurs yeux, d'où la divine étincelle est partie,
Comme s'ils regardaient au loin, restent levés
Au ciel; on ne les voit jamais vers les pavés
Pencher rêveusement leur tête appesantie.

Ils traversent ainsi le noir illimité,
Ce frère du silence éternel. O cité!
Pendant qu'autour de nous tu chantes, ris et beugles,
Éprise du plaisir jusqu'à l'atrocité,
Vois! je me traîne aussi! mais, plus qu'eux hébété,
Je dis: Que cherchent-ils au Ciel, tous ces aveugles?

Die Blinden

Betrachte sie, mein Herz; sie sind ein Grauen!
Den Gliederpuppen ähnlich; grundlos komisch;
Wie Somnambulen sind sie physiognomisch:
Wohin ergeht nur ihr umwölktes Schauen?

Ihr Augenpaar aus dem der Funke wich
Blieb mit fernspähender Geberde
Geöffnet stehn; nie sieht man sie zur Erde
Das Haupt gewendet und versenkt in sich.

Sie gehn durchs grenzenloseste Verließ
Den Bruder ewgen Schweigens. O Paris
Wo wir uns vom Gejohl begraben finden

Du welches Brunst zur Bestie werden ließ
Sieh her! so schleich auch ich! doch nahm mich dies
Oft Wunder: Was verrät sich Dort den Blinden?

(Benjamin 1991, 38–9)

Here one sees Benjamin not only dispatching the religious language of the original in a very systematic manner, but also de-energizing and desublimating the poem, rendering it altogether more earthly and secular. In line 1, 'mon âme' (my soul) becomes 'mein Herz' (my heart); in line 3, 'terribles, singuliers' (terrible, singular) all but disappears; in line 4, 'dardant' (flashing or shooting forth) becomes 'ergeht' (issues forth), and 'ténébreux' (dark, but referring us to *ténèbres* or *tenebrae*) becomes 'umwölktes' (clouded); in line 5, 'divine étincelle' (divine spark) becomes 'Funke' (spark); in lines 6–7, 'levés / Au ciel' (raised to the sky) becomes 'Geöffnet stehn' (stand open); in line 8, 'Pencher rêveusement' (incline dreamily) becomes 'zur Erde [...] gewendet' (turned towards the earth); in line 9, 'le noir illimité' (the limitless dark) becomes 'das grenzenloseste Verließ' (the most limitless abandonment); in line 11, Benjamin adds the idea of being buried ('begraben finden'); and, in line 14, 'Ciel' (Heaven) becomes 'Dort' (There).

But if Benjamin's translation enacts a literal desacralization of Baudelaire's poem, there appears to be scarcely any literality (*Wörtlichkeit*) of the kind he proposes in his foreword as the essence of good translation. There is very little evidence here of Benjamin producing a literal rendering of the syntax rather than transposing it to suit the target language. For instance, in line 2, 'Pareils aux mannequins' (like mannequins) is dispatched as 'Den Gliederpuppen ähnlich', rather than as the syntactically more literal 'ähnlich den Gliederpuppen'. And, in line 4, 'Dardant on ne sait où' (shooting one knows not where) becomes the unexceptionable 'Wohin ergeht nur'. Benjamin's practice of translation here is in principle closer, then, to Wright's than to Brodsky's translation of Beckett.

The relation between translation and original becomes rather less easy to read, however, when one turns to Benjamin's translation of the last two lines of Baudelaire's poem, which begin 'Vois!' ('Sieh her!'), hardly an insignificant command in a poem about blindness. In the 1860 version of the poem, published in *L'Artiste*, this 'Vois!' appears as 'Moi'; by 1868, the self in this poem has undergone its own translation, becoming the imperative to see. 'Vois!' – a command to see, then; but can we tell who is being called upon to see at this moment? The addressee of this imperative would appear to be the city itself, translated as a proper name by Benjamin. But who could say with any degree of certainty that the addressee of this imperative to see might not also be the reader, or the speaker himself, or the translator, or indeed the blind, as though both poetry and translation were precisely a calling upon the blind to see?

That these speculations are not simply to be dismissed is suggested by the fact that the poem's speaker compares himself to the blind. The speaker comparing himself to his subject, and thereby making of the poem quite explicitly a poem about the poet and poetry, is a gesture that is characteristic of many poems in *Les Fleurs du mal*. What is noteworthy in this particular instance, however, is both the similarity and the difference between the poet and the blind. The difference is introduced by the 'mais' ('doch') in the penultimate line of the poem: 'mais plus qu'eux hébété, / Je dis: Que cherchent-ils au Ciel, tous ces aveugles?' How is this to be translated? That there is a real problem for any translator of these last lines, despite their apparent lexical and syntactical simplicity, is evident from the range of English translations that they have elicited, some of which are little short of astonishing in their not even registering the command to see:

> But stumbling through the light I wonder what
> The blind keep looking for up in the skies?
> (Baudelaire 1997, 241;
> trans. Walter Martin)

> whereas I ...
> I too drag by, but wonder, duller still,
> what Heaven holds for them, all these blind men?
> (Baudelaire 1982, 97;
> trans. Richard Howard)
>
> see! I too drag myself along! But, more bewildered even than them, I say: What are they seeking in Heaven, all these blind men?
> (Rees 1992, 19;
> trans. William Rees)
>
> Look at me! Dragging, dazed more than their kind.
> What in the skies can these men hope to find?
> (Baudelaire 1998, 188;
> trans. James McGowan)

Although this may not have been his intention, McGowan's translation 'Look at me!' effectively translates both the 'Vois!' and the original 'Moi', granting the reader a synchronic vision of the poem's genesis; however, this translation also strips the poem of any possible ambiguity as to what the addressee of the imperative is being called upon to see, syntactically connecting the 'Vois!' and the 'je', which are merely juxtaposed in the original. In addition to the problems they experience when faced with the imperative 'Vois!', a command to see that some of them do not appear to see, the translators also vary considerably in their translation of the verb *chercher*. To translate it as 'looking for' (as Martin does) is particularly hazardous, given that it refers to the blind and therefore is presumably not to be taken literally, but both 'holds for' (Howard), which renders the blind passive, and 'hope to find' (McGowan) depart considerably from the apparently most literal translation: 'seeking' (Rees), which still retains the notion of *chercher* as a kind of seeing, to both eye and ear.

However, none of these translations is as adventurous as Benjamin's: 'doch nahm mich dies / Oft Wunder: Was verrät sich Dort den Blinden?' (but I have often wondered at this: What reveals itself There to the blind?). Gone is the sense of idiocy, stupidity, or even intoxication communicated by the word 'hébété'. Gone, too, is any comparison between the speaker and the blind. In their place is the sense of the miraculous, the marvellous, the astonishing, together with the source of wonder being not Heaven (*Ciel*) but 'There' (*Dort*), a deixis that would, of course, be particularly difficult for the blind to interpret. It is as though Baudelaire's blind have been granted sight by Benjamin, as though 'There' is enough for them. And this bestowal of sight, this unblinding of Baudelaire's 'aveugles', is reinforced by Benjamin's dispatching of 'cherchent-ils' as 'verrät sich'. Not only does the verb *verraten* introduce the thought of betrayal (*Verrat*) into the translation, and thus the familiar play on *tradutorre/traditore*, but it also changes everything by presupposing that there is indeed something that manifests itself (*verrät sich*), makes itself visible there, to the blind. If there is uncertainty in Benjamin's translation, then it is the speaker's uncertainty as to *what* is seen, not whether there is anything to be seen.

'Que cherchent-ils au Ciel, tous ces aveugles?' How is one to read this question?

On the one hand, Baudelaire's poem seems to end with a very Hölderlinian question, and one that Benjamin, who in his foreword has identified Hölderlin as the literal translator *par excellence*, does not ask: What remains to be seen in a sky from which the gods have fled? Surely only the blind, only those from whose eyes the divine spark (*divine étincelle*) has departed, would look for something where there is nothing. Only the blind (in other words, only the naïve) would not see that there is nothing to be seen now in that empty *Ciel* reflecting their empty eyes. Only the blind would not see that we moderns, we inhabitants of the *cité*, find ourselves in the time of nihilism, the time of history, the *indessen* of the gods' absence. And is it not this very blindness to the nothing-to-be-seen that prevents any passage beyond nihilism, beyond the nihilism which consists precisely in looking for something where there is nothing, in failing to *see* that there is in fact nothing to be seen?

On the other hand, however, the poet's question, 'Que cherchent-ils au Ciel, tous ces aveugles?', might be read to mean: What are the blind looking for? Is there something there? Did the gods never leave? And am I, the poet, the one who fails to see them, the one who is in fact blinder than they, just as I am 'plus qu'eux hébété'? Can only those who are literally blind, or those who are blind to the literal, or those who, like Oedipus, have practised self-blinding (in other words, self-translation), see something there where this poet sees nothing? Is blindness to the literal the precondition of seeing, of being able to read, and of being able to translate? In other words, is translation, as self-blinding to the literal, perhaps the act by which true seeing is accomplished?

What is negated in Benjamin's dispatching of Baudelaire's poem is the indecision within the original as to how that final question is to be read, the indecision between threat and promise, a doubt that does not necessarily unite threat and promise in a tragicomic economy. And this translation of the original is not so surprising, if also not so ethical, since Benjamin's own theory of translation depends upon the translator being in a position to distinguish clearly the literal from the non-literal. From this one might argue that, were he to *see* this indecision in Baudelaire's poem, then Benjamin would have to reopen the question of whether one can ever be sure that one is seeing or not seeing the literal. But then who has the authority to rule out the possibility that Benjamin himself wishes to have us, his would-be readers, see what happens to his own theory of literal translation when it is put into practice, not least when it is put into practice on a poem entitled 'Les Aveugles'?

Anethical translation

Having watched Benjamin translating Baudelaire one is left, then, with the question of who, if anyone, is seeing, and where, if anywhere, the literal might be. Perhaps translation is nothing other than the opening of this question. Were that the case, then Umberto Eco's declaration of the ethical obligation that governs translation proper – that the translator must respect 'what the author has written' – becomes less a point of departure than a stumbling-block. And Benjamin's practice of translating 'Les Aveugles' casts doubt, too, on Blanchot, de Man, and Derrida's belief that translation discloses an irreducible difference preceding all identity. By insisting upon such an irreducible difference within the original, by conceiving of translation in terms of necessity and impossibility, they underestimate the difficulties involved in determining whether alterity is there at all, and if so, where. Beyond this, they underestimate the difficulties involved in determining what it might mean to respect or disrespect this alterity, not to mention how one might justify this alterity as a value, and thereby make of it the foundation for an ethics.

In the wake of Benjamin's translation of 'Les Aveugles', one is left with neither a theory nor a practice of ethical and unethical translation, but rather with the thought of what might be termed *anethical* translation. The prefix *an-* serves a double purpose here, indicating both 'privation' in the manner of the Greek *an-* (a productive prefix; as in 'analgesia') and also 'by way of' in the manner of the Latin *an-* (a non-productive prefix; as in 'announce' or 'annul'). In its anethicality, translation would take place in the meantime between theory and practice, between the poetic (*Dichtung*) and the sacred (*heilig*), between difference and reconciliation. Through this particular 'in other words', the distinction between seeing and not seeing, between the literal and the figurative, between nihilism and resistance to nihilism, would be dispatched to us in such a manner as to unsettle, if only in passing, any sense of where value might lie, and of what is ethical or unethical in any given act of translation, however respectful or disrespectful that act might appear to be. With this thought of the anethical in mind, we may now turn to consider what is undoubtedly one of the most remarkable instances of self-translation in modern literature.

2
Translation and Negation
Beckett and the Bilingual *Œuvre*

Telling 'translation proper'

How is one to tell whether a given text is a translation or, more precisely, whether it is the result of what Roman Jakobson terms 'interlingual translation' or 'translation proper' (Jakobson 1987, 429)? If this is a question only rarely asked in translation studies, it remains of some importance despite its apparent naïvety, since only when a text has been satisfactorily identified as the result of such a practice can one begin to analyse translation effects as distinct from other kinds of intertextual effect. Clearly, even a close resemblance between two texts in two languages is not enough to guarantee that the relationship between these texts is one of translation proper. Something more is needed. According to Jakobson, this something more is an intentional act of interpretation, across the limited difference between two historically existent languages – French and English, for instance. Now, there are two very obvious ways, one external, the other internal, in which this intentional act is generally indicated, and both of them bear upon the ethics of translation.

If a given text is the result of translation proper, one can expect – and this is in most instances both a legal and an ethical expectation – an explicit and very literal stating of the fact accompanying the text. Such a statement (a *translated from* and/or *translated by*) would be external to the translation in the sense that it would not translate anything in the original, even if that original is itself already a translation. In some cases, however, in addition to such an external designation, the translator may also have inscribed the translatedness of the text within the translation itself, producing a work that marks or remarks upon itself as a translation: a kind of translationese, the defamiliarizing effect of which would be to remind the reader not only that the text in hand is a translation, but also that one language cannot simply be mapped unproblematically onto another, that there is not necessarily any general principle of equivalence between languages. Not only would this internal marking be rather less common than the external designation, but, depending on the theory of translation being applied, it might even be considered undesirable. If, as is most often the case, the translator's aim is for the translated text to read as though it had been written in the target language, any such internal marking would of course be a sign of bad or failed translation. Be it external or internal, however, the mark of translation would always point elsewhere: to an original text that would necessarily precede the translation. That said, these two forms of referral back to the original do not necessarily guarantee the ethicality of the translation, if ethicality is defined as respect for the other in its otherness. For, insofar as it assumes a principle of general equivalence between languages, translation risks the unethical at every moment, and this risk is all the greater for the fact that translation raises the question of who has the authority to judge whether – and, if so, where – the alterity of the original has been respected in translation.

If the guaranteed ethicality or unethicality of a given translation remains far from easy to determine, even when that translation is marked as a translation externally and/or internally, what is one to make, for instance, of Samuel Beckett's translation of Proust, which in some instances contains neither a framing designation nor any obvious internal marking: no quotation marks, no italics, no evident translationese? Such a practice would certainly appear to be unethical in the extreme, since it would not even acknowledge the existence of the original, let alone respect the differences between languages.

Covert translation: Beckett translating Proust

There are two preliminary objections that might be made to any analysis of Beckett as a translator of Proust. The first is that, unlike Walter Benjamin, Beckett never published a translation of any of Proust's works.[1] What this objection leaves out of account, however, is that in his first book-length publication, the 1931 monograph on Proust's *À la recherche du temps perdu*, not only does Beckett include explicit translations from Proust's novel, contained within quotation marks and identified in Beckett's foreword as his own, but he also engages in acts of undisclosed, fragmentary, and highly condensing translation, a kind of dispatching that, while bearing a close resemblance to what Jakobson defines as 'translation proper', is quite unlike the regulated and ostensibly respectful translation of Proust subsequently undertaken by Scott Moncrieff and Terence Kilmartin.[2] Leslie Hill sees the covertness of Beckett's translation of Proust 'almost as a token of his respect for the Proustian text and his detachment from it' (Hill 1990b, 165), but what, one might ask, would it mean for something to be *almost* a token of respect? It would perhaps be more accurate, or at least less rhetorically evasive, to describe the effect of Beckett's practice of translation in *Proust* as a putting into question of the very distinction between respect and disrespect, ethicality and unethicality, in the translation of another.

Even if one accepts that Beckett is a covert translator of Proust, however, it might still be objected that the analysis of Beckett as a translator of others is a far cry from any analysis of his activities as a self-translator, and it is the latter that the majority of commentators have taken to be the most significant side to Beckett's practice of translation, if not his practice as a writer. However, this second objection takes for granted an assumption that is subjected to unremitting pressure in Beckett's *œuvre*, namely that a clear and systematic distinction can be maintained between self and other, identity and difference, and thus between translation and self-translation. Furthermore, Beckett's dispatching of *À la recherche du temps perdu* is hardly extrinsic to his own practice as a writer of literary texts, the evidence for this being that some of the key statements in *Proust*, statements that are in fact examples of Beckett the translator, have repeatedly been taken by commentators as expressions of his own theory of art and literature. Not least among these is the following description of the voice of Proust's narrator's grandmother on the telephone, part of a sequence in which the birth of aesthetic expression is related to a negation that takes the form of the speaker's death, as though this death were itself the precondition of art:

> a grievous voice, its fragility unmitigated and undisguised by the carefully arranged mask of her features, and this strange real voice is the measure of its owner's suffering. He hears it also as the symbol of her isolation, of their separation, as impalpable as a voice from the dead. (Beckett 1987, 27)

Now, this passage, which anticipates the voices to be heard in many of Beckett's own later works, is in fact Beckett's dispatching into English of the following passage in *Le Côté de Guermantes II*:

> cet isolement de la voix était comme un symbole, une évocation, un effet direct d'un autre isolement, celui de ma grand'mère, pour la

première fois séparée de moi [...] cette voix, fantôme aussi impalpable que celui qui reviendrait peut-être me visiter quand ma grand'mère serait morte. (Proust 1954, ii. 136)

Among the many other, less adventurous but none the less significant examples of Beckett's dispatching of Proust is the following from *Le Temps retrouvé*, in which Beckett substitutes 'Proust' for the 'writer' to whom the narrator refers, thereby collapsing the very difference between artist and artefact, factual and fictional being, that is posited so emphatically in Beckett's own foreword:[3]

> For Proust, as for the painter, style is more a question of vision than technique. (Beckett 1987, 87–8)
>
> car le style, pour l'écrivain, aussi bien que la couleur pour le peintre, est une question non de technique mais de vision. (Proust 1954, iii. 895)

That Beckett's dispatching of Proust can also exhibit disrespect through the rather more brutal means of simply reversing the sense of the original is evident in his translation of Proust's narrator's description of his grandmother (in an experience of involuntary memory after her death) as 'une présence inconnue, divine' (Proust 1954, ii. 755). Beckett's translation domesticates this strange presence into a 'divine *familiar* presence' (Beckett 1987, 41; emphasis added).

Perhaps the most significant of all Beckett's dispatchings of Proust into English, however, is the following statement, which so clearly anticipates the procedure of Beckett's own postwar trilogy:

> The only fertile research is excavatory, immersive, a contraction of the spirit, a descent. The artist is active, but negatively, shrinking from the nullity of extracircumferential phenomena, drawn in to the core of the eddy. (Beckett 1987, 65–6)

This characterization of the artist's *via negativa* is Beckett's dispatching of a statement made by Proust's narrator in *Le Temps retrouvé*:

> le travail de l'artiste [est de] chercher à apercevoir sous de la matière, sous de l'expérience, sous des mots quelque chose de différent. (Proust 1954, iii. 896)

With Proust's 'quelque chose de différent' becoming Beckett's 'core of the eddy', translation threatens – or promises – to turn something into nothing. This raises the question not only of the extent to which translation of the Beckettian variety might constitute a negation of the original, but, more generally, what the relationship might be between translation and negation in Beckett's œuvre.

That Beckett's approach to translation will from the outset be characterized by a certain reversibility, in which negation is not simply opposed to affirmation, is evident in his dispatchings back into French of extracts from *Proust* in the academic spoof 'Le Concentrisme', presented by Beckett at Trinity College Dublin in November 1930 as a paper on a French writer, Jean du Chas, an invention of Beckett's who bears more than a passing resemblance to his inventor, not least in his having produced a Descartes-parodying *Discours de la Sortie*.[4] As Ann Beer observes,[5] the phrase 'an art that is perfectly intelligible and perfectly inexplicable' (Beckett 1987, 92), which appears in *Proust* and might well be applied to some of Beckett's own works, is translated in 'Le Concentrisme' as 'cet art qui [...] est parfaitement intelligible et parfaitement inexplicable' (Beckett 1983a, 42), and the sentence 'Swann is the cornerstone of the entire structure' (Beckett 1987, 34) is dispatched into French as 'Le concierge [...] est la pierre angulaire de mon édifice entier' (Beckett 1983a, 36), a comic diminution not just of one of the most significant characters in Proust's novel but of the novel in its entirety.

Radical transformations: Beckett translating Chamfort

While Beckett's covert dispatchings of Proust lie somewhere between interlingual translation, paraphrase, interpretation, and transformation, he was also responsible throughout his career for a large number of quite explicit translations of others: from modern French poets (and, in particular, Paul Éluard and others for the Surrealist Number of Edward Titus's review, *This Quarter*, in 1932), through to Mexican poetry for the 1959 *Anthology of Mexican Poetry* edited by Octavio Paz, to 'Huit Maximes' by the eighteenth-century French writer Sébastien Chamfort in the mid-1970s, almost half a century after *Proust*, under the title 'Long after Chamfort'. If Beckett's translations of Chamfort are long after *Proust*, they are, as their title suggests, even longer after Chamfort. Indeed, to refer to Beckett's dispatchings into English of Chamfort's maxims as translations is not only to expand the very genre of translation to a point at which it threatens to lose all specificity, but also to render the relationship between original and translation a highly paradoxical one. This is particularly evident in the case of Beckett's treatment of the seventh maxim:

> Vivre est une maladie dont le sommeil nous soulage toutes les seize heures. C'est un palliatif; la mort est le remède.

As Christopher Ricks observes,[6] the poet W. S. Merwin has translated this maxim with ostensibly literal respect for the original as:

> Living is an ailment which is relieved every sixteen hours by sleep. A palliative. Death is the cure. (Chamfort 1969, 128)

In his far more radical, far less obviously literal dispatching of Chamfort, not only does Beckett recast Chamfort's prose as poetry, but he also opens up new semantic possibilities and relates manner to matter in a way quite alien to Chamfort:

> sleep till death
> healeth
> come ease
> this life disease
> (Beckett 2002, 189)

As so often in his analysis of Beckett as a translator of French into English, Ricks celebrates Beckett's dispatching of Chamfort for the distance it achieves from the original – which is to say, for its independence from, one might even say its unethical negation of, that original. Beckett's translation is, he declares, not just long after Chamfort but 'splendidly' so, in striking contrast to 'the minimal distance secured by Chamfort's straighter translator'. Beckett, he concludes, turns Chamfort's aphorism into an 'elegiac prayer' (Ricks 1993, 14), which would seem to accord perfectly with Beckett's own definition of poetry in his review of his friend Thomas MacGreevy's *Poems* (1934): 'All poetry, as discriminated from the various paradigms of prosody, is prayer' (Beckett 1983a, 68).[7] What remains unremarked upon by Ricks, however, is the fact that Beckett is here translating an aphorism that is itself about a certain kind of negating translation, namely that from life to death. The dispatching of Chamfort's maxim suggests, then, that in Beckett there will be an intimate relation between the art of translation and the art of death, with the definition of 'translation proper' becoming an easing, liberating negation.

So many bilingual couples: Beckett translating Beckett

If Beckett's dispatchings of other writers appear on occasion to put considerable strain upon the distinction between respect and disrespect in translation, the complications only increase when one turns to his practice of self-translation. As has often been observed, Beckett's *œuvre* is perhaps unique in its bilinguality. It may be distinguished from Nabokov's, for instance, despite the many apparent similarities. Like Beckett, and at roughly the same historical moment, Nabokov switched from his mother tongue (Russian) to a foreign tongue (English) in mid-career, and, like Beckett, he engaged in the translation of his own earlier works, and indeed the works of others (including Pushkin and Lermontov into English, and Lewis Carroll into Russian), while continuing to produce new work. Unlike Beckett, however, Nabokov did not continue to produce his own works in both languages, and did not systematically translate his English-language works back into Russian. As a result, the bilinguality of Beckett's *œuvre* differs from Nabokov's in that for most of Beckett's works there are two texts produced by the author (one in English, often Irish-English, and one in French), not to mention his contributions to the German translations undertaken by Elmar Tophoven and others, and his directorial involvement in German-language productions of his plays at the Schiller-Theater, Berlin, in the 1960s and 1970s. The exceptions are, for the most part, English texts that Beckett did not translate into French, and include two very early works, *Dream of Fair to Middling Women* (written in 1931–32, but published posthumously) and *More Pricks Than Kicks* (1934), and one very late work, *Worstward Ho* (1983). As for works written in French and not translated into English by Beckett, the most substantial is *Eleutheria*, his first completed play, written in early 1947, over a year before *En attendant Godot*, but unpublished and unperformed during Beckett's lifetime.

Beckett's first major act of self-translation was the dispatching into French of his first published novel, *Murphy* (1938), which he undertook in 1938–40 with the aid and encouragement of his friend Alfred Péron,[8] who died shortly after his liberation from a German concentration camp in 1945 and to whom the translation of *Murphy*, published by Bordas in 1947, is dedicated. With this initiation into self-translation, combined with the writing of original works in both French and English, an extremely complicated process begins to unfold, making it very difficult to sustain any simple or consistent distinction between original and translation. Not only does Beckett come to write both in English and in

French, and to translate his English works into French, and his French works into English, but on occasion he modifies the original work in the light of the translation – as is the case for *Company* (1980) / *Compagnie* (1985)[9] – and even, in the case of *Bing* / *Ping* (1966), produces the English translation not from the original text as published but from draft versions of the original, something that the translator of another's work would scarcely dream of doing. Given his taking of these kinds of liberties, Beckett's bilingual *œuvre* constitutes a major challenge to the contrary positions taken by two of the founding fathers of modern translation theory, Friedrich Schleiermacher and A. W. Schlegel.

According to Schleiermacher, a writer 'can produce original work only in his mother tongue' (Schleiermacher 1992, 50). To argue that not only Beckett's self-translations into French but also those works originally written in French – including the postwar trilogy (*Molloy*, *Malone meurt*, and *L'Innommable*) and the plays *En attendant Godot* and *Fin de partie* – are not 'original work' would seem ridiculous, unless, that is, one were intent upon reconceiving the very concept of originality. And as for the notion of a mother tongue (*Muttersprache*), upon which Schleiermacher relies, the belief that literature is ever written in the author's mother tongue is placed in question by Beckett as early as his 1929 essay in defence of Joyce's *Work in Progress*, in which he claims that both Dante and Joyce produce 'synthetic' languages, unique to their works and spoken by 'no creature on heaven or earth' (Beckett 1983a, 30). Before attempting to determine whether or not Beckett's works in French are original works, then, one would first have to consider the possibility that he too might be attempting to produce, like Dante and Joyce before him, one more synthetic language (or languages), neither maternal nor paternal, neither native nor foreign. In Beckett's case, this synthetic language would, after the false start of *Dream of Fair to Middling Women*, increasingly come to be governed not by the synthesizing principle of paronomasia that underlies *Finnegans Wake*, drawing linguistic multiplicity into palimpsestic unity, but by an analysing principle that generates textual couples as self-divided as Beckett's characters, couples that seem to belong neither apart nor together, as though each were calling to its other: 'Lève-toi que je t'embrasse' / 'Get up till I embrace you' (Beckett 1952, 10; 1990, 11), only to recoil again in disgust.

If Beckett's bilingual *œuvre* constitutes an obvious challenge to Schleiermacher's radical distinction between translation and original work, it poses a no less formidable, although less often recognized, challenge to A. W. Schlegel's counter-claim that 'it is easy to demonstrate that objective poetic translation is true writing, a new creation'.[10] This position has found numerous modern advocates, including Henri Meschonnic, who argues that properly literary translation is productive, not reproductive.[11] At first glance, Beckett's self-translations into both English and French might seem to accord far more readily with this conception of literary production. Indeed, if only implicitly, many of Beckett's commentators accept Schlegel's view, since they often analyse his works either in English or in French, without concerning themselves unduly with whether or not the text in question is a translation, working instead on the assumption that Beckett's self-translations are originals in a way that, say, Brodsky's and Wright's translations of *Eleutheria* are clearly not. On closer examination, however, Schlegel's claim is no less problematical than Schleiermacher's when applied to Beckett, for the simple reason that Beckett repeatedly subjects the distinctions between original and copy, primary and secondary, creation and repetition, production and reproduction, to question, not least in the opening sentence of *Murphy* – 'The sun shone, having no alternative, on the nothing new' (Beckett 1938, 1) – where the difference between new and old, originality and cliché, Scripture and scripture, is already hard to maintain. If Beckett's self-translations are not simply secondary, neither are they simply original. Rather, in an *œuvre* that both thematizes and is governed by a principle of repetition that is very rarely pure, these translations dispatch the originals by repeating them in a manner that recasts them. How, then, are we to conceive of these textual couples that go to make up an *œuvre* that itself both thematizes and is structured by numerous dualities?

In the wake of Derrida's deconstructive theory of general textuality – the most economical expression of which being the claim that 'there is nothing outside of the text' (*il n'y a pas de hors-texte*) (Derrida 1976, 158) – a number of commentators have argued that Beckett's bilingual *œuvre* deconstructs the binary oppositions that structure most theories of translation, and effects a liberation of the text from the myth of any extratextual origin. According to Meschonnic, who is not referring to Beckett in particular, one simply cannot maintain the distinction between original and translation by appealing to the latter's greater proximity to such an extratextual realm: 'dire que l'écrivain va du réel au livre, et le traducteur d'un livre à un livre, c'était méconnaître ce qu'on sait aujourd'hui, qu'il y a toujours déjà eu des livres entre l'expérience et le livre' (Meschonnic 1973, 360). And, according to Steven Connor, Beckett's self-translations are exemplary in their disclosure of a difference that is always already at work in the original: 'translation is a "supplement" or sequel to the original text which, while appearing to guarantee the integrity of that original, actually subverts that integrity by opening up areas of absence or "lack" in it'; translation discloses 'the inherent self-division of an original text which is itself a process of internal repetition and self-translation' (Connor 1988, 113–14). Leslie Hill takes a similar line.[12]

So, Beckett's bilingual *œuvre* would obey the paradoxical logic of supplementarity formulated by Derrida in his reading of Rousseau in *Of Grammatology* (1967): the translation supplements an original that not only calls for translation but depends upon translation in order to be a work in the first place. The aporetic law of translation both governing and disclosed by Beckett's bilingual *œuvre* becomes, but for the translation, no original; and yet, given the translation, no original. The original's condition of possibility is also its condition of impossibility. One of the most persuasive and well-evidenced versions of this argument is to be found in Brian Fitch's *Beckett and Babel* (1988). According to Fitch, the two versions of almost all Beckett's works constitute an interdependent couple in which there is simply no '*prime instance*' (Fitch 1988, 140), no identifiable original that would then be reproduced in the merely secondary form of translation. In Beckett's bilingual *œuvre*, there is nothing but degrees of secondariness and supplementarity. Rather than the translation relying wholly, and not just chronologically, upon the original, in Beckett the translation discloses a lack, difference, or dependence in the original that denies it the very authority of the original. Interdependence, then, means that the original depends on the translation to be what it is. According to Fitch – and here Derrida's influence is particularly evident – the couple is to be thought in terms of an aporia of necessity and impossibility. In his analysis of the relation between *Bing* and its translation into English under the title *Ping*, for instance, Fitch concludes that 'Given the necessity and, at the same time, the impossibility of effecting a synthesis of any kind enjoying a textual status, such a synthesis can only be situated in the realm of the hypothetical: it remains unrealized – indeed, unrealizable – and yet necessary for any adequate account to be given of the status of these two texts' (Fitch 1988, 138). Before putting this theory of the interdependent couple to the test by considering some of Beckett's acts of self-translation, however, it is perhaps worth considering Beckett's own characterization of English and French in his early works, not least because from the outset he sets these two languages in opposition to one another, finding neither equivalence nor complementarity, but radical disparity.

Beckett's two languages

In 'Dante ... Bruno . Vico . . Joyce' (1929), Beckett dismisses the English language as being 'abstracted to death', by which he means that it lacks any properly mimetic relation between form and content. His scarcely coincidental example of such deathly abstraction is the English word 'doubt', which he contrasts with Joyce's coinage 'in twosome twiminds', an expression that gives us the 'sensuous suggestion of hesitancy, of the necessity for choice, of static irresolution' (Beckett 1983a, 28). Commentators have often sought to apply this principle of sensuous suggestion to Beckett's own works, with Martin Esslin going so far as to claim that all Beckett's works are 'poetry' because 'the manner of saying and the matter said completely and organically coincide' (Esslin 1967, 60). What this conception of Beckett's language (or languages) leaves out of account, however, is not only the fact that his bilingual œuvre will testify again and again to a writer 'in twosome twiminds', shuffling between languages, but also that being 'abstracted to death' is repeatedly presented in his works as something devoutly to be wished, and that translation may well be one means of enacting that abstraction. Far from being simply rejected as non-literary, an abstracting or deadening language promises a negation akin to the one promised by that other great deadener: habit. That, from the outset, Beckett will be drawn to such a deadening language, a language defined negatively and in its negativity, is clear from the would-be writer Belacqua's reflection in *Dream of Fair to Middling Women* that 'Perhaps only the French language can give you the thing you want', namely a language 'without style', a language free from the 'flower value' of English (Beckett 1992, 48). Among Beckett's own various responses to the question of why he began writing in French immediately after the Second World War, there is one that echoes Belacqua's reflection in *Dream*: French, Beckett is reported to have told Niklaus Gessner, is a language in which it is 'plus facile d'écrire sans style' (Gessner 1957, 32 n.). Indeed, Beckett repeatedly thinks the switch from English to French in terms of negation: as weakening, impoverishment, reduction, separation, self-denial, ascesis.

Following Beckett's lead, those commentators who have compared the English and French versions of his works in detail have tended to characterize the latter as for the most part more impoverished than the former. Where they have not followed Beckett, however, is in the value that is repeatedly placed on such impoverishment in his works. According to Fitch, for instance, in the works either first written in or translated into French there is far less 'textual activity', which is to say 'far less ambiguity, less word-play, whether in the form of puns, linguistic permutations, or simply alliteration' (Fitch 1988, 38). As a result, the French texts often serve to clarify or to limit the ambiguity of the English, even supplying an interpretation of, or commentary on, them. For example, *Le Dépeupleur* (1970) clarifies its own translation into English as *The Lost Ones* (1972). Despite the seemingly obvious exceptions – the 1974 English translation of *Mercier et Camier* (1970), for instance, which is much shorter than the original French – Beckett's self-translations into French and into English may be distinguished from each other as impoverishing to enriching.

Like Fitch, although with even fewer reservations, Ricks too argues that Beckett's French texts (irrespective of whether they precede or follow the English) are generally 'more abstract, less corporeal' than their English counterparts (Ricks 1993, 64), the latter not only more fully incarnating their meaning, binding form to content in a more tightly mimetic fashion, but also being semantically richer, more ambiguous, more playful. Relying upon the definition of the aesthetic as an 'incarnation' in T. S. Eliot's *Notes Towards the Definition of Culture* (1948) and (although he does not acknowledge this particular debt) in Hegel's *Aesthetics*, Ricks can conclude his analysis of a passage from *Comment c'est* (1961) / *How It Is* (1964) with the claim that, 'As often in Beckett, his original French reads like a highly talented translation of a work of genius, and not as the thing itself' (Ricks 1993, 4). Whereas Fitch would bracket the question of value in his analysis of impoverishment and enrichment in translation, Ricks has no qualms at all about celebrating the greater aesthetic value of Beckett's English texts, irrespective of whether they are translations or not. What neither Fitch nor Ricks takes into account, however, is the justifiability of either bracketing the question of value when considering self-translation in Beckett, or championing the English texts on aesthetic grounds (for their greater 'incarnation' of meaning), given that, far from being bracketed, value in Beckett's *œuvre* is repeatedly thought in terms of negation. Furthermore, to bracket the question of value altogether or to celebrate semantic enrichment and the incarnation of meaning in Beckett's English texts is to ignore the fact that, if it is to be ethical, translation must exhibit a respect for the other, a respect that is not necessarily evident in translations that enrich, any more than it is in those that impoverish. Although enrichment and impoverishment are generally thought in opposition to each other, in the case of self-translation they are both forms of negation, since both would negate the alterity of the original. Only when this more general negation, preceding the very distinction between enrichment and impoverishment, has been taken into account can one proceed to consider whether one form of negation promises a value that the other does not.

Translating the negative: impoverishment and enrichment

Let us now take a closer look at what happens when this more general negation of alterity is not taken into account in the analysis of Beckett's acts of self-translation. In his commentary on the opening paragraph of Beckett's French translation of *Murphy*, Fitch finds nothing but losses everywhere, his own rhetoric militating against the possibility that the French text may have a value that the English does not. Overall, he concludes that the French translation 'fails to capture the full impact' and 'loses much of the effectiveness of the original' (Fitch 1988, 38). This impoverishment is apparent not least in the translation of 'the nothing' that makes its first appearance in the novel's opening sentence: 'The sun shone, having no alternative, on the nothing new', translated by Beckett with apparent fidelity to the original as 'Le soleil brillait, n'ayant pas d'alternative, sur le rien de neuf'. Among the impoverishments that Fitch identifies here are the loss of the original's 3/7/5 syllabic structure, the change in tense (with the imperfect being far less novel an opening to a novel than the radical punctuality of the simple past). As for Beckett's translation of 'the nothing new' as 'le rien de neuf', Fitch claims that the use of the definite article in the English has a defamiliarizing effect, whereas in the French 'le rien' is much less remarkable, given that in French the definite article is often used where it is not in English. Here, though, Fitch is arguably seeing losses in 'the nothing' where there are none, for there does exist in French, as a common expression (a cliché even), the phrase 'il n'y a rien de neuf' ('there's nothing new' or 'there's no news'), in which the 'rien' functions as an indefinite pronoun and is not preceded by an article. Given that the phrase 'il n'y a *le* rien de neuf' is not grammatically correct, the French expression 'le rien de neuf' is arguably no less strange than the English it translates.

This particular 'nothing new' is itself nothing new, or, more precisely if also more paradoxically, it is a new version of the 'nothing new', being Beckett's redispatching of a well-known phrase from Scripture: 'there is no new thing under the sun' (Ecclesiastes 1.ix; King James Version). Referring us back to Ecclesiastes, the opening sentence of the English original is itself already a kind of translation. In Benjaminian terms, it is the translation of Scripture into scripture (literature), a departure from the sacred (*heilig*) that is orientated towards the sacred. Having begun with this redispatching of 'the nothing new', Beckett's novel proceeds to chart its protagonist's attempts to free himself from it by translating himself into 'the Nothing', which very briefly becomes an object of experience for him shortly before his tragicomic death:

> Murphy began to see nothing, that colourlessness which is such a rare postnatal treat, being the absence (to abuse a nice distinction) not of *percipere* but of *percipi*. His other senses also found themselves at peace, an unexpected pleasure. Not the numb peace of their own suspension, but the positive peace that comes when the somethings give way, or perhaps simply add up, to the Nothing, than which in the guffaw of the Abderite naught is more real. (Beckett 1938, 246)

For this conception of 'the Nothing' and, in particular, the theory that 'naught is more real' than this 'Nothing', Beckett is drawing, as he indicates, on the atomist theory of Democritus of Abdera, one of the pre-Socratics on whom he took extensive notes in the early 1930s. In a letter to Sighle Kennedy of 14 June 1967, he identifies the idea that nothing is more real than nothing as one of two 'points of departure' for the study of his novel, the other being '*Ubi nihil vales, ibi nihil velis*' (where you are worth nothing, there you should want nothing) from the *Ethics* (1665) of the Belgian Occasionalist Arnold Geulincx: 'If I were in the unenviable position of having to study my work my points of departure would be the "Naught is more real ..." and the "Ubi nihil vales ..." both already in *Murphy* and neither very rational' (Beckett 1983a, 113). The Democritean atomist paradox, as it is often termed, maintains that being consists of atoms (*atomoi*, or indivisibles) and void (*apeiron*, or the unlimited), and that the void is in fact no less real than the atoms. It is an idea that also finds its place in *Malone Dies* (1951), where its apparent paradoxicality is identified as a threat to thought itself: 'I know those little phrases that seem so innocuous and, once you let them in, pollute the whole of speech. *Nothing is more real than nothing*' (Beckett 1959, 193), the original French reading: '*Rien n'est plus réel que rien*' (Beckett 1951a, 30). Beckett's 1930s notes on the pre-Socratics, now in Trinity College Dublin, are drawn from a range of sources, including Wilhelm Windelband's *History of Philosophy* and John Burnet's *Greek Philosophy, Part 1: Thales to Plato*. However, the particular phrasing of the atomist paradox both in Beckett's notes[13] and in *Murphy* suggests that he also consulted Archibald Alexander's *Short History of Philosophy*, which is the only one of these works to include the word 'naught' in the formulation of the atomist theory: 'Aristotle, in his account of the early philosophers, says, "Leucippus and Democritus assume as elements the 'full' and the 'void'. The former they term being and the latter non-being. Hence they assert that non-being exists as well as being." And, according to Plutarch, Democritus himself is reported as saying, "there is naught more real than nothing" ' (Alexander 1922, 38–9).

Now, in Beckett's French translation of *Murphy*, the phrase 'to the Nothing, than which in the guffaw of the Abderite naught is more real' is translated as 'au Rien, ce Rien dont disait le farceur d'Abdère que rien n'est plus réel' (Beckett 1965, 176), the difference between the signature 'naught' and the colourless 'nothing' being reduced to zero, and with it all trace of Beckett's source. Furthermore, the capitalized 'Rien' arrives doubly unexpectedly (at least to those familiar with the original), coming before the capitalized 'Nothing' in the English, the phrase 'Murphy began to see nothing' being dispatched as 'Murphy se mit à voir le Rien'. With Beckett's translation of *Murphy* into French, then, we have not only the translation of an attempt at self-translation, with self-translation's trajectory here being, from the outset, the passage from 'the nothing new' to 'the Nothing', but also an acceleration of that passage, as though French granted quicker access to the experience of 'the Nothing' (*le Rien*). Simply to insist upon Beckett's translation of *Murphy* into French as an impoverishment is to leave out of account the paradoxically enriching effect of negation so characteristic of Beckett's works, the experience of 'the Nothing' in *Murphy* itself being described as a 'positive peace' (*paix positive*).

If impoverishing translation from English into French is more paradoxical than it might at first appear, paradoxicality is also evident in Beckett's enriching translations from French into English. Whereas *Murphy* was translated into French shortly after its publication in English, two of Beckett's early postwar French texts, *Mercier et Camier* and *Premier amour* (both written in 1946), were not translated into English until over 20 years later, and then only as a result of publishers' demands upon Beckett for texts in the wake of his being awarded the Nobel Prize for Literature in 1969.[14] Beckett's belated translation of *Premier amour* is significant not least because the British edition, which follows the American, contains a revised translation of one sentence that epitomizes the kind of enriching incarnation, or increased corporealization of meaning, that Ricks sees as characteristic of Beckett's practice of self-translation into English, the kind of enriching incarnation of meaning that would make of his English texts 'works of genius', to be distinguished from those 'highly talented translations' that his works in French always are. In the original French, the sentence in question begins: 'Personnellement je n'ai rien contre les cimetières, je m'y promène assez volontiers qu'ailleurs, je crois, quand je suis obligé de sortir' (Beckett 1970d, 8). In the first American edition, this is translated with seemingly literal respect for the original as: 'Personally I have nothing against graveyards, I take the air there willingly, perhaps more willingly than elsewhere, when take the air I must' (Beckett 1974a, 11). In the British version, however, 'I have nothing against graveyards' is redispatched as 'Personally I have no bone to pick with graveyards' (Beckett 1995a, 25). With this introduction of cliché, the literal sense of which is reactivated by the context, there is undoubtedly both a tightening of the bond between language and meaning and an increase in textual activity. However, increased activity, textual or otherwise, is precisely what the narrator of this story wishes to avoid, and he might therefore be said to be less at home in the revised English translation than he is in both the original French and the American texts. The dispatching of 'rien contre' ('nothing against') by 'no bone to pick with' may bring form and meaning closer together, but it does so at the cost of separating the narrator from the very 'nothing' that he takes to be his true home.

In this story, expulsion into an intolerable outer realm follows upon the death of the father, and this outer realm is figured as an encounter with the feminine: the prostitute named first Lulu (a type-name for a prostitute, to be found in Wedekind's 'Lulu' plays), then Anna. Love – or at least love of a woman, as distinct from love of a father – is presented here as the very paradigm of exile: 'Ce qu'on appelle l'amour c'est l'exil' / 'What goes by the name of love is banishment' (Beckett 1970d, 22; 1995a, 31). And this exilic encounter with the feminine is the precondition for a very literal – and, for the hapless narrator, intolerable – incarnation: the story ends with the narrator fleeing the cries of childbirth. Beckett's revised English translation, which negates by enriching the 'rien contre' ('nothing against'), only increases a liveliness that in the text itself eventually takes the form of those rending cries, which play the role of the Furies here, as though to punish the narrator for playing the paternal role in his turn: 'Ils me poursuivirent jusque dans la rue' / 'They pursued me down the stairs and out into the street' (Beckett 1970d, 55; 1995a, 45). The narrator's aestheticizing response to these cries anticipates that of Beckett the self-translator: 'Je me mis à jouer avec les cris un peu comme j'avais joué avec la chanson, m'avançant, m'arrêtant, m'avançant, m'arrêtant, si l'on peut appeler cela jouer' / 'I began playing with the cries, a little in the same way as I had played with the song, on, back, on, back, if that may be called playing' (Beckett

1970d, 55; 1995a, 45). Here, Beckett's 'syntax of weakness'[15] – that appended qualifying phrase, 'si l'on peut appeler cela jouer' / 'if that may be called playing' – is itself an aestheticization that tells against such aestheticizing negation, which gives way to another rhythmic negation, one that is less evident in translation: 'Tant que je marchais je ne les entendais *pas*, grâce au bruit de mes *pas*' / 'As long as I kept walking I didn't hear them, because of the footfalls' (Beckett 1970d, 55, emphasis added; 1995a, 45). Even though the word 'footfalls' works in a manner that 'steps' would not, in the original French the word 'pas' works doubly, as both a noun and a particle of negation, in a deadening repetition with a difference.

Incarnation, aestheticization, increased liveliness – be it literal or textual – are thematized in this story as cries that both repeat and exacerbate the initial expulsion of the narrator following the father's death. Far from being an unambiguous value, to be celebrated by those readers and commentators who would define the aesthetic as a particular incarnation of meaning, the aesthetic is associated here with suffering and failed negation. It produces not the 'positive peace' enjoyed all too briefly by Murphy, but a negating flight whose end remains very much in question: 'Pendant des années j'ai cru qu'ils allaient s'arrêter. Maintenant je ne le crois plus' / 'For years I thought they would cease. Now I don't think so any more' (Beckett 1970d, 56; 1995a, 45). If there are lessons to be drawn from this story, then one of them would be that, *pace* Schopenhauer, the aesthetic may itself be an exacerbation of the very condition it promises to alleviate or even overcome, and that any unambiguous celebration of the value of the aesthetic in Beckett's works of self-translation is nothing less than an attempt to silence those cries, which are themselves the cries of one more enriching, incarnating translation.

But this is still too simplifying a reading of the story, since, as we have seen, when the narrator gives up the aesthetic (gives up playing with the cries), relying instead upon walking to silence them, the French text is arguably more textually active than the English: the 'pas' being semantically and rhythmically richer than the 'footfalls', working to achieve a repetition (*pas ... pas*) that is not quite one, since the two deadening *pas* are in fact different parts of speech. If aestheticization is presented here as an exacerbation of the very suffering that it promises to alleviate, it seems as though any flight *from* the aesthetic (from playing with the cries to walking away from them) is also a flight *into* the aesthetic, back into the richer vein of the French *pas*. Furthermore, the original French text is already marked by (and as) translation, and thus as itself an instance of (linguistic) exile, in a way that the final English translation is not, for the French contains three lines that disappear altogether in the process of translation, lines that refer to the two characters' non-native pronunciation of the French language: 'N'étant pas française elle disait Loulou. Moi aussi, n'étant pas français non plus, je disais Loulou comme elle. Tous les deux, nous disions Loulou' (Beckett 1970d, 17). The final English translation, in which this indication that the story is narrated in a language that is not the narrator's mother tongue is simply erased, might therefore be seen to be paradoxically both more and less alienating than the original French.

If, as numerous commentators have sought to demonstrate, Beckett's *œuvre* abounds in enriching translations into English akin to the one to be found in Beckett's revised English translation of *Premier amour*, in each of these instances one might again hear those cries of incarnation from which the narrator of that story flees. These enrichments can take many forms, even, paradoxically, that of an apparent impoverishment. This is the case, for instance, in Beckett's English translation of the short prose text *Sans* (1969) as *Lessness* (1970). Here, when translating the negative, Beckett negates the various particles of negation in the original French: 'sans', 'pas', and 'rien' are all translated as 'no', such that the line 'Ciel gris sans nuage pas un bruit rien qui bouge terre sable gris cendre' (Beckett 1972, 70, 74) is dispatched as 'Grey sky no cloud no sound no stir earth ash grey sand' (Beckett 1995a, 197, 199); 'sans prise' is translated as 'no hold'; 'sans bruit', 'pas un bruit', and even 'silence' are all translated as 'no sound'; and 'rien qui dépasse' is translated as 'no relief'. Indeed, 'no' is even introduced into the text where there is no equivalent for it in the French: the words 'No sound no stir' are added in the translation of the line 'Gris cendre ciel reflet de la terre reflet du ciel' (Beckett 1972, 69, 73) as 'No sound no stir ash grey sky mirrored earth mirrored sky' (Beckett 1995a, 197, 199); and 'no sound' is also added in the translation of the line 'Jamais ne fut qu'air gris sans temps chimère lumière qui passe' (Beckett 1972, 69, 74) as 'Never was but grey air timeless no sound figment the passing light' (Beckett 1995a, 197, 200).

However, if 'no' translates a range of negatives in the French, one of those negatives ('sans'), which serves as the title of the French text, is also translated as 'lessness' or 'less'. Both '-ness' and '-less' are very frequent suffixes in the English text, but 'lessness' also resembles a substantive in the English title, creating a hesitation – a grammatical 'in twosome twiminds' – between substantive and suffix. Other instances of 'sans' being translated not as 'no' but as '-less' include 'sans fin' ('endless'), 'sans issue' ('issueless'), and 'sans temps' ('timeless'). The prevalence of the suffix '-less' or '-lessness' is also achieved through the translation of 'lointains' as 'endlessness', of 'infini' as 'endless', of 'sans relief' as 'flatness', and of 'inchangeant' as 'changelessness'. In the English translation of *Sans*, then, the 'no', the '-less' and '-lessness' serve to produce a text far more obviously governed by repetition than is the original French. And this seems only appropriate for a work that not only contains a very large amount of lexical and phrasal repetition in the original French, but is also repeated in its entirety, albeit in a different order.

Beckett's marked preference for the negating particle 'no' in the English translation of *Sans* is not simply a preference for repetition and reduction, but also a preference for a word that includes the possibility of palindromic reversal, negation, and affirmation housed within the same elements: 'no'/'on'.[16] As already observed, in Beckett's French texts a similar effect is achieved through the double sense of the word 'pas' (as both noun and particle of negation), a doubleness of which Blanchot too takes advantage in the title of his 1973 work, *Le Pas au-delà*.[17] The negating/affirming reversibility of 'no'/'on' lies at the very heart of one of Beckett's last works, *Worstward Ho* (1983), whose 'impossible prose' – as he terms it in a letter of February 1982 to Alan Schneider (Harmon 1998, 421) – Beckett was to leave untranslated. This would make *Worstward Ho* one of Beckett's few non-bilingual works, were it not for the fact that the English text – itself written in what, following Beckett on Dante and Joyce, might well be termed a 'synthetic' language – already presents itself as both an act and a result of translation: 'Say for be said. Missaid. From now say for be missaid' (Beckett 1983b, 7).[18]

The 'losing battle': translation as negation

The reversibility of negation and affirmation that is explored perhaps most exhaustively by Beckett in *Worstward Ho* returns us to the more general question of the relation between self-translation and negation in his œuvre. From relatively early in his career as a self-translator, Beckett inscribes the practice of translation within an economy of double failure. In a 1957 letter to Thomas MacGreevy, he declares: 'How sick and tired I am of translation and what a losing battle it is always. Wish I had the courage to wash my hands of it all, I mean leave it to others and try to get on with some work.'[19] Here, in addition to the unsurprising sense of his having failed to achieve self-translations that satisfy him, there is also the sense of his having failed to abandon that attempt. But what, in Beckett's eyes, would make of an act of self-translation a success? And what of the very clear distinction he appears to insist upon here between 'translation' and 'work'? Given the very deliberate manner in which he so often deploys, in order to reactivate, clichés in his own works – and, as we have seen in the case of *Premier amour / First Love*, on occasion adds them in the process of self-translation – one might begin to seek an answer to these questions by considering the specific cliché upon which Beckett relies here to characterize his relation to the act of self-translation. To wash one's hands of something, as Pilate washed his hands of all responsibility for the Crucifixion: it is as though self-translation were akin in some way to the authorizing of a killing, and the killing not simply of a god, at once the most original and unoriginal of origins, but rather of an incarnation, of an original work of art defined as incarnated meaning. It is as though, for Beckett, a successful translation would have to be, not a perfect reflection or reproduction of the original that adds nothing to and subtracts nothing from it, nor even a redispatching of the original in all its originality, but rather a murderous dispatching of the original, out of which would emerge another original, in another language, freed from any dependence upon the work from which it none the less derives. It is as though, for Beckett, the perfect translation would negate the intertextual difference between the original and the translation. If this reduction to nothing of difference is the ideal, however, in Beckett's letter to MacGreevy the emphasis falls upon its failure.

Now, it is precisely this experience of negation's failure that is limited by Ricks in his celebration of Beckett's translations into English, and negated altogether by Fitch when he argues that the process of self-translation in Beckett is the consummating moment in a project the aim of which is the production of literary texts that have been freed from all referential, representational, or mimetic function, texts that are no longer dependent upon, derived from, or directed towards any extratextual point of origin (see Fitch 1988, 191). This conception of Beckett's *œuvre* is shared by all those commentators who would situate his works squarely within the postmodern.[20] Works that accomplish the negation of the extratextual, or its reduction to nothing but a textual effect; works that nullify the referential function of language: we have, of course, already encountered such nihilating rhetoric in Blanchot's and de Man's readings of Benjamin's 'The Task of the Translator', for both of whom Benjamin theorizes translation as a radical negation of the original, the pure, and the sacred. Like Blanchot and de Man before him, Fitch relies upon Benjamin to support his theory of self-translation's aim and function in Beckett. Benjamin, he claims, is 'the only writer, to my knowledge, whose account of translation could possibly throw any light on the situation we are examining, however indirect that light may prove to be!' (Fitch 1988, 181). The Benjamin he invokes here is precisely the one dispatched to us by de Man, who in turn invokes the Benjamin dispatched by Carol Jacobs, for whom Benjamin's notion of a pure language (*reine Sprache*) accords perfectly with a poststructural conception of pure textuality. In her analysis of Harry Zohn's English translation of Benjamin's essay, Jacobs reveals the manner in which Zohn supplies organic metaphors for Benjamin's figures (for instance, 'flowering' for the German 'Entfaltung'), and takes this to be one of the key means by which the humanistically inclined Zohn obscures the essential point of Benjamin's essay, which is that translation 'denies the linear law of nature in order to practice the rule of textuality' (Jacobs 1975, 757). The pure language to which Benjamin refers us, she concludes, 'does not signify the apotheosis of an ultimate language but signifies rather that which is purely language – nothing but language' (Jacobs 1975, 761).

This, then, is the interpretation of Benjamin's foreword to his own translations of Baudelaire's 'Tableaux parisiens' that underlies the deconstructive conception of self-translation in Beckett. As we have seen in the previous chapter, however, de Man's reading of Benjamin fails to take account of that strange logic whereby translation would paradoxically constitute not the consummation but the threat and the promise of nihilism. Similarly, Fitch's theory of self-translation in Beckett fails to take account of the manner in which Beckett's acts of self-translation are conceived by Beckett himself as 'losing battles' that may well be orientated towards the production of a work that would be constituted by nothing but 'expressionless, meaningless, and productive language', a *reine Sprache* thought as the inhuman rather than the sacred, but that, in Beckett's eyes (be they blinded or not), enact the failure of that productive language to come into being, the failed negation of the extratextual other. To take account of this failure is not to make of it the proof of an irreducible alterity or referentiality. Despite Beckett's own declaration, in his 1938 review of Denis Devlin's *Intercessions*, that 'art has nothing to do with clarity, does not dabble in the clear and does not make clear' (Beckett 1983a, 94),[21] Carla Locatelli maintains in an argument governed throughout by a rhetoric of revelation and demonstration that in his later works Beckett 'articulates with extreme lucidity the impossibility of totally escaping from representation and from interpretation' (Locatelli 1990, 36). But, of course, to take the enacted failure of negation to be a disclosure of the irreducibility of the referential is no less negating of the 'battle' structuring the relation of original and translation, textual and extratextual, than is the argument of Fitch and others that in Beckett self-translation constitutes an absolute negation of the referential.

From textual couple to anethical 'pseudocouple'

That Beckett's works are structured in terms of couples and dualities (light and dark, speech and silence, body and mind, spirit and matter, for instance) requires little emphasis. That those works are also populated by numerous couples (Mercier and Camier, Molloy and Moran, Vladimir and Estragon, Pozzo and Lucky, Hamm and Clov, Nagg and Nell, Winnie and Willie, Reader and Listener, to name only a few) requires even less. These couples are conceived by Beckett not only as interdependent but also as antagonistic, each party being at war with the other.[22] Thus, if the translation accomplishes the work of the original in its negation of the tie to the extratextual, then the original–translation couple would be a couple apart in Beckett, utterly distinct from all others.

Now, by the time of *L'Innommable* (1953) / *The Unnamable* (1959), the couple is being thought as the 'pseudocouple' (Beckett 1953, 16; 1959, 299), which raises the question of what the difference might be between the couple and the pseudocouple, and what light this particular difference might shed upon the relation between original and translation. As a remark of Beckett's in a letter of 29 December 1959 to Alan Schneider makes clear, not only is the pseudocouple at war with itself, but its two elements belong neither together nor apart: *'nec tecum nec sine te'*.[23] If the strange logic of the pseudocouple is applied to Beckett's self-translations, then we find ourselves precisely with enactments of negation that are not irreversibly determined as either possible or impossible. In the pseudocouple of original and translation, and indeed across the series of pseudocouples produced throughout Beckett's career, we would have a series of unaccomplished negations. The *dispatching* of both the textual and the extratextual would become the end towards which these pseudocouples, and indeed these series of pseudocouples, are orientated.

Resting neither in English nor in French, but passing to and fro between them, abiding in neither, inhabiting what in the short prose text 'neither' (1979) – another of those works that remained untranslated by Beckett – is termed the 'unheeded neither' (Beckett 1995a, 258), this self-translating writer inhabits, if anything, a collapsing *indessen* or *inzwischen*, in between times and places, in between the difference between time and place, between languages, between original and translation, between letter and spirit, literal and figurative. This collapsing between is also the place of both the threat and the promise of an end, and thus akin to what Hölderlin in his 1802 ode 'Bread and Wine' terms a 'time of dearth' (*dürftige Zeit*), and Adorno in *Negative Dialectics* a 'no man's land' (*Niemandsland*). However, this region is not necessarily the place in which negation is known in its impossibility or in which difference is revealed in its irreducibility.[24]

If Beckett's practice of negating translation can be said to be anethical, then this is because it repeatedly finds itself pursuing the ethical by way of the unethical, and the unethical by way of the ethical. Paradoxically, this anethical dispatching of the other involves the attempted reduction to nothing of that other – be it the other as a textual or an extratextual entity – in the name of the other, just as it involves the attempted disintegration of identity in the name of identity. If Beckett's bilingual *œuvre* does not necessarily accomplish the reduction to nothing of alterity, that reduction is none the less both the promise and the threat of self-translation. Beckett's collapsing pseudocouples testify, then, to the dream of the other's annihilation, the reduction to nothing not just of the textual or the extratextual but of all alterity. Beyond the distinction between freedom and fidelity, beyond the distinction between reduction, addition, and modification, Beckett's practice of translation may itself be translated as a nihilation, but a nihilation that is governed by a reversibility that is the trait of anethical dispatch.

Part II

The Laugh of the Other: On the Ethics of Comedy

3
Pratfalls into Alterity
Laughter from Baudelaire to Freud and Beyond

There would seem to be something about the comic that attracts cliché, and there is arguably no claim about the comic more clichéd than that it ultimately resists analysis, always outwits its interlocutors, and is what Simon Critchley terms a 'nicely impossible object for a philosopher' (Critchley 2002, 2). Together with this paradoxical thought of the comic's resistance to philosophy goes a no less universalizing insistence upon its resistance to translation. Critchley, for instance, is only repeating Paul Valéry, among others, when he argues that humour 'resists direct translation and can only be thematized humourlessly' (Critchley 1997, 157).[1] Humour, then – its difference from the comic being one to which we shall have reason to return – becomes the most absolute of idioms, the ultimate shibboleth. And yet, if (as Henri Bergson argues) cliché, as an instance of mechanicity in language, is itself but one form of the comic, then to say that the comic attracts cliché is to say that it attracts itself, that it doubles itself, feeds on itself, exponentially. As if to prove this very point, in *Jokes and Their Relation to the Unconscious* (1905) Freud claims that the notion of translation's impossibility, and the unethicality that this impossibility imposes upon every would-be translator, has itself become the subject of a joke: 'An admirable example of a modification joke [...] is the well-known cry: "*Traduttore – Traditore!*" The similarity, amounting almost to identity, of the two words represents most impressively the necessity which forces a translator into crimes against his original [*der Notwendigkeit, die den Übersetzer zum Frevler an seinem Author werden läßt*]' (Freud 1960b, 33–4).

Now, to argue that the comic resists both thought and translation is to identify it not merely as the purest of idioms but as marked by an irreducible alterity, and the thought of its relation to alterity certainly haunts three of the most influential modern theorizations of the comic: by

Baudelaire, Bergson, and Freud. And yet, as we shall see, if it often seems as though the laughter prompted by the comic is being conceived by these writers as a laughter *at the other*, a means of reinforcing the difference between same and other, this notion of laughter being directed at the other serves, paradoxically, both to hide and to disclose a sense that laughter is in fact always the laughter *of the other*. Whether or not either of these kinds of laughter can be said to be ethical is the question that will guide the analyses that follow.

The pantomime of unknowing: Baudelaire

In his seminal essay 'On the Essence of Laughter' (1855), Baudelaire argues that laughter (*le rire*) is alien to both absolute knowledge and absolute power, that it is 'generally the apanage of madmen', and that it 'always implies more or less of ignorance and weakness' (Baudelaire 1995, 149). Like so many of those who come after him, Baudelaire thinks the comic in terms of a fall (*chute*), a debasement, a lowering, and a loss. Seeing the other fall (be that fall literal or figurative), one laughs, and one does so in order both to express and to insist upon the difference between the one who falls and the one who witnesses that fall. Crucially, however, while laughter is prompted by a fall that testifies to a lack of, or limit to, knowledge and power on the part of the one who falls, this laughter is itself impossible without there being ignorance or delusion also on the part of the one who laughs: 'Laughter comes from the idea of one's own superiority. A Satanic idea, if ever there was one! And what pride and delusion [*aberration*]! For it is a notorious fact that all madmen in asylums [*tous les fous des hôpitaux*] have an excessively overdeveloped idea of their own superiority: I hardly know of any who suffer from the madness of humility. Note, too, that laughter is one of the most frequent and numerous expressions of madness' (Baudelaire 1995, 152). For Baudelaire, then, laughter is essentially postlapsarian and intimately related to madness. Only the fallen can laugh, and that at which they laugh is precisely the fall of the other, whom they, in their ignorance, take to be unlike themselves. Thus, while Baudelaire's theory of the comic may fall squarely within what John Morreall, in his tripartite division of the theorization of the comic, terms the superiority theory of laughter, as distinct from the relief theory and the incongruity theory,[2] the sense of superiority felt by the one who laughs is itself the sign of an erring (*aberration*) closely akin to madness.

The two conditions of possibility for laughter, as Baudelaire theorizes it, are that only the fallen can laugh and that the fall at which they laugh is always taken to be the fall of the other. Laughter, then, is always in error, is grounded in misrecognition or forgetting, since the one who laughs has to forget his own fallenness. Laughter is possible only on the condition that the one who laughs fails to see that the other is no other – or, more precisely, that the self who laughs is already other than itself, fallen from the self it aberrantly takes itself to be. Paradoxically, then, no one can laugh at the self (as a laughing being), the madman least of all, even though, in fact, one can only laugh at oneself. Indeed, according to Baudelaire, the very definition of madness becomes an absolute mistaking of the other, an absolute resistance to the truth of the identity of fallen self and fallen other. It is the madman who makes the greatest distinction of all between fallen self and fallen other, reducing the world as such to the status of the absolutely inferior other, and therefore a reason for endless laughter. No one has more reason to laugh than the madman, since for the madman Being itself is alterior. Baudelaire's madman is nothing but a laughing mouth, a gaping hole in Being.

The laughter of the madman is not, however, absolute laughter, as becomes clear when Baudelaire distinguishes between the philosopher (*le philosophe*) and the madman (*le fou*) on the grounds that the philosopher alone is able to laugh at himself knowingly. Strangely, this distinction makes Baudelaire's philosopher madder than his madman, for the philosopher laughs at himself, not because he sees beyond the difference between self and other, or because he sees the self in the other, but precisely because he can make of the self an other. Baudelaire's philosopher is, then, less the antithesis of his madman than a further stage in the madness of laughter. While the madman sees the whole world as other, the philosopher can see even the self that laughs as other: 'The man who trips would be the last to laugh at his own fall, unless he happened to be a philosopher, one who had acquired by habit a power of rapid self-division [*la force de se dédoubler rapidement*] and thus of assisting as a disinterested spectator at the phenomena of his own ego' (Baudelaire 1995, 154).

However, while the philosopher goes one crucial step beyond the madman through an act of self-division (*dédoublement*), if he is to be able to laugh he must remain, just like the madman, in possession of a laughing self, which is to say, a self that mistakes itself, that takes itself to be essentially different from the other at which it laughs. In his very act of self-division, the philosopher remains tied to the delusion that there can be an unfallen, laughing self. In acknowledgement of this, Baudelaire has to proceed to distinguish both the philosopher and the madman, on the one hand, from the wise man (*le Sage*) on the other. The latter alone possesses absolute knowledge, and therefore does not – indeed *cannot* – laugh.

It is, then, the mirthless *Sage*, not the *philosophe*, who is the antithesis of the endlessly laughing *fou*.

Given that, according to Baudelaire, both laughter and the laughable are possible only where there is delusion, ignorance, limitation, it would seem reasonable to assume that the wise man, as both the unlaughing and the unlaughable, will therefore possess both absolute knowledge and absolute power. However, he certainly lacks something, namely the power to laugh, and, indeed, Baudelaire emphasizes the childlike nature of the wise, who, 'through the contemplative innocence of their minds, approach a childlike state [*se rapprochent de l'enfance*]' (Baudelaire 1995, 154). For the wise man, the comic itself has become the absolutely other, and thus, paradoxically, both laughable and that at which he could laugh only at the expense of his wisdom.

For Baudelaire, then, the comic is absolute knowledge's absolute other. Associated with both madness and philosophy, it is alien to absolute knowledge and marks the limit of absolute power. The comic alone is laughable for absolute knowledge, and yet it is precisely that at which such knowledge cannot laugh. It is this thought of the comic as the limit to, or the rupture within, absolute knowledge that recurs in the work of Georges Bataille, who, like Baudelaire before him, conceives of laughter not only in terms of falling, but also precisely in terms of a fall into alterity: 'Someone falls to the ground like a bag: he's isolated from the system of things by falling. [...] In any kind of *joking* [plaisanterie], a system that's given as absolute [*se donnant pour isolé*] liquefies, falls suddenly into another' (Bataille 1988, 140). It is to this thought of a laughter that interrupts the system that Derrida draws attention in his early essay on Bataille and Hegel. According to Derrida, Bataille's is a laughter that, like the trace, like *différance*, 'exceeds dialectics and the dialectician', is that 'almost-nothing into which meaning sinks' (Derrida 1978a, 256). Such laughter is alterior, then, to both being and nothingness.

Returning to Baudelaire: although the comic is alien to knowledge, it none the less has both a history and a teleology. The philosopher goes beyond the madman in being able, through a rapid *dédoublement*, to make of the self a laughable other, while remaining aberrantly tied to a laughing self. The more philosophical one becomes, the more of that self becomes alterior. The consummation of this process is the absolute alterification of the self, the rendering laughable of the self in its entirety, the leap from philosophy to wisdom: 'As the comic is a sign of superiority, or of a belief in one's own superiority, it is natural to hold that, before they can achieve the absolute purification promised by certain mystical prophets, the nations of the world will see a multiplication of comic themes in proportion as their superiority increases' (Baudelaire 1995, 154). Just as Hölderlin is a paradigmatic figure for Benjamin in his taking of translation to the limit where meaning is threatened with its own disappearance, so Melmoth, from Charles Maturin's *Melmoth the Wanderer* (1820), is a paradigmatic figure for Baudelaire. In his terrible laughter (*rire terrible*), Melmoth is an essentially liminal being, at once the most alienated and the most nearly purified of figures: 'the outcast of society [*l'être déclassé*], wandering somewhere between the last boundaries [*limites*] of the territory of mankind and the frontiers of the higher life' (Baudelaire 1995, 156). Of course, the rendering laughable of the self in its entirety would coincide with the absolute disappearance of any laughing self, and thus the disappearance of laughter as such. When Being in its entirety has been rendered laughable, laughter itself disappears. Borrowing the term from Benjamin, this moment is the *Jetztzeit* of laughter's consummation and overcoming. The absolute laugh, the laugh for which Being itself is laughable, is the *last laugh*. And this last laugh is also precisely the laugh that no one laughs. In short, it is the laugh of absolute alterity.

Baudelaire casts the passage towards this last laugh, which threatens madness and promises wisdom, in terms of the distinction between two kinds of laughter. On the one hand, there is the ordinary or significative comic (*le comique significatif*); on the other, the absolute comic (*le comique absolu*). In both the ordinary and the absolute comic, laughter is the expression of an idea of superiority: in the former, superiority over other men; in the latter, superiority over nature. The absolute comic, however, is closer to the non-rational, non-dialectical leap or reversal of the last laugh from laughter to joy, from ignorance to knowledge, from guilt to innocence. The laughter of the absolute comic 'has about it something profound, primitive and axiomatic, which is much closer to the innocent life and to absolute joy than is the laughter caused by the comic in man's behaviour' (Baudelaire 1995, 157). And the purest form of the absolute comic is pantomime: 'The pantomime is the refinement, the quintessence of comedy; it is the pure comic element, purged and concentrated' (Baudelaire 1995, 161).

Given that pantomime is an art, it is a certain kind of artist who is most closely associated with this last laugh. Situated beyond both the madman and the philosopher, but on this side of the wise man, this artist is able not only to treat the self as other but also to disguise his delusive knowing (which the philosopher fails to do), to present himself as unknowing – in other words, as laughable – while having the last laugh on those who laugh. On the one hand, this artist is the incarnation of absolute knowledge: 'an artist is only an artist on condition that he is a double man [*à la condition d'être double*] and that there is not one single phenomenon of his double nature of which he is ignorant' (Baudelaire 1995, 165). On the other hand, he *presents* himself as unknowing. Unlike the madman, the philosopher, or the wise man, the artist negotiates the difference between knowing and unknowing by producing that which appears not to know. And, for Baudelaire, this *appearance of unknowing* is the very definition of art. His model for such playing at unknowing is E. T. A. Hoffmann: 'I would say that when Hoffmann gives birth to the absolute comic it is perfectly true that he knows what he is doing; but he also knows that the essence of this type of the comic is that it should appear to be unaware of itself [*l'essence de ce comique est de paraître s'ignorer lui-même*] and that it should produce in the spectator, or rather the reader, a joy in his own superiority and in the superiority of man over nature' (Baudelaire 1995, 165).

Baudelaire's theory of the comic is, then, profoundly dualistic, not least in its being grounded in the possibility of doubling (*dédoublement*), if also orientated towards its own disappearance (in the last laugh), when the very difference between self and other would be negated, and with it the comic as such. He distinguishes between two basic kinds of comedy (ordinary and absolute), and defines the comic as both Satanic and saving, mad and philosophic, threatening and promising. Furthermore, laughter is grounded in an aberrant distinction between self and other, which in turn reflects what Baudelaire terms 'a permanent dualism [*une dualité permanente*] in the human being – that is, the power of being oneself and someone else at one and the same time' (Baudelaire 1995, 165). To the questions: Who laughs? At whom or at what do they laugh? And to what end? Baudelaire's response is that only the unknowing self can laugh, that it can laugh only at the self mistaken for the other, and that the end of laughter is the wisdom that does not laugh. As for the last laugh, however, this is not a laugh *at the other* but the laugh *of the other*, a laugh that is produced only in that liminal space of knowing-unknowing, of apparent unknowing, or, more precisely, of unknowing's appearance, for which Baudelaire's name is *art*. If the artist never laughs in person, then that is because this last laugh survives only for as long as it comes from no one and nowhere, to inhabit the liminal space of pantomime.

Art, alterity, and the laughing machine: Bergson

In *Laughter: An Essay on the Meaning of the Comic* (1900), Henri Bergson follows Baudelaire in conceiving of the comic as a fall, at once literal and figurative – the confusion between literal and figurative itself being an instance of the comic, according to Bergson. Indeed, he even repeats Baudelaire in choosing the man who falls over in the street as his example of the literal fall. The figurative fall, however, is theorized by Bergson as a departure of consciousness into unconsciousness, of the organic into the mechanical, of the living into the non-living, of the human into the non-human. It soon becomes clear that this figurative fall may itself be subdivided into the literal and the figurative. Bergson's 'central image' of the comic event is a consciousness that 'gives us the impression of being a thing' (*nous donne l'impression d'une chose*) (Bergson 1999, 56). The comic is produced by consciousness lapsing into unconsciousness or automaticity: 'Rigidity, automatism, absentmindedness [*distraction*] and unsociability are all inextricably entwined; and all serve as ingredients to the making up of the comic in character' (Bergson 1999, 133). And, just as for Baudelaire, so for Bergson, the comic must be – more precisely, it must give the impression of being – completely unaware of its comicality. The comic is not just a lapse into unknowing, then, but a lapse into unknowing that appears to occur unknowingly.

If the comic is a lapse of consciousness, what laughs is the awareness of unawareness, the consciousness of unconsciousness. If Bergson is no less dualist in his approach than Baudelaire, he is unlike Baudelaire in conceiving of the comic lapse into alterity as a lapse of *genuine* knowing into unknowing, genuine consciousness into unconsciousness, whereas for Baudelaire it is a lapse of *apparent* knowing into unknowing, and, in pantomime, the highly paradoxical *apparent unknowing* of unknowing. For Bergson, then, comedy is directly related to the question of knowledge, not feeling. Indeed, he insists that if our feelings are aroused by what we see in a theatrical performance, then that performance simply cannot be comic: 'Unsociability in the performer and insensibility [*insensibilité*] in the spectator – such, in a word, are the two essential conditions' (Bergson 1999, 131). And, following Baudelaire's theory of *dédoublement*, Bergson argues that one can laugh at oneself only if one is divided from that self by the gulf separating genuine consciousness from unconsciousness, genuine knowing from genuine unknowing. In short, one can only laugh at the absolutely other. To laugh at the self is possible only when that self is taken as other. Only on the condition of our being able to distinguish clearly and unambiguously between the human and the non-human, the living and the non-living, knowing and unknowing, is the comic possible. Close as he is to Baudelaire, then, Bergson insists that the laughing consciousness is not deluded, is not itself fallen.

That things are slightly more complicated than this summary suggests, however, becomes evident as soon as one considers the figures Bergson deploys to communicate the comic fall. For his conception of the comic is scarcely reconcilable with that rhetoric of parasitism upon which he relies when describing how consciousness can lose itself to unconsciousness, the living to the unliving, the spontaneous to the mechanical, the unique to the repetitive: 'a person is never ridiculous except through some mental attribute resembling absentmindedness, through something that lives upon him without forming part of his organism, after the fashion of a parasite [*par quelque chose qui vit sur elle sans s'organiser avec elle, à la manière d'un parasite*]' (Bergson 1999, 152). If this parasite upon consciousness is itself the non-living, as Bergson repeatedly insists, then this introduction of the living–non-living intruder (*intrus*) marks a hesitation between fall and parasitism, between a lapse that originates in consciousness itself and a loss that is brought about by something beyond consciousness, which returns us to a preliminary question that Bergson's entire argument might be said to have been designed to obscure, or to disclose through its exclusion, namely how it is possible for consciousness ever to become unconsciousness, or for the living ever to become non-living, or for the human ever to become non-human – in other words, how something can ever become other than itself.

Were there no fall into alterity, were life to remain unremittingly mindful of itself, purely self-identical, there would be nothing comic, no laughter at all. There can be nothing comic either for or about a consciousness that never lapses from absolute self-knowing or that never serves as the unwitting host for unknowing:

> The rigid mechanism which we occasionally detect, as a foreign body [*comme un intrus*], in the living continuity of human affairs is of peculiar interest to us as being a kind of *absentmindedness* on the part of life. Were events unceasingly mindful of their own course, there would be no coincidences, no conjunctures and no circular series; everything would evolve and progress continuously. [...] The comic is that side of a person which reveals his likeness to a thing [*ce côté de la personne par lequel elle ressemble à une chose*], that aspect of human events which, through its peculiar inelasticity, conveys the impression of [*imite*] pure mechanism, of automatism, of movement without life. (Bergson 1999, 81–2)

As though to prove that one cannot write on the comic without oneself being subject to it, Bergson proceeds to repeat again and again that the comic lies in unknowing repetition, and to do so in sentences that are themselves, in both their content and their syntax, exercises in repetition. Following his own argument, however, this repetition would be comic only if we could be sure that he is repeating himself unknowingly or, more problematically, if we could be sure that he is consciously aiming to give the impression that he is repeating himself unknowingly. Were we to know that he is consciously repeating himself, without any intention to give the impression of unawareness, then his repetition would not be comic, even if Bergson himself makes no allowance for conscious or 'living' repetition and does not consider the possibility that ageing and indeed dying might be seen as the becoming-comic of the living, the increasing repetitivization of that which is living only because it can repeat itself.

Leaving out of thematic account these and other complicating possibilities to which his own rhetoric can scarcely help but direct the reader, Bergson struggles to maintain a dualist structure whereby we have, on the one hand, the living consciousness defined as a changing stream (*cours changeant*) in which there is nothing rigid, nothing fixed, nothing that repeats itself, and, on the other hand, the non-living defined as the mechanical in which there is no freedom, no spontaneity, nothing but lifeless repetition. And yet, not only can the living consciousness lose itself to an alterity in the form of an intruder (*intrus*) or parasite that is itself in some sense living, but that consciousness can save itself from that alterity, defend itself against the living–non-living intruder, and it can do this by laughing at itself – more precisely, by laughing at itself *in the guise of the other*. Although Bergson does not articulate the strange logic at work here, it is clear that it is not simply a question of living consciousness being able to lose itself to the alterity of the mechanical, but rather of it *having to be able* to lose itself to the mechanical. A living consciousness that could not lose itself in this way would not be a living consciousness at all.

Now, if laughter is prompted by consciousness's loss of itself to the alterity of the machine, that which laughs, and thus recalls consciousness to itself, is precisely the consciousness that has not lost itself, but which observes the loss of consciousness from a dramatic distance. Therein lies laughter's function: to recall consciousness to itself, to save the living from the non-living, the human from the non-human. It is in his analysis of the comic in character, which follows upon his analyses of the comic in general, the comic in situations, and the comic in words, that Bergson theorizes this saving function. The comic in character is not merely one in a series of types. Rather, it is the synthesis and consummation of the comic in situations and in words, that form in which they lose themselves, as though having to submit to a comic fate: 'the comic in words follows closely on the comic in situations and is finally merged [*vient se perdre*], along with the latter, in the comic in character' (Bergson 1999, 118).

In his analysis of the comic in character, Bergson argues that, for all the various forms taken by the comic, laughter is always a corrective (*une correction*), its function being simply to recall consciousness to itself. Essentially conservative in nature, laughter recalls that which has fallen into, or been inhabited by, alterity. Yet again, however, we are returned to the highly problematical nature of this fall or this invasion. If laughter is directed to that consciousness which has automatically (*automatiquement*) lost itself to alterity, then this depropriation occurs unconsciously. In other words, the one who falls into or is inhabited by alterity has already to be unconscious in order to become unconscious, alterity having to be always already on the scene: 'Any individual is comic who automatically goes his own way [*qui suit automatiquement son chemin*] without troubling himself about getting in touch with the rest of his fellow-beings. It is the part of laughter to reprove his absentmindedness and wake him out of his dream' (Bergson 1999, 121). Breaking automatically with the world of work and sanity, the comic character turns towards play and idling: 'to remain sensible is, indeed, to remain at work. But to detach oneself from things [*se détacher des choses*] and yet continue to perceive images, to break away from logic and yet continue to string together ideas, is to indulge in play or, if you prefer, in *dolce far niente* [*voilà qui est simplement du jeu ou, si l'on aime mieux, de la paresse*]' (Bergson 1999, 175).

Laughter, then, is a critique of that which loses itself to an alterity that has to be always already present, the fall into automaticity being itself automatic. And, as a corrective, laughter is the negation of that alterity which prevents consciousness from being itself. And yet – and again the rigorous dualism of Bergson's argument is threatened here – if living consciousness is definable as the 'negation of repetition', and thus a flow of absolutely unique singularities, the alterity of unconsciousness is also a singularity in its very mechanicity. That this is the case is suggested by Bergson's characterization of the fall into alterity as a fall away from the norm, the group, the *genera*: 'Now, it is the business of laughter to repress any separatist tendency [*tendances séparatistes*]. Its function is to convert rigidity into plasticity, to readapt the individual to the whole [*de réadapter chacun à tous*], in short, to round off the corners wherever they are met with' (Bergson 1999, 158). Paradoxically, the art of comedy offers general types (*types généraux*), but general types of that which in its unsociability departs from the norm, departs from the very generality of the social. Moreover, the peculiarity that characterizes the comic figure in its mechanicity lies in a prioritization of the very consciousness from which it departs, for the comic figure places thought above thing, the comical consisting 'in seeking to mold things on an idea of one's own, instead of molding one's ideas on things – in seeing before us what we are thinking of, instead of thinking of what we see [*à voir devant soi ce à quoi l'on pense, au lieu de penser à ce qu'on voit*]' (Bergson 1999, 165).

At this point it is certainly tempting to claim that Bergson's strictly dualist argument is itself comic in its rigidity. And yet, that rigidity is subject to disturbances of a kind that render the very distinction between the comic and the non-comic problematical, to say the least. We have already seen how the non-living is presented as a living parasite or foreign body, and how the lapse away from the singularity of consciousness into repetitive mechanicity is itself a lapse away from the norm. Similar disturbances affect Bergson's conception of the relation of the comic to its antithesis, which is not the serious but the graceful. The more mechanical, the more like a puppet (*pantin*), the body becomes, the more comical it becomes: '*The attitudes, gestures and movements of the human body are laughable in exact proportion as that body reminds us of a mere machine* [une simple mécanique]' (Bergson 1999, 32); 'it might be said that all *character* is comic, provided we mean by character the *ready-made* element in our personality, that mechanical element which resembles a piece of clockwork [*mécanisme*] wound up once for all and capable of working automatically' (Bergson 1999, 134). The antithesis of the puppet's mechanical body is the graceful body. Here, Bergson might appear to be completely at odds with the Kleist of 'On the Marionette Theatre' (1810), for whom grace is exhibited precisely in the marionette, on account of its being without self-consciousness. And yet, the difference between Bergson and Kleist is far from being so simple, since Bergson's non-comic consciousness, freed from all alterity, is nothing other than that 'infinite consciousness' which Kleist presents as the marionette's double: 'Grace appears most purely in that human form which either has no consciousness or an infinite consciousness' (Kleist 1994, 12). Where Kleist might be said proleptically to outwit Bergson, however, is in his suggestion that absolute unconsciousness, pure mechanicity, is indistinguishable from infinite consciousness.

Just as, for Bergson though not for Kleist, the graceful body is the body freed from all mechanicity, all repetition, and all unconsciousness, so graceful language is achieved through an absolute mindfulness of the speaker to the spoken. Graceful language is governed by absolute consciousness, does not lapse into, is not inhabited by, automaticity. For the life of thought – that living thing (*chose qui vit*) – to be preserved in language as that which translates thought (*qui traduit la pensée*), language itself must live (Bergson 1999, 109). When language lapses into the alterity of lifelessness, it becomes comic. Clichés – 'ready-made formulas and stereotyped phrases' – are always comic, as, more generally, is any disparity between language and idea: '*A comic meaning is invariably obtained when an absurd idea is fitted into a well-established phrase-form*' (Bergson 1999, 104). When Bergson claims that the unconscious confusion of the literal and the figurative is comic, one is left uncertain whether one is supposed to laugh or not: all depends here upon how literally he means the claim that graceful language is no less alive than the consciousness it translates.

In addition to clichés, puns are identified as another form of linguistic gracelessness. The pun (*calembour*) is a case of the 'reciprocal interference of series', here between two entirely distinct sentences and ideas: 'In the pun, the same sentence appears to offer two independent meanings, but it is only an appearance; in reality there are two different sentences made up of different words, but claiming to be one and the same because both have the same sound' (Bergson 1999, 111). The gracelessness of the pun lies, then, in this radical difference, or, more precisely, in the superficial blurring of this difference. More generally still, Bergson argues that any play upon words is a case of language departing – or at least appearing to depart – from its proper function, turning against the human, losing its own consciousness: 'the play upon words makes us think somehow of a negligence [*laisser-aller*] on the part of language, which, for the time being, seems to have forgotten its real function [*destination véritable*] and now claims to accommodate things to itself instead of accommodating itself to things' (Bergson 1999, 111). Just as the comic absurd lies in privileging thought over thing (despite the fact that the comic has been defined as thought's loss of itself to the thing), so here the comic in language lies in the privileging of language over the thing. In each case, a fundamental binary distinction – between tragic and comic, tears and laughter, pure individuality and pure generality, consciousness and thing, living and non-living – is subjected to a pressure that impels both the comic and the non-comic towards that most hybrid of forms, the tragicomic. It is only appropriate, then, that Bergson's example of the comic absurd should be Don Quixote, the tragicomic figure *par excellence*, not least because in this figure the difference between comedy and insanity is at stake.

Following Baudelaire, Bergson touches upon the relation between the comic and madness towards the end of his essay, only to argue strenuously for a clear line of demarcation between the two. That inversion of consciousness and thing which characterizes the comic absurd is indeed to be found 'in certain types of insanity' (Bergson 1999, 166). Bergson insists, however, that insanity itself is never comic, since it provokes an emotional response in those who witness it, namely pity. All depends here, then, on our being in a position to know whether we are faced with the comic absurd or with insanity, for the comedian cannot be insane, or at least cannot be taken for insane. What makes such a position of knowledge so difficult to achieve is that, for Bergson, the logic of the comic absurd is the same as the logic of insanity: both share the logic of dreams. And the very distinction that Bergson claims to wish to retain between the comic absurd and insanity is abandoned in his analysis of the madness (*démence*) that is particular to dreams. This madness involves the experience of alterity in the form of an other self, inhabiting the living consciousness:

> We allude to the strange fusion that a dream often effects between two persons who henceforth form only one and yet remain distinct. Generally one of these is the dreamer himself. He feels he has not ceased to be what he is; yet he has become someone else. He is himself, and not himself [*C'est lui et ce n'est pas lui*]. He hears himself speak and sees himself act, but he feels that some other 'he' has borrowed his body and stolen his voice [*il sent qu'un autre lui a emprunté son corps et lui a pris sa voix*]. (Bergson 1999, 171)

The dreamer is inhabited, then, by the self as other, and this other is in fact neither consciousness nor thing, neither living nor dead, but rather the hybrid conscious-unconscious, living-dead. The strange nature of this particular other is evident in Bergson's example, taken from Mark Twain's remarkable 'Encounter with an Interviewer' (1874), in which the writer claims (in the manner of the comic absurd, according to Bergson) that he and his twin 'got mixed in the bath-tub when we were only two weeks old, and one of us was drowned [...] that was *me*' (Twain 1994, 88; quoted in Bergson 1999, 172–3).[3] The one who speaks here, belonging properly to neither the living nor the dead, neither consciousness nor unconsciousness, neither the self nor the other, is the *artist*.

If the series of dualist distinctions shaping Bergson's argument – in a manner that we now have reason to hesitate terming strictly mechanical – leads to the emergence of an other as *artist*, inhabiting the place of the living consciousness, what of laughter itself? Here, too, Bergson's argument heads towards a tragicomic breakdown of the distinction between the spontaneous and the automatic. Having defined laughter as a corrective response to the automatic lapse of consciousness into the alterity of the mechanical, towards the end of his essay he identifies this corrective response as itself mechanical, indeed as mechanicity *par excellence*: 'Now, laughter is simply the result of a mechanism [*l'effet d'un mécanisme*] set up in us by nature or, what is almost the same thing, by our long acquaintance with social life. It goes off spontaneously and returns tit for tat [*Il part tout seul, véritable riposte du tic au tac*]. It has no time to look where it hits' (Bergson 1999, 177). Here, the difference between spontaneity and automaticity, between pure life and pure lifelessness, is itself what lapses.

Bergson's thesis on laughter may be summed up, then, as follows: laughter, as a mechanical effect, is always laughing at itself, and in so doing dividing itself from itself, producing or being produced as its own other. The laughing self (as mechanical other) is laughing at the other (as another mechanical self). Laughter is the mechanical negation of the mechanical. When it comes to laughter, it would seem that there is nothing but alterity. Life itself, living consciousness, is always other than itself in its very act of marking its difference through laughter from all laughable alterity. If consciousness alone can laugh – the comic figure, the object of laughter, is, or at least always *presents itself as*, absolutely serious – this consciousness is nothing but an endlessly repetitive mechanical fall into mechanicity.

As with Baudelaire, so with Bergson, these complications come to a head around the question of the *art of comedy*. Initially, the very relation between art and comedy is presented as one more in a series of oppositions. Art is defined as that which reveals a reality beyond the general, a reality that is unique, the absolute singularity of a here and now: 'art always aims at what is *individual*. What the artist fixes on his canvas is something he has seen at a certain spot, on a certain day, at a certain hour, with a colouring that will never be seen again. What the poet sings of is a certain mood which was his, and his alone, and which will never return' (Bergson 1999, 144–5). Properly speaking, there cannot be an art of comedy, since, whereas art deals only in singularities, comedy deals only in types: 'It takes note of similarities. It aims at placing types before our eyes. It even creates new types, if necessary. In this respect it forms a contrast to all the other arts' (Bergson 1999, 146).

If there is an art of comedy, then its essence lies not in the nature of that which is revealed, but rather in a certain feigning. Given that the object of laughter is always that which has lapsed into absentmindedness (*distraction*), the comic figure must by definition always *present itself* as unknowing, as unaware of its condition. If there is to be a comic art, then the distinction between *real* unconsciousness and *feigned* unconsciousness has, paradoxically, both to disappear and to remain in place. If the spectator or reader is simply aware that the comic figure is feigning unconsciousness, then laughter will not be provoked; and yet, if the comic figure is really unconscious, then there will be laughter but there will not be art. The spectator or reader of the comic has, then, both to know and to forget that the artist of the comic is feigning. And that forgetting on the reader's or spectator's part, which is the precondition of laughter, is itself a lapse from absolute consciousness. Again, we are returned, *as though* mechanically, to the conclusion that the laugh laughs only at the laugh. In this instance, the one who laughs at the art of comedy is himself laughable in his absentmindedness. Bergson leaves us, then, with a highly problematical series of collapsing distinctions between insanity, dream logic, and art, between the comical and the deranged, between what is conscious and what is unconscious, between life and automatism. These distinctions can scarcely help but bring to mind Freud, to whom we may now turn for further reflections upon the relationship between comedy and alterity, and for a further turn of that screw which leads unremittingly towards the thought that both the subject and the object of the last laugh is a figure whose alterity is of a kind that defies all the categories by which it might be known.

Death, deception, and the sublime humorist: Freud

In both *Jokes and Their Relation to the Unconscious* (1905) and 'Humour' (1927), Freud aims to overcome the fundamental confusions besetting all previous treatments of the topic, and to establish a 'sharp conceptual and material distinction' between the joke (*Witz*) and the comic (*Komische*) (Freud 1960b, 212), and ultimately between these and humour (*Humor*). However, his procedure proves to be very different in these two works, not simply because the paper on 'Humour' was written after the development of his second topography of the mind, but also because, while in 'Humour' he enters without hesitation into an identification of both what humour shares with jokes and the comic, and what distinguishes it from them, in *Jokes* he presents 'the problem of the relation of jokes to the comic' as something that 'we intended to evade' (*das wir zu umgehen trachteten*) (Freud 1960b, 65). Given that the final chapter of *Jokes* is devoted almost entirely to the clarification of this very relation, the reader is left wondering whether

Freud's confession of such an intention to evade is itself intended to be taken seriously or not.

Such uncertainty as to Freud's intention here may seem to be beside the point only if we in our turn evade the question of intentionality that lies at the very heart of his definition of the joke. For, according to Freud, an unintended joke is simply impossible. It is unsurprising, then, that he should eventually find himself obliged to address the question of precisely how one is to tell if an intention to joke is in fact present in a given utterance. Postponing this question of intentionality until after he has analysed the technique and the purpose of jokes, however, Freud argues that the psychical processes to be found in jokes are the same as those operating in dreams, namely condensation, displacement, and indirect representation. The invariable task (*Ausgabe*) of both jokes and dreams is to deal with (*erledigen*) an inhibition. In both jokes and dreams these psychical processes work upon unconscious material in such a way as to permit a relaxation of the mechanisms of repression upon that material. However, while the purpose of jokes is the attainment of pleasure (*Lusterwerb*), the purpose of dreams is predominantly the avoidance of unpleasure (*Unlustersparnis*). A further crucial difference between jokes and dreams is observable in their modes of construction. While the dream-work relies principally upon the technique of displacement (*Verschiebung*), in the joke-work displacement plays only a subordinate role. Unlike dreams, jokes are purely linguistic entities, relying upon the potential for a play (*Spiel*) in language that is owing to its essential doubleness: 'Nothing distinguishes jokes more clearly from all other psychical structures than this double-sidedness [*Doppelseitigkeit*] and this duplicity in speech [*Doppelzüngigkeit*]' (Freud 1960b, 172).

The activation of this doubleness can take two basic forms: the innocent (*harmlos*) and the tendentious (*tendenziös*), the latter being 'the highest stage' (*die höchste Stufe*) of jokes (Freud 1960b, 173). While both innocent and tendentious jokes are necessarily intended (*beabsichtigt*), the difference between them lies in the nature of the pleasure they afford. The pleasure produced by innocent jokes derives purely from the technique of the joke, whereas the pleasure afforded by the tendentious joke is a compound, deriving from both the technique and the economy in expenditure on inhibition or suppression of an instinct or drive (*Trieb*). If it is clear that there can be nothing ethical about tendentious jokes, even innocent jokes are not free of the unethical when they are considered from the point of view of their motivation: 'The motive force [*Triebfeder*] for the production of innocent jokes is not infrequently an ambitious urge [*Drang*] to show one's cleverness, to display oneself – an instinct [*Trieb*] that may be equated with exhibitionism in the sexual field' (Freud 1960b, 143). Within the general category of tendentious jokes, however, there are certainly degrees of unethicality. Of the four kinds of tendentious joke – the obscene (*obszön*), the hostile (*feindselig*), the cynical (*zynisch*), and the sceptical (*skeptisch*) – the obscene and the hostile are more obviously unethical than the cynical and the sceptical. Indeed, cynical jokes bear a certain resemblance to humour as Freud will come to define it in the final pages of *Jokes*. Unlike obscene or hostile jokes, they can appear to take the self (that is, the joker) as their object: 'A particularly favourable occasion for [cynical] tendentious jokes is presented when the intended rebellious criticism is directed against the subject himself, or, to put it more cautiously, against someone in whom the subject has a share – a collective person, that is (the subject's own nation, for instance)' (Freud 1960b, 111). Jewish jokes – when told by Jews – are perhaps the most common instance of such joking. As the above quotation suggests, however, such jokes do not quite take the subject as the direct object of the joke. Even in cynical jokes, the butt of the joke is alterior to the joke-teller. As for sceptical jokes, these Freud describes as the rarest of all jokes. What distinguishes them from all other forms of tendentious joke is that the object of their attack is neither a person nor an institution but 'the certainty of our knowledge itself' (*die Sicherheit unserer Erkenntnis selbst*) (Freud 1960b, 115). This attack on knowledge will always be limited, however, by the fact that, for such a joke to be recognized as a joke, there must be no uncertainty at all about the intention to joke. It is to this question of intentionality that Freud turns in his attempt to establish that distinction which he claims to have intended to evade (*umgehen*), namely the difference between jokes and the comic.

One of the principal distinctions between jokes and the comic is that, whereas jokes require a third person (the joke's hearer), in addition to both the subject (the teller) and the object (the butt or victim) of the joke, the comic requires only two persons (the subject and the object of the comic): 'If one comes across something comic, one can enjoy it by oneself. A joke, on the contrary, must be told to someone else [*ist man mitzuteilen genötigt*]' (Freud 1960b, 143). Unlike the comic, a joke always comes with the exigency to communicate it to this third person, the reason for this being that it is impossible to tell oneself a joke, or, more precisely, impossible to get any yield of pleasure from telling oneself a joke, since the joke cannot function as a joke must, which is to say, it cannot surprise the hearer with a play (*Spiel*) that is unanticipated and thus with a genuine lifting of an inhibition. It is this essential sociality of the joke that distinguishes it very clearly from that 'completely asocial' (*vollkommen asoziales*) mental product, the dream (Freud 1960b, 179). A second key difference between jokes and the comic lies in the nature and the origin of the pleasure they afford. The pleasure afforded by jokes is located in the unconscious, whereas the pleasure in the comic is located in the preconscious. Whereas the pleasure afforded by a joke derives from an economy in the expenditure of energy on the inhibition or suppression of an unconscious *Trieb*, the pleasure afforded by the comic derives from a difference in expenditure (*Aufwanddifferenz*) that comes to light through a comparison. For his introductory example of comic pleasure, Freud selects pantomime (*Pantomime*), as an intended (*beabsichtigt*) form of the comedy of movement. As we have seen, for Baudelaire, pantomime is the 'quintessence of comedy', the 'pure comic element, purged and concentrated'. For Freud, it is 'the most primitive kind of stage performance' (*die primitivste Bühnendarstellung*). The laughter provoked by pantomime is owing to the fact that the clown's movements strike us as exaggerated or pointless (*zwecklos*), as an unnecessary and indeed inexplicable expenditure (Freud 1960b, 190). The comic, then, is intimately related to an experience of inexplicability and apparent purposelessness in the other.

Among Freud's other examples of the comic of movement there is one that we have already encountered in both Baudelaire and Bergson, and which haunts almost all reflections on laughter, as though it demanded not simply explanation but justification, as though the question of the ethics of laughter were focused here more precisely than anywhere else. That example is, of course, the fall, in all its literality and alterity: 'For instance,' Freud declares, 'if someone slips in the street and falls down we laugh because the impression – we do not know why – is comic. A child laughs in the same case from a feeling of superiority [*Überlegenheitsgefühl*] or from *Schadenfreude*: "You've fallen down, I haven't" ' (Freud 1960b, 224). If children are quite simply without any feeling for the comic (*Gefühl für Komik*), if a child's laughter at the sight of another's fall originates purely in a sense of superiority or *Schadenfreude*, there is none the less always something infantile about the comic, as there is about jokes and even humour. If the adult laughs at the sight of another's fall because it is comic, this comicality arises precisely because the one who falls appears to the adult as childlike (*kindisch*). As an adult, 'I laugh at the difference in expenditure between another person and myself, every time I rediscover the child in him [*wenn ich in dem anderen das Kind wiederfinde*]' (Freud 1960b, 224).

The point at which the comic bears its closest resemblance to jokes, however, is in the naïve (*Naive*), and it is with the naïve, identified by Freud as a marginal case (*Grenzfall*) of the joke, that the question of intentionality returns as a problem. Like the pleasure derived from jokes, the pleasure derived from the naïve arises through the lifting (*Aufhebung*) of an internal inhibition, but here the *Aufhebung* is not partial but absolute, the value (*Größe*) of the censorship having been reduced to zero (Freud 1960b, 185). If the pleasure afforded by both jokes and the naïve is identical in its origin and nature, however, the fundamental difference between the two lies in the fact that the naïve is never made, is never the result of an intention (*Absicht*). In order to know that we have a case of the naïve rather than a joke, in order to know that we have the lifting of an internal inhibition that is not intended, we have to know that the one who produces the naïve lacks the inhibition that is the prerequisite of any yield of pleasure from it. Furthermore, for the naïve to occur, not only must its producer not intend it, not only must this producer lack the internal inhibition, but s/he must derive absolutely no pleasure from it. Here, Freud is in fact following Kant, who in the *Critique of Judgement* (1790) argues that naïvety is 'the breaking forth of the ingenuousness originally natural to man, in opposition to the art of disguising oneself that has become a second nature', and that 'an art of being *naïf* is a contradiction' (Kant 1952, 202–3). Unsurprisingly, then, the naïve is to be found most often in children, although Freud sees it also being 'carried over to uneducated adults [*in weiterer Übertragung dann beim ungebildeten Erwachsenen*], whom we may regard as childish so far as their intellectual development is concerned' (Freud 1960b, 182).

Can we be as confident as Freud appears to be, however, in our ability to distinguish between jokes and the naïve? Leaving aside his comparison of the uneducated adult to a child, what of jokes that are intended, but that are intended precisely to appear to be unintended? Are they still jokes? All depends here on our being in a position to know, and indeed on our being in a position to know whether or not we can know. That such knowing will be no easy task, that it involves telling the difference between being and appearance, between the serious and the playful, and indeed between the fictional and the non-fictional, becomes evident when Freud argues that the joke-teller must only *appear* to be serious while the producer of the naïve must in fact *be* serious: 'It is merely a question of [*Er handelt sich nur darum*] whether we assume that the speaker has intended [*beabsicht*] to make a joke or whether we suppose that he – the child – has tried in good faith to draw a serious conclusion on the basis of his uncorrected ignorance [*unkorrigierten Unwissenheit*]. Only the latter case is one of *naïveté*' (Freud 1960b, 183). Despite that reassuringly dismissive 'merely' (*nur*), Freud proceeds to acknowledge that telling the difference between the joke and the naïve is not always easy, not least given the existence of misleading (*mißverständlich*) naïvety, in which the faux-naïve speaker presents what is in fact a joke as the naïve: 'We may assume in the child an ignorance that no longer exists; and children often represent themselves as naïve [*und Kinder pflegen sich häufig naiv zu stellen*], so as to enjoy a liberty that they would not otherwise be granted' (Freud 1960b, 184). Now, if it is always possible to represent oneself as naïve, if it is always possible to feign naïvety, to make an art of the natural, either to deceive or to reserve the joke for those with the acumen to detect such feigning, and to appreciate the joke that would lie precisely in the act of feigning itself, then any clear distinction between jokes and the comic becomes problematical, to say the least. And if jokes are never ethical, in that they always originate in the unconscious and always take an other as their target, then neither is such feigned naïvety, any more than is the childish naïvety of the child or the uneducated adult.

In Freud's attempt to distinguish jokes from the naïve, and indeed from all other forms of the comic, all depends, then, on whether the producer is knowing or unknowing, on whether s/he is prompting laughter intentionally or not; in short, on whether that producer knows what s/he is saying or doing, and whether the one who laughs knows whether or not the intention to provoke laughter is present or not. And if the problems besetting Freud's distinction between jokes and the comic appear formidable, these problems are only compounded when he turns to the question of humour at the very end of *Jokes* – one might even say, at the death of the joke book, given that humour will for Freud be very much a response to death.

The difference between jokes and the comic on the one hand, and humour on the other, is, above all, an ethical one. Humour is 'one of the highest psychical achievements', and an achievement that 'enjoys the particular favour of thinkers' (Freud 1960b, 228). Not only does humour enjoy this intellectual distinction, but it also possesses a grandeur (*Großartigkeit*) and magnanimity (*Seelengröße*) that is alien to both jokes and the comic. From the outset, Freud employs a rhetoric of the sublime in his reflections on humour. Whenever it is a question of humour, it will also be a question of heights, elevations, grandeur, greatness. What places humour above both jokes and the comic is not least that it is related to suffering (*Leiden*), and to a pleasure achieved in the face of suffering, which is to say a pleasure that depends upon, and yet constitutes a resistance to, suffering. Unlike the comic, humour is 'a means of obtaining pleasure in spite of the distressing affects that interfere with it [...]. The conditions for its appearance are given if there is a situation in which, according to our usual habits, we should be tempted to release a distressing affect and if motives then operate upon us which suppress that affect *in statu nascendi*' (Freud 1960b, 228).

That humour is a response to, and more precisely a defence against, suffering is evident from the fact that both in *Jokes* and, over 20 years later, in 'Humour', Freud's principal example is gallows humour (*Galgenhumor*). Although he insists that this is the crudest form of humour, just as pantomime is the crudest form of the comic, it is also the purest form of humour, that form in which humour's very essence is disclosed, since, for Freud, there is a fundamental relation between humour and death, between humour and the absolute destruction of the ego. That he considers the example of gallows humour indispensable is evident not least from the fact that in 'Humour' it becomes the sole example included in his analysis, the particular instance of gallows humour upon which he comments there being drawn from his earlier work, in which it is presented as follows:

> A rogue [*Spitzbube*] who was being led out to execution on a Monday remarked: 'Well, this week's beginning nicely.' This is actually a joke, since the remark is quite apt in itself, but on the other hand, is misplaced in a nonsensical way, since for the man himself there would be no further events this week. But humour is concerned in the *making* of such a joke [*Es gehört aber Humor dazu, einen solchen Witz zu machen*] – that is, in disregarding what it is that distinguishes the beginning of this week from others, in denying the distinction [*den Unterschied zu leugnen*] which might give rise to motives for quite special emotions. (Freud 1960b, 229)

If this example of humour also involves a joke, what clearly distinguishes the humorist from the joker here is that the former makes a joke at his own expense – or, more precisely, makes a joke that is itself the denegation of his own situation, a denegation of the fact that the joker is about to die, a denegation of the distinction between the day of the joker's death and any other day, the sign of an astonishing indifference (*Gleichgültigkeit*) that interrupts that pity (*Mitleid*) which we would otherwise feel for the condemned man.

What Freud does not observe in either *Jokes* or 'Humour', however, is that his very identification of this joke-making as an example of humour is grounded in a number of assumptions about the nature of the person responsible for the remark 'Well, this week's beginning nicely'. These assumptions include, but are certainly not limited to, the following: that the one who is making this remark is intending a joke; that he is aware he is about to die; that he is not mad; that he does not wish to die; that he believes in the possibility of his own death; that he believes that the execution will indeed take place, and is confident that it will not (like Dostoevsky's and Blanchot's, for instance) be called off at the last moment or be prevented from taking place by a breakdown in the machinery of execution. Perhaps the strangest of Freud's assumptions, however, is one that does not directly affect the claim that what we have here is both a humorist and a joker, but which none the less returns us to the question of the ethics of humour. This assumption is that the humorist is not the victim of a miscarriage of justice, that he is unquestionably a rogue (*Spitzbube*) or a criminal (*Delinquent, Verbrecher*) who is on the point of undergoing capital punishment for a crime that is unspecified but that is assumed by Freud to have taken place. In other words, both in *Jokes* and in 'Humour', Freud's humorist is taken to be guilty, to be responsible for a crime for which the punishment is capital, a death that is precisely not a natural death but an execution (*Exekution*) carried out in the name of the law. That this assumption is scarcely a coincidence, that humour has everything to do not just with death but also with the law and with ethics, and indeed with the relation between death and ethics, becomes evident when Freud goes on to argue that the humorist is necessarily a deceiver.

In both *Jokes* and 'Humour', Freud defines humour as a defensive process (*Abwehrvorgang*), indeed as the highest of the defensive processes. In 'Humour', this process is analysed in terms of Freud's second topography of the mind. Here, humour is identified as a defensive process that protects the ego from the real, and is to be situated 'among the great series of methods which the human mind has constructed in order to evade the compulsion to suffer [*dem Zwang des Leidens zu entziehen*] – a series which begins with neurosis and culminates in madness and which includes intoxication, self-absorption [*Selbstversenkung*] and ecstasy' (Freud 1964, 163). Now, the greatest compulsion to suffer, the greatest threat to the ego, is death itself, which is why gallows humour cannot be just one example among others. Humour's time is death's imminence.

If humour is ultimately a response to a death that, in Freud's example, is far from simply natural, and if it has the remarkable power to protect the ego from the reality of this death, that power is exercised in the production of an illusion. The super-ego convinces the ego that its death is not to be taken seriously, that this death is something towards which the ego can be completely indifferent (*gleichgültig*). How does the super-ego achieve this end? The answer lies not simply in the ego's childish readiness to believe that it is not threatened with death, but also, and indeed principally, in the authority of the super-ego, in the fact that the super-ego's power over the ego is that of a parent over a child. Indeed, the super-ego's authority is directly linked, here as elsewhere, to its origin in the parental agency. And yet, for all its maturity and authority, the super-ego exerts a power over the ego that takes the form of a repudiation (*Abweisung*) of the real and a submission to illusion: 'in bringing about the humorous attitude, the super-ego is actually repudiating reality and serving an illusion [*die Realität abweist und einer Illusion dient*]' (Freud 1964, 166). The reality in question here is death; the illusion being served is the belief that the ego is invulnerable. If Freud characterizes this liberating super-ego as no less of a parental figure than the super-ego in its more usual role as severe master (*gestrenger Herr*) or conscience (*Gewissen*), then this particular parent, this particular father-humorist, is one who is absolutely irresponsible in that, while it has no power to prevent the literal death of the ego, it does have the power to delude the ego into thinking itself invulnerable. Indeed, if the super-ego treats the ego like a child for fearing the death that threatens it, if it reassures this child-ego by refusing to take the real seriously, by making fun of the ego's own fears, it can do so only because it is itself playing the child. And this childishness is compounded by what bears a close resemblance to madness, in that humour, like madness, involves a complete detachment of the ego from the real defined as the external world (*Außenwelt*). It is all the more striking, then, that Freud should insist that, unlike childishness, unlike madness, unlike criminality, and unlike jokes and the comic, humour has dignity (*Würde*), the pleasure it affords possessing 'a character of very high value' (Freud 1964, 166). What are we to make of this claim? What could possibly make humour superior in value to all other forms of resistance to the real?

In *Jokes*, and even more insistently in 'Humour', Freud relies heavily upon a rhetoric of the sublime, and the sublimity of humour lies precisely in its denegation of the real; in other words, in its reduction to nothing of the real, which in gallows humour takes the form of an absolute negation, a death that, far from being natural, is a punishment meted out by a law whose validity is precisely what is not questioned by Freud when he identifies the gallows humorist as a criminal. Humour, then, is the artful negation of a non-natural negation:

> Like jokes and the comic, humour has something liberating [*etwas Befreiendes*] about it; but it also has something of grandeur and elevation [*etwas Großartiges und Erhebendes*], which is lacking in the other two

ways of obtaining pleasure from intellectual activity. The grandeur in it clearly lies in the triumph of narcissism, the victorious assertion of the ego's invulnerability [*Unverletzlichkeit*]. The ego refuses to be distressed by the provocations of reality, to let itself be compelled to suffer. It insists that it cannot be affected by the traumas of the external world [*Außenwelt*]; it shows, in fact, that such traumas are no more than occasions for it to gain pleasure. This last feature is a quite essential element of humour [*ist für den Humor durchaus wesentlich*]. (Freud 1964, 162)

Freud's rhetoric, together with the emphasis upon death as a real threat to the ego that is imagined not to be a real threat, returns us to Kant's analytic of the sublime. According to Kant, the elevation of the subject in the experience of the sublime discloses to the subject its 'power of resistance' to the 'seeming omnipotence of nature' (Kant 1952, 111). However, this empowerment is possible only if the subject experiences a threat to its natural being that is not in fact a real threat, that is purely hypothetical or imagined:

> we may look upon an object as *fearful*, and yet not be afraid *of* it, if, that is, our estimate takes the form of our simply picturing to ourselves the case of our wishing to offer some resistance to it, and recognizing that all such resistance would be quite futile. [...] One who is in a state of fear can no more play the part of a judge of the sublime of nature than one captivated by inclination and appetite can of the beautiful. He flees from the sight of an object filling him with dread; and it is impossible to take delight in terror that is seriously entertained. (Kant 1952, 110)

In Freud's analysis of humour, however, this threat is of course a real one, although the illusion that it is not one is what the super-ego grants the ego. For Kant, the aesthetic of the sublime negotiates the gap between the understanding (nature) and reason (freedom), between knowledge and ethics. For Freud, however, humour may possess a dignity (*Würde*) absent from both jokes and the comic, but it can scarcely be said to be ethical. For all its dignity, its liberating effect originates in the super-ego's repudiation of reality and its childish serving of illusion. That Freud assumes the guilt of his humorist, that this humorist is a criminal facing capital punishment, the justification for which goes without saying here, suggests that this illusion is closer to a lie than to a fiction.

Things are no less complicated when it comes to the role of alterity in humour. Freud argues that, unlike jokes and the comic, humour requires no other: 'It completes its course within a single person [*in einer einziger Person*]; another person's participation adds nothing to it [*fügt nichts Neues zu ihm hinzu*]' (Freud 1960b, 229). At first glance, then, it would seem that in humour there is simply no place for alterity, as there is in the case of jokes (the butt, victim, or object of the joke) and the comic (that which produces the comic effect being alterior to that which appreciates it). However, if humour is characterized by a certain asceticism in this respect, if it appears to spare the other, this is only because the humorist, that single and indeed most singular of beings, is, like Baudelaire's philosopher, internally divisible, into ego and super-ego, and is therefore already more than one. In fact, it is the ego that plays the role of the other, in the sense that it is led to accept an illusion by a subject (the super-ego) that knows the real and can master the ego's response to it. As for the ethicality of humour, then, all depends here on whether the super-ego may in fact be said to be making fun of the ego, not only on account of the ego's fears in the face of the real, but also through convincing the ego to accept an illusion. Is the super-ego making a joke at the expense of the ego? It is with this question in mind that we can turn to a recent attempt to conceive of an ethical laughter on the basis of Freud's theory of humour.

Literature and ethical humour, or the laugh beyond all other

In *On Humour* (2002), Simon Critchley attempts to establish a rigorous distinction between ethical and unethical humour – that is to say, between laughter at the expense of another and laughter at the expense of no one, between laughter that victimizes the other and laughter that is liberating and consoling for the self. Ethical laughter – or 'true humour' – does not exceed the economy of the self in search of an object: 'true humour does not wound a specific victim and always contains self-mockery. The object of laughter is the subject who laughs' (Critchley 2002, 14).

In theorizing such 'true humour', Critchley draws explicitly on Freud's 1927 essay, in which, as we have seen, humour is distinguished from both jokes and the comic through its involving a single person and operating by way of the split between ego and super-ego. In order to derive a theory of properly ethical humour by way of Freud, however, Critchley has first to cleanse Freud's theory of those traits which tie it to a superiority theory of laughter. But this cleansing does not make of ethical laughter a laughter without object. Rather, the object becomes the self's (which is to say, the ego's) own finitude: its weakness, its limitations, its lack of mastery. Things are not quite so simple as this statement suggests, however, for if the ethical laugh is the 'quiet acknowledgement of one's own limitedness' (Critchley 2002, 109), it is also paradoxically a cognitive mastery of one's own lack of mastery. That the ethical laugh is a knowing of unknowing, a mastery of unmastery, and thus a negation of the negative, is evident from the fact that it affords a transcendence closely akin to that achieved in the experience of the Kantian sublime. As the 'highest laugh', the ethical laugh 'does not bring unhappiness, but rather elevation and liberation, the lucidity of consolation' (Critchley 2002, 111). In contrast to that Nietzschean laughter echoed in Bataille, ethical laughter 'insists that life is not something to be affirmed ecstatically, but acknowledged comically. This is the sardonic and more sarcastic comedy of someone like Sterne, Swift or Beckett which arises out of a palpable sense of inability, impotence and inauthenticity' (Critchley 2002, 106).

Critchley also follows Freud in theorizing humour as a response to real suffering. However, whereas Freud insists that humour involves both a recognition and an unresigned (*nicht resigniert*), rebellious (*trotzig*) denial of the real, Critchley lays the emphasis squarely upon the moment of recognition, leaving out the repudiation of reality and the serving of an illusion that Freud includes in the economy of liberation and elevation, and which leads him to qualify his remark on the liberating and elevating nature of the experience by tracing it back to the triumph of narcissism and insisting that the pleasure generated by the humorous attitude is one that we regard as possessing a 'very high value' – without our rightly knowing why (Freud 1964, 166). The consequence of Critchley's exclusion of the moment of repudiation and subservience to illusion is that his ethical theory of humour comes to bear a very close resemblance to humour as theorized by Kierkegaard in his *Concluding Unscientific Postscript* (1846), in which it is identified as 'the border between the ethical and the religious', involving a resignation or acceptance that the tragic does not: 'Humour has its justification in its tragic side, in the fact that it reconciles itself to the pain that despair seeks to abstract from, although it knows no way out' (Kierkegaard 1968, 459).

If there is something problematical about the experience that lies at the heart of Critchley's theory of ethical humour – namely the acknowledgement of finitude, which negates itself in its very occurrence – then this is a problem that returns us to the question of the role of alterity in his theory of laughter. Laughter remains ethical only for as long as it is at the expense of no other, only for as long as it respects the other. And yet, one of the aspects of Freud's theory of humour that Critchley accepts without suspicion is that of the split within the self between ego and super-ego, and also between two kinds of super-ego, namely the severe master and the gentler parent. It is clear, however, that this split is structured as one more form of the self–other relation, grounded in Freud's rigorous distinction between inner world and outer world, and that were this not the case it would not be possible for the super-ego to reassure the ego through its serving of an illusion. Indeed, Critchley conceives of the ethical laugh – more precisely, the ethical smile – as being a 'smile of knowing self-mockery and self-ridicule' (Critchley 2002, 107). From this it is clear not only that the ethical smile is grounded in knowledge, and in an uncritical acceptance of the inner world–outer world distinction, but that for it to take place the self (as ego) must function as an other that is no less alterior than the other at whose expense the most unethical of laughter would take place. That the difference between ego and super-ego can be maintained as a case apart, clearly distinguishable from all other forms of self–other relation, including that of parent and child, is precisely what Freud's own work places in question. The relation between ego and super-ego can scarcely be said to be ethical, then, any more than Critchley's theory of humour can be said to go beyond the theory of laughter as being at the expense of the other. In what he theorizes as ethical laughter, there is no less violence directed at the other than there is in unethical laughter, and no less insistence upon the cognitive supremacy of the one who laughs than there is in a superiority theory of laughter of the kind proposed by Baudelaire.

Now, one possibility that Critchley does not consider in his attempt to theorize an ethical humour – a possibility that has emerged in our readings of Baudelaire and Bergson – is that it may in fact only ever be the other who laughs, that the one who laughs (be it the philosopher, the madman, the living being, the ego, or the super-ego) only laughs on the condition that it is subject to the law of the other. Were this the case, then, strange as it may seem, it would never be true to say 'I am laughing'. And if it is only ever the other who laughs, then the very notion of an ethical or an unethical laugh is rendered highly problematical, at least for as long as the ethical is conceived in terms of a respect for the other. Furthermore, as we have seen, for his examples of ethical laughter Critchley turns to literature, and in particular to Sterne, Swift, and Beckett, to a kind of humour that appears to be self-mocking and, one might argue, bears a closer resemblance to what Freud terms cynical joking, so evident in 'stories created by Jews and directed against Jewish characteristics' (Freud 1960b, 111), than to what he later theorizes as humour. Indeed, Critchley's conclusion is that the theory of the *'risus purus'* (or pure laugh) in Beckett's *Watt* (1953) is nothing less than a theory of ethical laughter, and this despite the fact that this *'risus purus'* is defined, in distinction from the 'ethical laugh' (which takes that which is 'not good' as its object), as the self-reflexive 'dianoetic laugh', whose object is the laugh itself (Beckett 1963, 46–7). It is this ethical laughter that Critchley hears in Beckett's works, and principally in what Beckett refers to as his 'syntax of weakness'.[4] We are left, then, to consider the validity of this particular literary example. Is Beckett's humour indeed ethical in its acknowledgement of finitude? Is it a humour at the expense of no other? Is it a humour of the self, rather than a laughter of the other? Is it a laughter above and beyond all other kinds of laughter, with a value beyond the laughter of superiority, victimization, and mastery, and beyond even the laughter of sovereignty as theorized by Bataille? Is it a laughter that can be known to be liberating, elevating, and consoling? These are the questions that will guide our reading of the strange fate of the comic in Beckett's works.

4
Last Laughs
Beckett and the *'risus purus'*

Arming the mind with laughter

That the comic will have a significant role to play in Beckett's *œuvre* is evident as early as the first page of his first novel, *Dream of Fair to Middling Women*, a work described by Beckett in its early stages of composition as his 'German comedy'[1] and in which the celebrated Swiss clown Grock is not only repeatedly invoked but also identified as the 'faithful philosopher' of the novel's would-be-writer protagonist, Belacqua (Beckett 1992, 136).[2] From the outset, however, Beckett casts doubt upon the very possibility of any faithful relation being maintained in the highly paradoxical art of the clown. As we have seen in the previous chapter, the most obvious aspect to this art's paradoxicality lies in the fact that, at its best, it is an art that must appear to be no art at all. In Beckett's clowns, however, the distinction between a disguised art of unmastery and sheer naïvety becomes increasingly difficult to maintain. On the one hand, his clowns can appear to be mere victims, their comic suffering the wholly unanticipated concomitant of blind desire. On the other hand, that suffering can itself appear to be the object of what is never simply a masochistic drive, as though the clown were the most knowing of all victims, the one for whom a comic reversal is the most anticipated of all eventualities, the one who dreams of mastering the art of unmastery, turning the tears of the self into the laughter of the other.

Across the first page of *Dream*, an apparently naïve and still energetic young Belacqua pedals furiously through a sub-Proustian landscape ('a frieze of hawthorns') in unexplained pursuit not of a *jeune fille en fleur* but of a horsedrawn van, only to find the object of this pursuit evacuating its bowels in his face, as though to punish him for a desire that both suffers and would make suffer, and that, as Beckett's later works suggest, is tied to birth, death, sex, and neurosis: 'Whip him up, vanman, flickem, flapem, collop-wallop fat Sambo. Stiffly, like a perturbation of feathers, the tail arches for a gush of mard. Ah ...!' (Beckett 1992, 1). In that abrupt shift from one voice to another, from one style to another, and from one rhythm to another, the comic emerges in the form of what, much later, Beckett will term a 'wordshit'.[3]

At *Dream*'s opening, then, Belacqua appears to serve as an example of the purely unwitting clown-victim, a Beckettian object, a figure who has yet to make an art of unmastery. Only a few years later, in 'Yellow', the penultimate story in *More Pricks Than Kicks* (1934), Beckett has Belacqua attempt to pass from unwitting to witting clown, placing his faith this time not just in Grock and the Russian clowns Bim and Bom, but also in the 'laughing philosopher', Democritus of Abdera,[4] whom he would prise free of his lachrymose pre-Socratic double, Heraclitus. Belacqua's aim is to turn the comic to his advantage, to have it at his disposal, to make of humour a resource, refuge, or defence against the worst. He would resist any reversible coupling of the comic and the tragic, laughter and tears. The entire scene is structured, however, as a sequence of reversals, no doubt ironic, but less clearly either comic or tragic, Democritean or Heraclitean:

> Here, as indeed at every crux of the enterprise, he sacrificed his sense of what was personal and proper to himself to the desirability of making a certain impression on other people, an impression almost of gallantry. He must efface himself altogether and do the little soldier. It was this paramount consideration that made him decide in favour of Bim and Bom, Grock, Democritus, whatever you are pleased to call it, and postpone its dark converse to a less public occasion. This was an abnegation if you like, for Belacqua could not resist a lachrymose philosopher and still less when, as was the case with Heraclitus, he was obscure at the same time. He was in his element in dingy tears and luxuriously so when these were furnished by a pre-Socratic man of acknowledged distinction. (Beckett 1970c, 176)

In this early story, then, the comic is treated quite explicitly as a form of self-negation. To wear the comic mask is, for Belacqua, to think of the other at the expense of what is 'personal and proper' to the self. It is to 'efface' the self, to negate that which comes most naturally to it, and to do so for fear of misreading, for fear, that is, of appearing 'yellow' in the eyes of the other:

> But weeping in this charnel-house would be misconstrued. All the staff, from matron to lift-boy, would make the mistake of ascribing

his tears, or, perhaps better, his tragic demeanour, not to the folly of humanity at large which of course covered themselves, but rather to the tumour the size of a brick that he had on the back of his neck. [...]

So now his course was clear. He would arm his mind with laughter, laughter is not quite the word but it will have to serve, at every point, then he would admit the idea and blow it to pieces. (Beckett 1970c, 176–7)

By thinking of the hospital as a charnel-house Belacqua's aim is to master the very principle of reversibility (to be distinguished from alternation) that governs the art of comedy, just as it governs the art of tragedy. And yet, as the story unfolds, it is precisely this reversibility that outwits him, the final (catastrophic) reversal, amid a blaze of exclamatives, being one that it would be precipitous to identify as either comic or tragic, since the reversibility governing both of these genres also structures the relation between them. Belacqua's attempt to side with the comic over the tragic ends in death, and more precisely in a death caused by the failure of others to listen to his heart – in other words, a failure to listen to that other within, over which he, anticipating the arrhythmic Murphy, can exert no mastery at all:

By Christ! He did die!
They had clean forgotten to auscultate him!
(Beckett 1970c, 186)

Deciding in favour of the comic mask rather than the (to him) more natural tragic, Belacqua sets himself up, or is set up, for a fall. 'Yellow' becomes, among other things, the story of a failure to master the comic, a failure to transcend a certain naïvety that sets one up for a fall, even when one is canny enough to try to co-opt the comic. It is as though the comic were taking its revenge on Belacqua here for thinking he can master it by assuming its mask or appearance. Convinced that he can simply adopt the comic, 'arm his mind with laughter', he is outwitted by it. Indeed, this early story suggests that to try to master the comic is to enter into a realm governed by a principle of reversibility that can make of the comic the tragic, and of the tragic the comic, and that it can do so by the abrupt literalization of a figure: derided as a charnel-house by Belacqua, the hospital becomes just that.

The literalization of a figure: the ostensibly comic will often take this form in Beckett, until the distinguishability of the literal and the figurative itself becomes problematic. In 'Yellow', Belacqua's own would-be comic reversal comes back at him, lays him flat. He places his faith in the apparent asymmetry of the relation between the comic and the tragic proposed by John Donne in one of his *Paradoxes and Problems*, quoted in 'Yellow': 'Now among our wise men, I doubt not but many would be found, who would laugh at Heraclitus weeping, none which would weep at Democritus laughing' (Beckett 1970c, 175).[5] This paradox suggests that the comic is the safer bet. 'Yellow' serves as early evidence, however, that in Beckett this will not necessarily always be the case. This story also suggests that in Beckett's hands the comic will be an art that defies decision, intention, and mastery, and that reverses reversals, making it particularly difficult to determine who, if anyone, would have the last laugh, and what the nature and function of that last laugh might be. As we shall see, however, none of this has prevented commentators from seeking in their turn to appropriate the comic in Beckett, making of it the most unambiguously ethical of modes.

Variations on the comic (1): the return of the abject body

The comic – or, more precisely, that which bears a resemblance to the comic – takes many forms in Beckett's *œuvre*, both visual and verbal, as though there were not only a comedy of the body and a comedy of the mind, but also a comedy of being divided into mind and body, of being divided by at least two kinds of comedy. Much of the ostensibly comic in Beckett would seem to fall neatly within Bergson's definition of the comic as a lapse of the living into the mechanical, although in Beckett this kind of comedy is both intensified and complicated by the mechanical itself proving to be so faulty. Indeed, his presentation of the body as a failing machine often takes the form less of what Freud terms the 'comedy of movement' than of what might be termed the comedy of movement's repeated failure.

As has often been observed by commentators, much of the comic business in Beckett's early plays belongs to a familiar comic tradition: the pratfalls and the routines echoing those to be found in the circus and vaudeville, including the hat-swapping routine, the falling trousers, and the collapsing bodies in *Godot*, Clov's stepladder-and-telescope routine in *Endgame*, and Krapp slipping on his own banana skin in *Krapp's Last Tape*. By the time of the later plays, however, the body has come to function quite differently. In *Footfalls* and *Quad*, for instance, movement has become obsessively repetitive, faultless in its form, and certainly not comic in any traditional sense. This turn towards the deorganicized, spectral body is preceded, however, by the experience of the abject body in Beckett's early prose fiction, and particularly in the postwar trilogy. This abject body is an alterity that marks the mind's finitude, but is never simply alterior in the sense of being an object. As Julia Kristeva argues in *Powers of Horror* (1980), 'The abject is not the ob-ject facing me, which I name or imagine. Nor is it an ob-jest, an otherness ceaselessly fleeing in a systematic quest of desire. [...] The abject has only one quality of the object – that of being opposed to *I*' (Kristeva 1982, 1). The subject's relation to the abject body is, then, essentially antagonistic. It is neither the peaceful coexistence of the indifferent nor a dialectical relation, dynamic in the sense that it can lead to an eventual synthesis of subject and object. If the abject body is hostile, it is never entirely foreign, not just because it offends against the conventions of a polite society that scarcely gets a look-in in Beckett's works, but also because the mind is constantly having to face its own failure to master the body.

In Beckett, the abject body is the clown's body, but the clown's body in its disintegration: coming apart, defying the power of thought, to which it is none the less tied, obedient only to a principle of decomposition. In its disintegrative unmasterability, this body is a thing of disgust, and if there is pantomime in Beckett, then it is a pantomime inflected with revulsion. Given this disgust, which in Beckett's early works is directed at the female body in particular, it might seem difficult, if not impossible, to argue that the body is assigned a value or that it constitutes the site of political or ethical resistance. Despite many apparent similarities, it would appear to be more than a little naïve to claim any real kinship between the abject body in Beckett and the grotesque body championed by Bakhtin in his study of Rabelais. According to Bakhtin, the Rabelaisian body both laughs and makes laugh, is essentially transgressive, forcing connections between realms held apart by the dominant ideology; it is 'unfinished, outgrows itself, transgresses its own limits. The stress is laid on those parts of the body that are open to the outside world, that is, the parts through which the world enters the body or emerges from it, or through which the body goes out to meet the world' (Bakhtin 1984, 26). For Bakhtin, this grotesque, laughing, and laughable body is the site of a radical resistance to the official culture. It functions within that carnival-grotesque form which accomplishes a liberation from all normativity, 'from the prevailing points of view of the world, from conventions and established truths, from clichés, from all that is humdrum and universally accepted' (Bakhtin 1984, 34).

If the Beckettian abject body is the repressed other of the official body, it does not possess the power of resistance to the official or normative that Bakhtin claims for the Rabelaisian body, if only because Beckett's creatures dream of negating it. And yet, despite this dream, recent studies of Beckett have repeatedly asserted its value. For example, while taking issue with Bakhtin's political 'romanticization and heroization' of the grotesque body, and insisting that the body which returns is not one with which we can ever quite identify (we 'have' rather than 'are' our bodies), Simon Critchley argues that the abject body in Beckett marks the finitude of the human in a manner that liberates us from the dream of transcendence, which is to say from the unethical dream of absolute mastery. While Beckett insists that his work is 'a matter of fundamental sounds (no joke intended)',[6] the comic is to be sought precisely where the mastery of intentions, paronomastic or otherwise, is exceeded. In *Molloy*, for instance, the fart is not just one among other forms of the body's return. It is the sign of the abject body as something essentially excremental, in which spirit (as *pneuma*) has become another kind of gas. As 'wordshit', literature itself becomes an abject body. Among the things that any such championing of abjection in Beckett must leave out of account, however, are: (1) the dream of disembodiment that recurs throughout Beckett's *œuvre*, a complete alterification of the body, beyond all spectrality; (2) the movement away from abjection in the later works; and (3) the movement towards what might be termed the posthumorous, when not only will the comic body be comic no more, but the very reversibility of, and between, the comic and the tragic would be subject to disintegration.

Variations on the comic (2): Beckett's 'syntax of weakness'

As Ruby Cohn was the first to demonstrate, in *Samuel Beckett: The Comic Gamut* (1962), the many visual, physical forms of the comic in Beckett's works are complemented by an extremely wide range of verbal forms, from the apparently deliberate telling of jokes to the innumerable confusions and misunderstandings, puns, word plays, anticlimaxes, and ironies, all of which fall within the broader category of Beckett's 'syntax of weakness'.[7] That the precise function of this syntax may well prove difficult to determine, however, becomes evident as soon as one considers that seemingly most identifiable form of verbal humour: the joke or, more precisely, what in *Endgame* is termed the 'funny story' (*bonne histoire*) (Beckett 1990, 101).

According to Cicero, in Book II of his *De Oratore*, the most common kind of joke works through the generation, and then the disappointment, of an expectation. However, for a joke to be recognized as a joke, one cannot simply by surprised by the non-arrival of the expected; rather, one has to expect that the expected will not arrive while also being surprised by the particular form taken by that non-arrival. It is precisely the teller's staging of the act of joke-telling, and an obedience to the general form or genre of the joke, that alerts the hearer to expect this non-arrival. In Beckett, this already complicated play with expectation and its disappointment is radicalized in various ways, with jokes being at the expense of the very genre of the joke and the repetition of jokes making the relation between expectation and its disappointment a challenge to thought itself.

To begin with a 'funny story' that does not quite get told: in *Godot*, the audience never hears the punchline to the story of 'the Englishman in the brothel', which in both its form and its content would seem to adhere to one of the most familiar forms of the joke. Here, in Beckett's 'nothing new', the incompletion of this joke is owing paradoxically to its already having been told. If Estragon wishes to hear Vladimir tell the story, it is in part because he already knows it, or at least knew it. Its not getting properly told is not the only unexpected aspect, however, even if this failure anticipates Godot's own repeated failure to arrive, for there is a joke of sorts (or at least a playing with expectation) at Vladimir's expense in Estragon's giving the impression that he is about to tell the story, only to foist the responsibility upon the other:

ESTRAGON: [...] You know the story of the Englishman in the brothel?
VLADIMIR: Yes.
ESTRAGON: Tell it to me.
VLADIMIR: Ah stop it!
ESTRAGON: An Englishman having drunk a little more than usual goes to a brothel. The bawd asks him if he wants a fair one, a dark one, or a red-haired one. Go on.
VLADIMIR: STOP IT!

(Beckett 1990, 17–18)

If there is humour here, in the joke's very failure to get told, and in Estragon's desire to be told a joke he already appears to know, and therefore from which (according to Freud, at least) no pleasure is to be gained, there is also suffering, and indeed a making suffer: Vladimir wishes neither to tell the story nor to hear it told.

What, though, of a 'funny story' that does get told, despite the other's resistance, as is the case with Nagg's story of the tailor in *Endgame*? In the English text, Nagg appears to begin with a question: 'Will I tell you the story of the tailor?' (Beckett 1990, 101), However, this is in fact less than a question, since Nagg ignores Nell's immediate response to it: 'No.' In the Irish-English 'Will I tell you [...]?', rather than the English 'Shall I tell you?', translating the non-interrogative French, 'Je vais te raconter l'histoire du tailleur', Beckett secretes the possibility that Nagg is not asking permission of the other, but speculating upon what will be the case, beyond any intention on his or any other's part. The unexpected is already there, then, in that question that is not quite a question, with which the possibility of telling the 'funny story' is introduced in translation.

The story itself is identified as one that has been told before: 'Let me tell it again' – a request that is not quite a request, translating the much more openly aggressive 'Écoute-la encore'. And if the telling of this story is a retelling, it is a highly dramatized one, a little play-within-the-play. Nagg adopts not only the diegetic voice of the 'raconteur', but also the mimetic voices of the customer and the tailor. For all that, to refer to this story as a little play-within-the-play is slightly misleading, since Nagg's 'Let me tell it again' refers us to a former telling or tellings that remain unheard and thus neither properly inside nor quite outside the play. And if it is dramatized, this story is also de-dramatized by its being interrupted, its little secondary world of tailor and customer being one from which the hearer is dragged back, to be reminded that both the telling and the told are a repetition, and that repetition here involves degradation: '[*Pause. Normal voice.*] I never told it worse. [*Pause. Gloomy.*] I tell this story worse and worse' (Beckett 1990, 102). This principle of exacerbation governs not only the telling of the joke, but also its effect. Nagg claims that Nell's laughter, while they were boating together on Lake Como, was owing not (as she claims) to happiness but rather to his story, and that this laughter almost proved fatal:

NAGG: You were in such fits that we capsized. By rights we should have been drowned.
NELL: It was because I felt happy.
NAGG: [*Indignant.*] It was not, it was not, it was my story and nothing else. Happy! Don't you laugh at it still? Every time I tell it. Happy!
(Beckett 1990, 102)

'Don't you laugh at it still? Every time I tell it': not only does Nell deny that her former laughter was prompted by Nagg's story, but she does not laugh when that story is repeated to her. Instead, the laughter we hear on stage is anything but the result of happiness, and anything but natural, it being Nagg himself, not Nell, who laughs here, with that laughter being as staged and as unnatural as the story that precedes it: *'Pause. He looks at* NELL *who has remained impassive, her eyes unseeing, breaks into a high forced laugh, cuts it short, pokes his head towards* NELL, *launches his laugh again'* (Beckett 1990, 103). Nell's impassivity, her blindness, is the sign of a flight into a world from which Nagg's aggressively forced laughter is excluded, a world of the past in which the purity of the lake's bed ('So white') is itself the sign of a death to which her laughter, prompted (she insists) by happiness, might have carried them. And if there is disagreement here over the cause of a specific laugh – was it Nell's happiness or Nagg's 'funny story'? – there is no less disagreement over the greatest source of laughter:

NELL: [...] Nothing is funnier than unhappiness, I'll grant you that. But—
NAGG: [*Shocked.*] Oh!
NELL: Yes, yes, it's the most comical thing in the world. And we laugh, we laugh, with a will, in the beginning. But it's always the same thing. Yes, it's like the funny story we have heard too often, we still find it funny, but we don't laugh any more.

(Beckett 1990, 101)

The joke, the funny story, unhappiness: in each case, the laughter they provoke dries up with their repetition, even if (according to Bergson) repetition may also provoke laughter and indeed characterize laughter itself.[8]

Jokes that do not quite get told; jokes that do get told, that are forced on others, but that have been told before, and that provoke no laughter other than a *'high forced laughter'* that is launched by the teller: these 'funny stories' belong within the larger category of Beckett's 'syntax of weakness'. Another form of this syntax is the sentence that loses its way and its energy, lapsing not only into anticlimax but also into the nothing of 'no matter', as in *The Unnamable*: 'The fact would seem to be, if in my situation one may speak of facts, not only that I shall have to speak of things of which I cannot speak, but also, which is even more interesting, but also that I, which is if possible even more interesting, that I shall have to, I forget, no matter' (Beckett 1959, 294). Although Cohn identifies the tone of *The Unnamable* as tragicomic (Cohn 1962, 139), it is precisely the disintegration of even this most hybrid of genres that is enacted here. A far more prevalent form of Beckett's 'syntax of weakness' than the sentence that loses its impetus, however, is the assertion whose authority is weakened or even contradicted by one or more qualifying clauses (the rhetorical figure of *correctio*). Indeed, the postwar trilogy is an almost unremitting instance of such rhetoric: 'I seem to speak, it is not I, about me, it is not about me. [...] I shall not be alone, in the beginning. I am of course alone. Alone. That is soon said' (Beckett 1959, 293). This principle of self-correction can extend beyond an earlier phrase or statement to embrace an entire narrative, as is the case when Moran ends his report with a denial of the truth of its beginning: 'It is midnight. The rain is beating on the windows. [...] It was not midnight. It was not raining' (Beckett 1959, 92, 176). Beckett's works undertake an ever more radical hyperbolization of *correctio*, a procedure that would leave nothing intact. It is for this reason that the isolation of any one statement results in its disfiguration. To quote from Beckett is to negate the very process of self-correction within which any statement is hazarded. It is to assume that a statement can be lifted from its context, even though the limits of that context may be precisely what the text is opening to question. Among the statements that would suffer particular disfiguration through their being isolated as foundational truths for Beckett's *œuvre*, none is more relevant to the topic of comedy than Nell's 'Nothing is funnier than unhappiness', which she claims comes from the other – 'I'll grant you that' – even though the other's response (Nagg's shocked 'Oh!') suggests he would assert no such thing. If this claim has served as the basis for a theory of ethical humour in Beckett, it has done so only through its having been ripped from a disintegrating context that places the ethicality of all humour in question.

Analysing the bull: the witting and the unwitting

While *correctio* is among the most important rhetorical features of Beckett's 'syntax of weakness', there is another feature – the 'bull' – that obeys not the still rational principle underlying *correctio* but a principle somewhere between flagrant self-contradiction and radical paradox. In his *Biographia Literaria* (1817), Coleridge defines the bull as 'the bringing together two incompatible thoughts, with the *sensation*, but without the *sense*, of their connection' (Coleridge 1907, 52 n.). In other words, the bull is itself an instance of what in *The Unnamable* is termed the 'pseudocouple': incompatibles united by sensation but not by sense. But if, as Coleridge asserts, the bull is an absurdity, this does not necessarily make it either meaningless or meaning-free. Rather, there is the possibility of a sense beyond the sensible. Furthermore, if it constitutes a pseudocoupling of incompatible thoughts, it is itself part of a pseudocouple – with wit.

As Christopher Ricks observes, among all the bulls in Beckett's *œuvre* there is perhaps none more telling than the little phrase 'Nothing is more real than nothing'. This particular bull – the so-called atomist paradox – first occurs in *Murphy* (1938), where it is explicitly attributed to Democritus (the 'laughing philosopher'): 'the Nothing, than which in the guffaw of the Abderite naught is more real' (Beckett 1938, 246). In his notes on Democritus from the early 1930s, Beckett faithfully glosses the phrase 'Naught is more real than nothing' as meaning simply that non-being is as real as being.[9] The radical paradoxicality of the phrase – which detaches the nothing from itself, opens a space within it, even as it posits the nothing as that which lies beyond all affirmation and negation – and the appropriateness of its being communicated in the empty space of a 'guffaw' by the 'laughing philosopher', is activated only when it finds its way into Beckett's fiction. It is in *Malone Dies* (1951), however, that the threat posed to thought by this particular bull is identified: 'I know those little phrases that seem so innocuous and, once you let them in, pollute the whole of speech. *Nothing is more real than nothing*. They rise up out of the pit and know no rest until they drag you down into its dark. But I am on my guard now' (Beckett 1959, 193). In the course of the trilogy, and despite all such wariness, that darkness grows, as the comedy becomes ever less evident, such that towards the end of *The Unnamable* not only has *correctio* become the very form of disintegration, but Beckett's 'syntax of weakness' as a whole is far less obviously aligned with the comic than it is in his earlier works: 'I'm in words, made of words, others' words, what others, the place too, the air, the walls, the floor, the ceiling, all words [...] and nothing else, yes, something else, that I'm something quite different, a quite different thing, a wordless thing in an empty place' (Beckett 1959, 390).

Now, despite this darkening or this weakening of the link between the bull and the comic, Ricks not only identifies the bull as the most important form of Beckett's 'syntax of weakness', but also insists upon its ethico-political value. Reflecting on the various definitions of the bull, he observes that, according to the *OED*, the inconsistency or absurdity of the bull is 'unperceived by the speaker', and that, according to E. Cobham Brewer's *Dictionary of Phrase and Fable* (1870), the bull is 'inadvertent'. In both cases, then, the bull is thought to be simply unintended. Hedging his bets, Samuel Johnson defines the bull as both a 'blunder' (that is, unintentional) and a 'contradiction' (which just might be intentional). Ricks argues, however, that the best bulls, which is to say those with 'penetrative power' (Ricks 1993, 190), are forms of absurdity that remain indeterminable as either intended or unintended, witting or unwitting. Whereas a joke (according to Freud) has to originate in an identifiable intention to joke, a bull is that form of verbal humour which, at its best, leaves the question of intentionality wide open. Ricks then proceeds to outline the ways in which this power may be appropriated, either as a weapon of oppression or as a weapon of resistance to oppression. However, for the bull to become a 'resource' for those struggling against oppression, and indeed for those doing the oppressing, the very indecision that situates it between the witting and the unwitting, between pretence and naïvety, between the intentional and the unintentional, has to disappear: 'The bull is the resource of a pressed, suppressed, or oppressed people, a people on occasion *pretending to be self-subordinated by foolishness* so as the better to keep alive a secret self-respect and to be insubordinate and even safely provocative' (Ricks 1993, 193; emphasis added). The bull can become a resource to the oppressed, then, only if we are in a position to know that pretence is taking place. And yet, as soon as it becomes identifiable as a resource, as soon as it is at our disposal, as soon as it is mastered by a knowledge, as soon as it is perceived to be feigned naïvety, the bull immediately loses its power. That said, without such a knowledge, the ethical value of the bull must surely remain in question.

The ethics of the pure laugh

Simon Critchley (1997, 2002) has sought to develop Ricks's argument on the comic as an ethical resource in Beckett, while defending deconstruction from Ricks's attack upon it in the final pages of *Beckett's Dying Words* (1993). Critchley bases his argument on what has proven to be the most influential theorization of the comic in Beckett's entire œuvre. The passage in question forms part of Arsene's 'short statement' in *Watt* (1953), where laughter is subdivided into the ethical, the intellectual, and the dianoetic:

> The bitter, the hollow and – haw! haw! – the mirthless. The bitter laugh laughs at that which is not good, it is the ethical laugh. The hollow laugh laughs at that which is not true, it is the intellectual laugh. Not good! Not true! Well well. But the mirthless laugh is the dianoetic laugh, down the snout – haw! – so. It is the laugh of laughs, the *risus purus*, the laugh laughing at the laugh, the beholding, the saluting of the highest joke, in a word the laugh that laughs – silence please – at that which is unhappy. (Beckett 1963, 47)

Less often noted is the earlier definition of these three kinds of laughter as 'successive excoriations of the understanding', a 'passage from the lesser to the greater, from the lower to the higher, from the outer to the inner, from the gross to the fine, from the matter to the form' (Beckett 1963, 46). The '*risus purus*', or pure laugh, is, then, the laugh of spirit in its absolute separation from matter. It is self-reflexive, self-knowing, and self-mocking.

Associating this pure, self-reflexive laugh with Beckett's aporetic 'syntax of weakness', Critchley identifies it as ethical on account of its being at the expense of no other: 'the object of laughter is the subject who laughs' (Critchley 2002, 50). Furthermore, countering Adorno's dour insistence that in *Endgame* humour evaporates 'along with the meaning of the punchline' (Adorno 1991, 258), he argues that humour in Beckett persists as an 'acknowledgement of finitude' (Critchley 1997, 159). Comedy of the Beckettian variety is, then, a particular form of knowing, a cognitive relation that is itself ethical. Indeed, beyond being simply an acknowledgement or recognition, the comic becomes a profoundly ethical undoing of illusion, a way of seeing that is our only reliable relation to both the good and the true: 'The undoubted felicities of Beckett's bull [...] engage in a massive and unrelenting critique and dismantling of the illusoriness of what passes for life, through which we can detect the faintest glimmer of a world transfigured by a messianic light' (Critchley 1997, 171). In what is not an entirely unsurprising irony, Critchley proposes an ethical theory of the comic that is grounded in the value of alterity, and in the respect owed to the other, but that none the less requires another masterable alterity that can become the object of a negation. Here, that other alterity takes the form of illusoriness. To negate this particular form of alterity would be the very essence of ethical action.

There is something strange, if not quite laughable, about a theory of ethical laughter (at the expense of no other) in which the function of that laughter is identified as the dismantling critique of illusion. In both laughter and the theory of laughter, there would seem to be an irreducible negativity. As we have seen in the previous chapter, from Baudelaire to Freud laughter is thought in relation to a fall, a lapse, a disclosure of absence: the living becoming mechanical, consciousness losing its mastery, the human lapsing into the non-human, the subjection of the self to the law of the other. And this negativity is present even when laughter and the comic are thought as liberating: Bakhtin, for instance, sees Rabelaisian laughter as challenging and even overturning official authority.

When laughter is defined in terms of bathos or anticlimax (as it is by Cicero and Kant), this negativity takes the form of a reduction to nothing of an expectation, the appearance of nothing in the place of an expected something:

> In jest [...] the play sets out from thoughts which collectively, so far as seeking sensuous expression, engage the activity of the body. In this presentation the understanding, missing what it expected, suddenly lets go its hold, with the result that the effect of this slackening is felt in the body by the oscillation of the organs. This favours the restoration of the equilibrium of the latter, and exerts a beneficial influence upon the health.
>
> Something absurd (something in which, therefore, the understanding can of itself find no delight) must be present in whatever is to raise a hearty convulsive laugh. *Laughter is an affection arising from a strained expectation being suddenly reduced to nothing* [ein Affekt aus der plötzlichen Verwandlung einer gespannten Erwartung in nichts]. (Kant 1952, 199)

This negation of the expected makes space for the absurd: that is, the unanticipated and unreasonable. As we have seen, however, in Beckett this playing with expectation can take a very complicated form, with the punchline to a 'funny story' being that which fails to appear. It is not the 'funny story' itself, but precisely the reduction to nothing of that story, that is 'funny'.

Now, according to Kant, 'the joke must have something in it capable of deceiving us' (Kant 1952, 201). However, not only is laughter (as the result of a deception) healthy in the effect it has upon the body, but it also functions as a compensation for suffering: 'Voltaire said that heaven has given us two things to compensate us for the many miseries of life, *sleep* and *hope*. He might have added *laughter* to the list' (Kant 1952, 201). We are left to reflect, then, upon a rather more complicated relation between humour, deception, and compensation than Critchley envisages. Far from simply dismantling the illusory, as Critchley argues, laughter, at least as Kant theorizes it, functions by way of illusion. However, anticipating an entire tradition, to which Critchley certainly belongs, Kant does his best to keep humour on the side of knowledge, and to distinguish between kinds of humour in ethical terms. The bond between the cognitive and the ethical, between the true and the good, remains unquestioned: '*Humour*, in a good sense, means the talent for being able to put oneself at will into a certain frame of mind in which everything is estimated on lines that go quite off the beaten track, (a topsy-turvy view of things,) and yet on lines that follow certain principles, rational in the case of such a mental temperament' (Kant 1952, 203). If laughter is provoked by the absurd (by that which goes against what reason would expect), humour (in the 'good sense') is none the less guided by 'certain principles'. The absurdity with which this kind of humour has to do is principled.

The absurd has generally been thought within the broader category of the comic, with not all comedy being reducible to it. The absurd involves an apparent transgression of the rational, an event of difference or incongruity, surprise, and a taking unawares. This would suggest, however, that the absurd could not become a style or a mode without ceasing to function. As soon as we expect the absurd, as soon as we anticipate it, as soon as we are familiar with its rules, principles, or logic, it is no longer absurd, which is why there will always be something dubious about references to Absurdism or to a theatre of the Absurd. Certainly, Beckett himself has no time for the idea of a 'theatre of the absurd' of the kind to which Esslin believes he belongs. And Beckett's objection to the idea of absurdism has everything to do with his objection to judgements of value. To Charles Juliet's contention that 'the artistic enterprise is inconceivable without rigorous ethical standards', Beckett responds: 'What you say is correct. But moral values [*les valeurs morales*] are not accessible and not open to definition. To define them, you would have to make value judgements [*un jugement de valeur*], and you can't do that. That's why I have never agreed with the idea of the theatre of the absurd. Because that implies making value judgements' (Beckett in Juliet 1995, 148–9).

Laughter and the experience of unknowing

The various generalizing claims for the ethicality of Beckett's humour rely not only upon the assumption that his 'syntax of weakness' is an ethical way of both knowing and respecting the human in its real finitude, but also upon the assumption that in Beckett one is left in a position to establish who is laughing, at what they are laughing, and why. As we have seen, the properly ethical laugh is a cognitive laugh (a pure laugh of pure mind) that is self-reflexive and thus at the expense of no other: its economy is that of the absolutely self-regulating being. It is for this reason that the 'dianoetic' laugh is situated above and beyond both the 'ethical' (more precisely, the moral) and the 'intellectual' in *Watt*. For these two forms of laughter, the object of laughter is still a form of alterity: the bad and the untrue.

The context for this theory of the pure laugh is not restricted, however, to Arsene's speech or even to *Watt* as a whole, for Beckett's *œuvre* contains other explicit theorizations of laughter, no less dramatized than Arsene's, in which it is presented as anything but a sign of higher life. There is, for example, Moran's conversation with Father Ambrose in part II of *Molloy*. Here, laughter is presented as a trait that distinguishes the human from both the animal and the divine:

> Like Job, haha, he said. I too said haha. What a joy it is to laugh, from time to time, he said. Is it not? I said. It is peculiar to man, he said. So I have noticed, I said. A brief silence ensued. [...] Animals never laugh, he said. It takes us to find that funny, I said. What? he said. It takes us to find that funny, I said loudly. He mused. Christ never laughed either, he said, so far as we know. He looked at me. Can you wonder? I said. There it is, he said. He smiled sadly. (Beckett 1959, 101–2)

Just as, in *Endgame*, Nagg's laughter at his own 'funny story' is '*forced*', so here Father Ambrose appears to laugh at his own comparison of the animal and the biblical: Moran's grey hen (which 'for the past month and more had done nothing but sit with her arse in the dust') and Job. Unlike Nagg, however, Ambrose's laugh is imitated by another, although this repetition of the 'haha' can scarcely be called natural; indeed, it might even be seen as a parody of the pure laugh in *Watt*. To argue that this is the case, however, would be to assume that we are in a position to determine the precise nature and object of Moran's 'haha', and there is little here to support such a limitation. Furthermore, if laughter is a 'joy', then it is one only 'from time to time', and even then it is not unambiguously a joy that is at the expense of no other. Indeed, it is upon the very strangeness and even the inexplicability of laughter that the emphasis falls here, not least through the play upon the two senses of the words 'peculiar' and 'funny' (translating the French *propre* and *drôle*). If Father Ambrose follows Aristotle in defining laughter as 'peculiar to man' (*le propre de l'homme*), in translation that peculiarity is also an oddity. Likewise, that which is 'funny' here is not simply comic but also strange, and part of that strangeness is that both the reason (or reasons) for, and the object (or objects) of, laughter remain under- or over-determined. Lastly, this passage charts the exhaustion of laughter: from 'haha' to sad smile.

Far from simply offering us a laughter bound to the good and the true, a laughter that would be ethical in its absolute respect for alterity, and aligned with truth in its acknowledgement of human finitude, Beckett's works repeatedly emphasize the strangeness of laughter, and raise the question of whether one can in fact tell when a joke is being told, whether one ever knows what one is laughing at, and why, and even whether one ever knows whether one is laughing or not. In *Endgame*, for instance, Clov appears to take Hamm's question 'We're not beginning to ... to ... mean something?' as a joke: 'Mean something! You and I, mean something! [*Brief laugh.*] Ah that's a good one!' (Beckett 1990, 108). However, when Hamm follows Clov's 'that's a good one!' with 'I wonder. [*Pause.*]', the audience is caught between the following possibilities, among others: (1) Hamm is the consummate comedian, who does not laugh at his own jokes; (2) he has not made a joke at all; (3) he has made a joke and now no longer sees it as a joke; (4) he has sought to catch Clov out by delivering a line that could be mistaken for a joke.

And even when it might seem that a joke is unambiguously intended, not only is laughter not the response, but one is left to contemplate the possibility that a joke might be among the more 'inhuman' means of inflicting rather than alleviating suffering.[10] Is Clov joking, for instance, when he responds 'It's too soon' to Hamm's request for 'my pain-killer', given that Clov will later claim that there is no more pain-killer, and is 'There's no more pain-killer' itself the punchline to this joke? But then, if, as may well be the case, all is merely played here, might not Hamm himself know that there is no more pain-killer even when asking for it? And what of a question that may once have been intended as a joke, but no longer elicits laughter, either because it has been made one too many times, or because neither the teller nor the hearer (even when they are one and the same person) is sure whether a joke has been made or not?

HAMM: [...] No phone calls? [*Pause.*] Don't we laugh?
CLOV: [*After reflection.*] I don't feel like it.
HAMM: [*After reflection.*] Nor I.

(Beckett 1990, 97)

The indecisions affecting humour extend beyond the limits of any given contextual level. When, for instance, to Clov's question 'Do you believe in the life to come?', Hamm responds: 'Mine was always that. [*Exit* CLOV.] Got him that time!' (Beckett 1990, 116), Hamm's joke, if that is what it is, is not only assumed by its teller to have caused suffering (just as laughter causes the one who laughs to suffer in *Godot*)[11] but can be seen as all too serious, being perhaps, among other things, an allusion to Jung's failure to help the suffering Lucia Joyce.[12] Humour, as a form of 'play', is inscribed here within a savage economy, such that one is led to ask whether it may not be the *risus purus*, the laughter that laughs at unhappiness, that, far from alleviating unhappiness, in fact ensures its perpetuation.

If laughter can be a joy that also inflicts pain, then what of the smile? Is it perhaps more ethical, if – or indeed because – less energetic, than the laugh? According to Vladimir in *Godot*, the smile is not only less than a laugh – as is suggested by the French *sourire* – but 'not the same thing' (Beckett 1990, 13). Given that they are less energetic than laughs, it is unsurprising that in Beckett's entropic world the smiles should outlast the laughs. But if the smile is not the same thing as a laugh, it is no less difficult to read. Indeed, to describe the smiles in Beckett's works as enigmatic would be to understate the case, for not only does the question of what a given smile might mean become very difficult to answer, but even telling whether there is a smile there to be seen can prove no minor feat. In *Watt*, for instance, although the narrator identifies one of Watt's expressions as a smile, that is certainly not how Mr Spiro reads it:

> Watt smiled.
> No offence meant, said Mr. Spiro. (Beckett 1963, 25)

And even if Watt's expression is indeed intended to be a smile, it is far from being either a pleasure in itself or the expression of pleasure, for it is at odds with that 'rest' which is the object of his desire and in the interests of which his own mental labours are undertaken. If the comparison of this smile with a fart strikes us as humorous, that comparison also serves as a trap for the reader, encouraging a smile that may then be read as the sign of a suffering inflicted on the self by another. Indeed, the smile becomes the register of a troubling alterity:

> Watt's smile was further peculiar in this, that it seldom came singly, but was followed after a short time by another, less pronounced it is true. In this it resembled the fart. And it even sometimes happened that a third, very weak and fleeting, was found necessary, before the face could be at rest again. But this was rare. And it will be a long time now before Watt smiles again, unless something very unexpected turns up, to upset him. (Beckett 1963, 25)

The smile, then, can be the sign of the smiler's suffering at the hands of an alterity that the smiler wishes to reduce to nothing. However, it can also function as the very form taken by this intolerable alterity, as it does in the second part of *Molloy*, in a scene where the distinction between one identity and another, and between perception and hallucination, begins to break down, and both the origin and the proper place of that alterity which takes the form of a smile remain in question, undetermined as either inside or outside the one who suffers it:

> He [Youdi] said to me, said Gaber, he said –. Louder! I cried. He said to me, said Gaber, Gaber, he said, life is a thing of beauty, Gaber, and a joy for ever. He brought his face nearer mine. A joy for ever, he said, a thing of beauty, Moran, and a joy for ever. He smiled. I closed my eyes. Smiles are all very nice in their own way, very heartening, but at a reasonable distance. I said, Do you think he meant human life? I listened. Perhaps he didn't mean human life, I said. I opened my eyes. I was alone. (Beckett 1963, 165)

Here, the smile, on the face of another that may be no other, is intolerable when not kept at a 'reasonable distance'. When it does appear at a distance, however, it provokes a labour of interpretation, and it is no coincidence that Beckett should show an increasing predilection for the terminal smile, marking the accomplishment of a negation, even a killing of the other. The German television productions of *Eh Joe* (1966) and *Ghost Trio* (1976), both directed by Beckett for Süddeutscher Rundfunk, end with smiles that do not appear in the published scripts,[13] and the stage play *That Time* (1976) also ends with a smile, this one being *'toothless for preference'* (Beckett 1990, 395). We are told neither what the terminal smile in *That Time* is meant to mean, nor why it should be toothless, but, unsurprisingly, this has only encouraged the play's commentators to fill in the blanks. The general consensus is that this particular smile is the sign of a conclusive achievement. Having first remarked upon its enigmatic nature, James Knowlson proceeds to read this smile not only as signalling a combination of 'wry reflection on the insignificance of the individual human existence' and 'serene acceptance' of the void, but as a 'startling human response' (Knowlson and Pilling 1979, 210), working on the assumption that the 'inhuman' has no place here, even if, as we have seen, the thought of the inhuman does intersect with the thought of humour in Beckett, as it does in Wyndham Lewis before him.[14] Rosemary Pountney suggests that the smile is prompted by a 'delight in the unbroken silence' (Pountney 1988, 41), and S. E. Gontarski argues that the smile is a 'crux' that can be resolved by a structural analysis of the play: 'What Listener appears to be responding to at the end of the play is not the content of the voices, but their pattern. [...] Listener can take some pleasure in the restoration of order, or at least a formal harmony' (Gontarski 1985, 158). For both Pountney and Gontarski, then, the smile would be rooted in pleasure (be it the pleasure of silence or of aesthetic form), and in this it would recall what Freud terms his 'one contribution' to the physiological explanation of laughter, a contribution that emphasizes the troubling resemblance (played upon in *Watt*) between the grimace and the smile: 'So far as I know, the grimace characteristic of smiling, which twists up the corners of the mouth, appears first in an infant at the breast when it is satisfied and satiated and lets go of the breast as it falls asleep. Here it is a genuine expression of the emotions, for it corresponds to a decision to take no more nourishment, and represents as it were an "enough" or rather a "more than enough" ' (Freud 1960b, 146–7 n. 2). Beyond any and all of these interpretations, however, in which the negation registered by the smile would scarcely be unambiguously ethical, Listener's smile may, of course, also be read as a hermeneutic challenge or trap despite its apparent toothlessness, a kind of 'Make sense who may' (Beckett 1990, 476) which aggressively draws the spectator into a labour of interpretation that would itself be an attempt to put the play to rest, to establish the meaning of the smile with which it ends, and thereby to reduce its alterity as an interpretable object to zero. This challenge or trap can only come from the other, even if it is a challenge to negate the other, as though the smile were a mode of encouraging or prompting the unethical.

That there may well be such a connection between smiling and a negation that is not necessarily ethical is suggested by Beckett's remarks upon a derisive smile in his unbroadcast radio script *The Capital of the Ruins* (1946). Not only is this smile hard to distinguish from a nihilism that would reduce to nothing all evaluative distinctions, but it is to be glimpsed only in the other. Were it to be glimpsed in the self, then it is imagination rather than perception that would bear the responsibility:

> What was important was not our having penicillin when they had none, nor the unregarding munificence of the French Ministry of Reconstruction (as it was then called), but the occasional glimpse obtained, by us in them and, who knows, by them in us (for they are an imaginative people), of that smile at the human conditions as little to be extinguished by bombs as to be broadened by the elixirs of Burroughs and Welcome – the smile deriding, among other things, the having and the not having, the giving and the taking, sickness and health. (Beckett 1995a, 277)

Coming from the other, but from an other that can scarcely be distinguished from the self – the difference between the two being far from clear in so many of Beckett's works – both laughter and the smile repeatedly provoke a labour of interpretation to which they are also a response. Not only can they be read as signs of suffering as well as joy, as acts of aggression as well as acts of compassion, but they can scarcely be distinguished from their opposites. Indeed, the very difference between laughter and tears, comic and tragic, becomes ever more difficult to maintain in Beckett's disintegration of difference: 'I thought she [Lousse] was going to cry, it was the thing to do, but on the contrary she laughed. It was perhaps her way of crying. Or perhaps I was mistaken and she was really crying, with the noise of laughter. Tears and laughter, they are so much Gaelic to me' (Beckett 1959, 37). Here, we may well have not just a joke at the joke, prompting a laugh at the laugh, but a self-negating, self-reproducing joke at the indistinguishability of laughter and tears, happiness and suffering, the comic and the serious. And if Beckett can be said to trouble the difference between laughter and tears, smiles and grimaces, happiness and suffering, then he can also be said to trouble the difference between the ethicality and unethicality of each of these.

Anethical humour and the posthumorous: Beckett after Mauthner

Faced with the complicated and often contradictory roles played by laughter and smiles, the comic, 'funny stories', and humour in Beckett's *œuvre*, it is unsurprising that commentators have sought an underlying principle of the kind proposed by Nell in *Endgame*. As we have seen, however, when it is reinserted into a context that cannot be limited to that play or even to Beckett's published *œuvre*, the notion that 'Nothing is funnier than unhappiness' is 'granted' in a manner that is far from unambiguously respectful of the other, and that prompts one to ask whether any theory of ethical humour can be based upon it. Furthermore, Nell insists on the exhaustion of laughter that occurs with its repetition, even if repetition of a kind also has a role to play in humour. And if laughter is exhausted, so is humour. In Beckett, then, the comic, in all its forms, has both a history and an end, if a highly paradoxical one.

In each of the early plays there is already a darkening of mood, a movement away from the comic. This is particularly evident in *Endgame* and *Krapp's Last Tape*. While both plays open with pantomimic comic business, there is a pronounced movement away from this in the course of each play, and both end with tableaux that can scarcely be described as comic. Furthermore, as James Knowlson observes of Beckett's own

1969 Schiller-Theater production of *Krapp's Last Tape*: 'Beckett was extremely wary of overstressing the clownish elements in Krapp's physique, dress and behaviour' (Knowlson 1992, xvi). As early as the first London production of the play, in 1958, the 'purple nose' was made less obvious than the published text suggests, and was subsequently omitted from all those productions of the play with which Beckett was associated. And in Beckett's later works, there is a radical reduction of the comic, such that by the time of his last play, *What Where* (1983), there can scarcely be said to be anything humorous at all, and this despite the use of flagrantly clownish names: Bam, Bem, Bim, Bom. If laughter, the comic, and humour – even what Freud terms 'the various forms of "broken" humour' (Freud 1960b, 232) – might have an end, then we are left to reflect once again upon the possibility of a last laugh that is not necessarily pure, a laugh opening not just onto the posthumous but also onto what might be termed the *posthumorous*.

In *The Comic Gamut*, published in 1962 and thus not treating Beckett's late works, Ruby Cohn characterizes the trajectory of the comic in Beckett as a passage from a predominantly 'illiberal' comedy (generating laughter at the expense of the other) to that 'dianoetic' laughter theorized by Arsene in *Watt*. Indeed, she sees *Watt*, the first of Beckett's major works to have been written after his concerted reading of Fritz Mauthner's *Beiträge zu einer Kritik der Sprache* (1901–02), as the decisive text in the history of the comic in his *œuvre*. The importance of Mauthner's critique of language (*Sprachkritik*) to Beckett's own development beyond *Murphy*, evidenced not least by the extensive verbatim notes from Mauthner in the 'Whoroscope Notebook' and the typed notes held at Trinity College Dublin, is now generally acknowledged by commentators.[15] Less often noted, however, is that towards the very end of the *Beiträge* there is a section entitled 'Laughter and Language'. Here, Mauthner argues that laughter is not only critique but 'the best critique' (*die beste Kritik*). The laughter that he has in mind here is not just any old laughter but 'a strong laughter, stronger than the laughter of Aristophanes and Lucian, of Rabelais and Balzac, of Lichtenberg and Heine' (Mauthner 1923, iii. 632–3).[16] Swift and Voltaire have come closest to achieving it, although both fail, albeit for very different reasons. This strong laughter comes only from those who have committed themselves to the impossible – in this case, to the critique of language through language, the kind of enterprise outlined by Beckett in his July 1937 German letter to Axel Kaun, in which he famously proposes a pself-undoing literature of the unword (*Literatur des Unworts*) directed against the veil (*Schleier*) of language in order 'to get at the things (or the nothingness) behind it' (Beckett 1983a, 52). Crucially, however, Mauthner does not rest satisfied with this strong laughter, instead concluding that the highest form of knowledge (*Erkenntnis*) lies neither in language nor in laughter, but in a critique of language characterized by a mood of cheerful resignation (*Resignation*) or renunciation (*Entsagung*) (Mauthner 1923, iii. 634).

Now, for Beckett, too, there will be such a step beyond the energetic 'guffaw of the Abderite', but this step will carry him not into cheerful resignation but into the regions of the posthumorous. In Beckett's late works, it is no longer the case that, as Adorno puts it, 'A dried up, tearless weeping takes the place of laughter', or even that humour is salvaged because the reader or spectator is infected with 'laughter about the absurdity of laughter and laughter about despair' (Adorno 1992, 252–3). It is not simply that laughter has been left behind, however, but rather that one is no longer in a position to determine whether there is anything to laugh at, and, if not, who, if anyone, might have had the last laugh. That indecision is neither ethical nor unethical, but rather anethical, and, in the posthumorous, it finds perhaps its most easily mistakable form, not least in those little phrases that constitute as they deconstitute so many of Beckett's later works, phrases such as the following, from *Stirrings Still* (1988): 'till nothing left from deep within but only ever fainter oh to end. No matter how no matter where. Time and grief and self so-called' (Beckett 1995a, 265). With Beckett, then, it is not enough to insist upon the relation of the comic to the experience of impotence and ignorance, since that very experience includes the comic, making of it a problem rather than a solution. If there is a trajectory of the comic in Beckett, then it is from the 'guffaw of the Abderite' to a voiding that is neither liberally nor illiberally humorous, but anethically posthumorous, in which one is left to ask not only 'does one ever know oneself why one laughs?' (Beckett 1995a, 54) but also whether there is any laughter there at all.

Part III

The Difference a Woman Makes: On the Ethics of Gender

5
Feminine Alterities
From Psychoanalysis to Gender Studies

The pure alterity of the feminine: de Beauvoir versus Levinas

Not just one form of alterity among others, but alterity at its most radically unsettling: this is the thought that has tended to characterize postmodern takes on the feminine, in which its classical subordination to the masculine is submitted to an operation and a logic that would break with, or at least interrupt, what Derrida terms 'phallogocentrism', and in particular the binarity with which phallogocentrism fixes the relation between identity and alterity, same and other. This attempt to challenge phallogocentrism from within is grounded in a familiar interpretation of the place of the feminine in Western thought of the kind reproduced by Levinas in *Time and the Other* (1948), in which he claims that 'The Eleatic [Parmenidean] notion of being dominates Plato's philosophy, where multiplicity was subordinated to the one, and where the role of the feminine was thought within the categories of passivity and activity, and was reduced to matter' (Levinas 1987, 92–3). Taking as their point of departure just such an identification of the binary hierarchization of the masculine and the feminine, and the philosophical tradition founded upon it, many recent theorists of the feminine have sought not simply to reverse this binary hierarchization but also to effect its displacement through a reinscription of the feminine as that which, in its radical alterity, both precedes and exceeds binarity as such. The formidable risks run by any such act of reinscription are evident in the work of, among others, Luce Irigaray, Hélène Cixous, and Julia Kristeva, for each of whom the feminine, and in particular the maternal feminine, remains a notion with a critical edge, the need for which is always more than merely heuristic. Responding not just to a philosophical but also to a psychoanalytic and a literary tradition, Irigaray, Cixous, and Kristeva all privilege the feminine in its alterity, deploying that alterity as a value in the struggle against what they take to be the nihilism of phallogocentrism. In what follows, my aim will be to assess these and other attempts to reinscribe feminine alterity within an ethical discourse, and in particular to reflect upon some of the complications arising from attempts to coordinate feminine alterity, ethics, and literature.

Just how difficult it might prove to affirm the value of the feminine without remaining tied to phallogocentrism is apparent in Levinas's own attempt to think alterity first and foremost in terms of the feminine in *Time and the Other*, in which he claims that it is in the feminine that 'the alterity of the other appears in its purity [*dans sa pureté*]', and that for this reason the feminine occupies an 'exceptional position' in the economy of being (Levinas 1987, 86). Unlike the difference between being and nothingness, sexual difference 'conditions the very possibility of reality as multiple, against the unity of being proclaimed by Parmenides' (Levinas 1987, 85). In his attempt to challenge what he sees as an entire philosophical tradition governed by the principle of identity, then, Levinas assigns an absolute priority to sexual difference: it precedes, and indeed makes possible, all other differences. That originary other which first appears as the feminine is quite simply inappropriable, unmasterable. It is that which is 'essentially other' (*autre essentiellement*), 'a mode of being that consists in slipping away from the light [*se dérober à la lumière*]' (Levinas 1987, 86–7). What characterizes the alterity of the feminine is, in short, the mystery (*mystère*) of modesty (*pudeur*), Levinas's gendered rewriting (against Heidegger) of Heraclitus' characterization of Being (*phusis*) as that which 'loves to hide' (*kruptesthai philei*).[1] If Levinas's feminine other is not Being (*Sein*), neither is it an existent (*Seiendes*), situated over against the subject. The subject's relation to this feminine other is not cognitive; it is not a relation of power, possession, or appropriation. Rather, it is an erotic relation before and beyond all intersubjectivity, a highly paradoxical relation without relation with that which remains always to come (*à venir*). It is just such a gendered relation without relation that Blanchot will seek to articulate in his postwar *récits*, including *Death Sentence* (1948), *The Madness of the Day* (1949),[2] and *When the Times Comes* (1951), in each of which he takes advantage of the grammatical gendering in French of thought (*la pensée*), the law (*la loi*), and death (*la mort*).

That an identification of the feminine as the pure form of alterity risks simply reproducing the phallocentrism it is supposed to challenge is made clear by Simone de Beauvoir in her critique of Levinas in *The*

Second Sex (1949). Anticipating in certain important respects Derrida's claim that not only Heidegger's fundamental ontology but also Levinas's critique of Heidegger remains phallocentric, she argues that even to frame the question 'What is a woman?' is to bear witness to the historical dissymmetry of the relation between the masculine and the feminine, since a man 'never begins by presenting himself as an individual of a certain sex', man representing 'both the positive and the neutral [...] whereas woman represents only the negative, defined by limiting criteria, without reciprocity' (de Beauvoir 1972, 15). If the conception of 'woman' as a negative alterity is common to an entire phallocentric tradition, then, ironically, by deploying the feminine as the pure form of alterity in his attempt to break with a philosophy of the same (the Parmenidean 'One'), Levinas is confirming his attachment to that tradition through the very gesture that would mark his detachment from it: 'When he writes that woman is mystery, he implies that she is mystery for man. Thus his description, which is intended to be objective, is in fact an assertion of masculine privilege' (de Beauvoir 1972, 16 n. 1). Not part of a reciprocal or intersubjective relation, the feminine as negative alterity is that which in Western thought and culture never occupies the position of the One (the subject). Far from breaking with phallogocentrism, Levinas would simply mark its untroubled continuation within post-Holocaust philosophy.

How is one to explain this recurrent conception of the feminine as alterior, which would characterize an entire philosophical – and not just philosophical – tradition? According to de Beauvoir, the subject has remained masculine on account of women's having lacked 'concrete means for organizing themselves into a unit which can stand face to face with the correlative unit. They have no past, no history, no religion of their own; and they have no such solidarity of work and interest as that of the proletariat' (de Beauvoir 1972, 19). In short, women have remained dispersed (*dispersées*), their relation having only ever been to men, never to other women. It is this disempowering dispersal that marks women's particularity, distinguishing them from all other historical figures of alterity: blacks, Jews, homosexuals, the proletariat, to name only some of the most familiar. If the oppressive alterification of women is to end, then women must themselves be permitted to occupy the position of the subject. Here – as many theorists of the feminine will observe in de Beauvoir's wake – an obvious problem arises. If the subject–object, self–other, identity–alterity model has always been the very form of the patriarchal, phallocentric tradition, then would not enabling women to occupy the position of the subject be simply to reproduce the very mechanism of oppressive alterification of which women have hitherto been the unremitting victims? De Beauvoir herself shows an awareness of this problem, and places the emphasis not upon a new subject–object relation for women but upon an intersubjective reciprocity (*réciprocité*). The subject (be it masculine or feminine) enters into a relation with alterity that is not fixed, since that subject recognizes itself to be not just a subject but also the other's other.

For there to be a subject, however, there must be a certain transcendence, and thus negative alterity of a kind, as becomes clear when de Beauvoir outlines her existentialist ethics, which is grounded not in responsibility (the key term in Levinas's own later thinking of the ethical) but rather in the freedom of a subject that may be either masculine or feminine, but which in its essence is neither one nor the other. For de Beauvoir, alterity, no longer figured as the feminine, none the less reappears as that absolute evil (*mal absolu*) which is the limitation of this subject's freedom:

> There is no justification for present existence other than its expansion into an indefinitely open future. Every time transcendence falls back into immanence, stagnation, there is a degradation of existence into the '*en-soi*' – the brutish life of subjection to given conditions – and of liberty into constraint and contingence. This downfall represents a moral fault [*faute morale*] if the subject consents to it; if it is inflicted upon him, it spells frustration and oppression. In both cases it is an absolute evil [*mal absolu*]. (de Beauvoir 1972, 28–9)

Whereas for Levinas there can be no ethics without the experience of that absolute alterity which in its purity first takes the form of the feminine, for de Beauvoir alterity as limitation is absolute evil, the history of women's alterification being the history of the unethical, and alterification itself, paradoxically, being that 'other' against which a war in the name of the ethical must be waged.

From Freud to Lacan, and the 'no such thing as Woman'

On the one hand, de Beauvoir undoubtedly anticipates one of the fundamental principles of the postmodern theorization of the feminine, and more generally of gender studies, when she claims that 'One is not born a woman; one becomes one' – in other words, that 'woman' is a construction. On the other hand, her critique of the alterification of woman, her insistence upon the taking of a subjective position by women (subjectivity being conceived here in terms of freedom and transcendence) and the existentialist ethics built upon this conception of the subject, and, above all, her conception of the ethical relation as intersubjective, tie her to a philosophical tradition from which recent theorists of the feminine have sought assiduously to free themselves. Indeed, working by way of a reversal of the masculine–feminine hierarchy, some of the most influential recent theorists of the feminine have simply rejected de Beauvoir's critique of feminine alterity, instead valorizing the feminine precisely in its alterity. This is undoubtedly owing in no small part to the influence of psychoanalysis, a discourse that in both its Freudian and its Lacanian manifestations might be largely phallocentric but which at the same time provides the conceptual framework for a theorization of the feminine as a radical negative alterity that promises to challenge phallogocentrism in all its forms.

The apparent phallocentrism of Freud's conception of the feminine scarcely requires emphasis. In his *New Introductory Lectures on Psycho-Analysis* (1933), Freud states that women's sexual development is 'more difficult and more complicated' than men's on account of the girl's having to 'change her erotogenic zone and her object – both of which a boy retains' (Freud 1960a, 117, 119). The theory of penis envy (*Penisneid*), first proposed in his paper 'On the Sexual Theory of Children' (1908), serves to explain how a girl develops into a 'normal' (heterosexual) woman – that is, how the vagina replaces the clitoris as her erotogenic zone, and how the father replaces the mother as her love-object. Whereas the boy experiences the castration complex as a result of seeing (in the female genitals) that the penis need not necessarily accompany the body – in other words, he recognizes a lack in the other, a lack which marks that other as not-male – the girl has to face that same lack in herself: she is not threatened with castration, but is already castrated, determined negatively in relation to the male child, possessor of the phallus. On this anatomical basis, Freud proceeds to make a series of all too familiar generalizations about both the nature and the history of women, for the most part simply reiterating within a psychoanalytic framework Schopenhauer's observations in his notoriously misogynistic essay 'On Women', in *Parerga and Paralipomena* (1851). According to Freud, the formation of the super-ego is much more difficult in women – 'it cannot attain the strength and independence which give it cultural significance' – and this explains why women 'have made few contributions to the discoveries and inventions in the history of civilization'. Governed by narcissism and envy, women have 'little sense of justice', are 'weaker in their social interests', and possess 'less capacity for sublimating their instincts than men' (Freud 1960a, 132–4). In all of this, Freud reaffirms the classical conception of the feminine as a negative alterity, the feminine being characterized in every sphere in terms of lack in relation to the masculine.

For all the radicality of Lacan's linguisticist 'return to Freud', this conception of the feminine as a negative alterity remains firmly in place, and, if anything, is carried still further. In his Seminar of 1972–73, later published under the title *Encore* (1975), Lacan claims that 'Woman can only be written with a bar through it. There's no such thing as Woman, Woman with a capital *W* indicating the universal. There's no such thing as Woman because, in her essence [...] she is not-whole [*elle n'est pas toute*]' (Lacan 1998, 72–3). Now, although it might seem difficult to imagine how this essentializing conception of the feminine as negative alterity might be appropriated as a form of resistance to phallocentrism, that is precisely what one finds in the works of both Irigaray and Cixous. Indeed, as Jacqueline Rose observes, it is in response to Lacan's theorization of the feminine – a theorization which remains profoundly 'implicated' in phallocentrism – that the feminine is reconceived as a 'resistance to a phallic organisation of sexuality', constituting nothing less than 'a refusal of that organisation, its ordering, its identity'.[3]

From 'woman as other' to the 'other woman': Irigaray

In her two major works of the 1970s, *Speculum of the Other Woman* (1974) and *This Sex Which Is Not One* (1977), Luce Irigaray aims not simply to expose the phallocentricity of both Freud's and Lacan's conceptions of female sexuality in terms of lack, but also to disrupt the entire phallocentric order to which their discourses belong, and to reconceive the feminine – and in particular feminine 'style' or 'writing', or 'woman-speak' (*femme-parler*), as she terms it – in a manner that is no longer determined by the masculine. This reconceptualization or, more precisely, reinscription of the feminine begins with an observation that echoes de Beauvoir's in *The Second Sex*: for Freud and the phallocentric tradition to which he belongs – a tradition that stretches back at least as far as Plato – the feminine is defined by a masculine discourse as secondary to, and dependent upon, an originary masculinity that presents itself (more accurately, disguises itself) as sexual indifference: '[woman's] lot is that of "lack" ["*manque*"], "atrophy" (of the sexual organ), and "penis envy," the penis being the only sexual organ of recognized value [*reconnu valeureux*]'

(Irigaray 1985b, 23). It is on the secure ground of this universalizing characterization of the thinking of value that Irigaray's own countermove will take place.

In addition to this claim that the feminine has always been determined as a negative alterity by a masculine discourse, Irigaray makes two further fundamental claims, which together determine her own procedure. First, following the logic of Derrida's attempted deconstruction of Western metaphysics in his works of the later 1960s and early 1970s, she insists that it is not enough simply to effect an overturning or reversal (*renversement*) of the phallocentric order that determines the feminine as negative other. For all its apparently liberating force, such a reversal would ultimately achieve nothing but the reproduction of the existing order: 'if [women's] aim were simply to reverse the order of things, even supposing this to be possible, history would repeat itself in the long run, would revert to sameness [*au même*]: to phallocentrism. It would leave room neither for women's sexuality, nor for women's imaginary, nor for women's language to take (their) place' (Irigaray 1985b, 33). Secondly, however, the phallocentric order cannot effectively be challenged from a position beyond its borders, since, strictly speaking, there is no possibility of theoretical discourse outside the phallocentric order. Now, this double ban would seem to negate all possibility of liberating the feminine from its domination and its determination by the masculine. As we shall see, however, Irigaray remains faithful to neither of these initial claims.

Given that there is no discursive space outside the phallocentric order, the only way in which successfully to challenge phallocentrism is to disrupt (*déranger*) it from within. Now – and it is here that both the originality and the risk of Irigaray's strategy become apparent – this liberating disruption is to be achieved through a mimicry (*mimétisme*) of the phallocentric version of the feminine from which the feminine would free itself. Irigaray distinguishes, however, in a neatly binary fashion between two absolutely heterogeneous kinds of mimeticism, both of which are to be found in Plato, although the former has, she claims, been suppressed throughout the history of Western philosophy: 'there is *mimesis* as production, which would lie more in the realm of music, and there is *mimesis* that would already be caught up in the process of *imitation, specularization, adequation,* and *reproduction*' (Irigaray 1985b, 131). The mimicry of feminine alterity advocated by Irigaray is, then, mimesis as production, productivity taking the form here of a countering valorization of feminine alterity. To be effective, however, this valorization must be accompanied by a laughter that is itself 'the first form of liberation from a secular oppression' (Irigaray 1985b, 163). Here, Irigaray aligns herself with a tradition that includes Nietzsche, Bataille, and Derrida, although, crucially, Irigaray's laughter is explicitly gendered: 'women among themselves begin by laughing. To escape from a pure and simple reversal [*renversement*] of the masculine position means in any case not to forget to laugh. Not to forget that the dimension of desire, of pleasure, is untranslatable, unrepresentable, irrecuperable, in the "seriousness" – the adequacy, the univocity, the truth ... – of a discourse that claims to state its meaning' (Irigaray 1985b, 163).

In mimicry, then, the phallocentric conception of the feminine as negative alterity is affirmed, but as a value in its own right: 'One must assume the feminine role deliberately. Which means already to convert a form of subordination into an affirmation, and thus to begin to thwart it' (Irigaray 1985b, 76). It is clear, however, that this reassigning of value to the feminine in its alterity risks being no more than an act of reversal, and it is for this reason that the mimicry must include a disruptive excess (*excès dérangeant*): 'repeating/interpreting the way in which, within discourse, the feminine finds itself defined as lack, deficiency, or as imitation and negative image of the subject, [women] should signify that with respect to this logic a disruptive excess is possible on the feminine side' (Irigaray 1985b, 78). Now, this disruptive excess constitutes an alterity that is irreducible to that negative alterity of the feminine produced by the phallocentric order. It is, in short, an *other* otherness, which is to say an alterity more radical than the one produced and mastered by phallocentrism. In fact, if feminine mimicry is not simply an internalization of the mechanisms of oppressive alterification, this is because the feminine is always already alterior, always already elsewhere, the locus of an alterity that is not assigned to it by the masculine: 'if women are such good mimics, it is because they are not simply reabsorbed in this function. *They also remain elsewhere*' (Irigaray 1985b, 76). The feminine, then, is not, and never has been, simply within the phallocentric order. It also, and always already, constitutes 'an "outside" that is exempt, in part, from phallocratic law' (Irigaray 1985b, 68).

Beyond the negative moment of disruption, Irigaray's aim is to '(re) discover' this elsewhere, this 'possible space for the feminine imaginary' (Irigaray 1985b, 164), a space that has hitherto remained subject to phallocratic repression. It is a matter, then, of passing beyond the phallocentric thought of the woman as negative other (the woman as that which is *not man*) to the hitherto repressed thought of the other woman (*l'autre femme*), which is to say, woman conceived by woman, *as her own other*. Now, this other woman is not simply the antithesis of the woman as man's other; rather, she can only be imagined through a valorization of the negative alterity of the woman as other. The problem with this valorization, however, is that it threatens to collapse the difference between the two kinds of mimesis, and with it the distinction between the other woman and woman as other. For instance, Irigaray's own attempt to affirm the feminine in its independent alterity mimics, but not necessarily productively, the phallocentric reliance upon the anatomical-physiological difference between the sexes that she herself identifies in Freud: 'his tendency to fall back upon anatomy as an irrefutable criterion of truth' (Irigaray 1985b, 70–1). Distinguishing in a decidedly binary fashion between male auto-affection (which requires an instrument: the hand) and female auto-affection, Irigaray concludes: 'As for woman, she touches herself in and of herself without any need for mediation, and before there is any way to distinguish activity from passivity. Woman "touches herself" all the time, and moreover no one can forbid her to do so, for her genitals are formed of two lips in continuous contact' (Irigaray 1985b, 24). Now, this unmediated auto-affection is not just one trait among others, since it is precisely on account of this anatomical incorporation of alterity that woman 'cannot be identified either as one person or two' (Irigaray 1985b, 26). From this it is clear that, not only does a 'phallocentric' binarity already characterize Irigaray's distinction between two kinds of mimesis, but her identification of 'woman' as that which resists the very principle of identity, that which resists proper nomination, that which resists both reason and language (as grounded in a principle of identity and essence), itself obeys the very principle of identity that she has set out to disrupt.

Shoshana Felman and Toril Moi, among others, have taken issue with Irigaray's strategies for liberating the feminine from the enslaving alterification wrought by the phallocentric order. Felman's question, concerning what possible position Irigaray herself can claim to be speaking from (given her insistence that all discourse is subordinated to the law of the father),[4] can, at least in part, be answered by an appeal to that outside (*dehors*) without which productive mimicry would be impossible, although this only returns us to the highly problematical status of that outside in Irigaray's own discourse. Moi, on the other hand, questions above all what she sees as the essentializing, idealizing tendencies evident in Irigaray's conception of mimicry, which takes no account of historically contextual differences, and of the feminine as a self-affirming alterity: 'having shown that so far femininity has been produced exclusively in relation to the logic of the Same, [Irigaray] falls for the temptation to produce her own positive theory of femininity' (Moi 1985, 139). What is at issue in this second objection is whether Irigaray succeeds in passing from the mimetic reversal to the displacement of the phallocentric order. In other words, does her affirmation of the feminine as plural, multiple, fluid, and resistant to all appropriation, nomination, and identification simply remain trapped within the binary logic and the general characterization of the feminine to be found in the phallocentric order from which it would take its distance?

As we have seen, it is certainly the case that, as soon as Irigaray attempts to identify the form taken by the feminine in its own right, which is to say the alterity of the feminine as something other than the negative alterity into which it is cast by the phallocentric order, the difference between the productive mimicry of phallocentrism and its mere reproduction threatens to collapse, and this threat is also apparent in her vacillation between an insistence upon the impossibility of any outside and a reliance upon just such an outside, be it in the form of an excess or a space properly alterior, and indeed anterior, to the phallocentric order. If the feminine is that which resists identification, nomination, essentialization, and thematization, then the very stating of these 'truths' negates the difference between 'woman as other' and the 'other woman'. Similarly, woman's relation to alterity is presented simply as the antithesis of man's. Whereas the male relation to the other is appropriative and mastering, woman's is incarnating: 'Woman always remains several, but she is kept from dispersion because the other is already within her and is autoerotically familiar to her. Which is not to say that she appropriates the other for herself, that she reduces it to her own property. Ownership and property are doubtless quite foreign to the feminine' (Irigaray 1985b, 31).

It is with this anatomically grounded notion of the feminine as a non-appropriative incarnation or incorporation of alterity that Irigaray makes the connection between the feminine, writing, and an ethics of alterity. Again, everything is organized in neat opposition to the masculine. Whereas masculine discourse is coherent, linear, monologic, and governed by the principle of identity, the language of the feminine leaves the masculine reader 'unable to discern the coherence of any meaning. Hers are contradictory words, somewhat mad from the standpoint of reason, inaudible to whoever listens to them with ready-made grids, with a fully elaborated code in hand' (Irigaray 1985b, 29). Woman's writing 'tends to put the torch to fetish words, proper terms, well-constructed forms'; it is fluid and 'resists and explodes every firmly established form, figure, idea or concept' (Irigaray 1985b, 79). This writing is governed not by a principle of identity but rather by that principle of contiguity which is to be found – and not just figured – in woman's anatomy, in the contiguity of the genital labia.

One of the many problems besetting such a theory of feminine writing is that the connection between the feminine body and feminine writing is itself established in accordance with the very principle of identity (in this instance, between form and content) from which Irigaray wishes to free the feminine: that which resists conceptuality, identity, the thetic, reason, will have to be expressed in a form that resists all of these. There is, in short, an at-oneness between the feminine body and feminine writing that is at odds with the very notion of the feminine as that which resists the principle of identity. Now, this contradiction is not simply to be explained away as characteristic of a thinking that abandons the principle of non-contradiction in favour of paradox. Rather, what it suggests, beyond the difficulties of thinking sexual difference in non-essentializing, non-binary terms, is that in her reconceiving of feminine alterity as the 'other woman' Irigaray never addresses the confusion, rather than the deconstruction, of fact and value that characterizes her own discourse. It is this confusion, rather than the identification of the various characteristics (unity and plurality; fixity and fluidity; identity and alterity) to be assigned to the masculine and the feminine, that both enables and disables Irigaray's thinking of the feminine in its alterity, and that continues to govern her argument in *An Ethics of Sexual Difference* (1984), in which she proposes a new, ethical relation between the sexes modelled on that between woman and herself as what in Beckett's *Rockaby* is termed 'her own other' (Beckett 1990, 441).

Love of the other and 'feminine writing': Cixous

Like Irigaray, Cixous sees the feminine as having been determined as a negative alterity by a phallocentric discourse that works by way of binary oppositions which are, in fact, always hierarchical. In that discourse, to which both philosophy and much of literature belong, the feminine is figured as passive, secondary, lacking – in short, as nothing in itself. Indeed, the feminine in itself has simply been silenced. Like Irigaray, too, Cixous aims to call this entire phallocentric tradition into question through a countering affirmation of the very alterity that has been assigned to the feminine. According to Cixous, this affirmation has both to free the feminine from all negativity – 'We have no womanly reason to pledge allegiance to the negative' (Cixous 1981, 255) – and to reconceive its alterity.

In 'Sorties' and 'The Laugh of the Medusa', two overlapping virtual manifestos published in 1975, Cixous both addresses, and identifies with, women to argue that this self-affirmation of the feminine, this writing of woman by herself – 'woman must write woman' (Cixous 1981, 247) – involves above all a reassertion of the value of bisexuality. While this might appear to echo Virginia Woolf's argument for androgyny in the writer, in *A Room of One's Own* (1929), Cixous insists in a manner that Woolf does not that bisexuality must be wrenched free from that 'fate classically reserved for it in which it is conceptualized as "neuter" ', in order to disclose an 'other bisexuality' (Cixous 1986, 84), which is to say a bisexuality specific to woman: 'In a certain way, "woman is bisexual"; man – it's a secret to no one – being poised to keep glorious phallic monosexuality in view' (Cixous 1981, 254). Unlike classical bisexuality, this other bisexuality 'does not annihilate differences' in the interests of unity (Cixous 1986, 85), but activates or pluralizes differences beyond the binary.

Cixous's affirmation of the feminine in its bisexuality is grounded in a revaluation of alterity as such. The phallocentric order can be challenged only through a relocation of value in alterity, and through an openness to that alterity, a relation to it that is neither appropriative nor resistant. The very passivity assigned to the feminine by the phallocentric order is revalorized by Cixous as just such an openness to the other: 'there is a nonclosure that is not submission but confidence and comprehension; that is not an opportunity for destruction but for wonderful expansion' (Cixous 1986, 86). In short, the feminine becomes that which opens hospitably to the other, that which grants a place to it, unconditionally. The paradigm for such ethical openness is the maternal relation, in which the child is 'the other, but the other without violence, bypassing loss, struggle' (Cixous 1981, 261). In strict opposition to the principle of hatred governing the relation to alterity in the phallocentric order, the mother–child relation is governed by a principle of love. Femininity keeps alive 'the other that is confided to her, that visits her, that she can love as other' (Cixous 1986, 86). This loving openness to alterity is also the defining characteristic of both the woman's body and woman's writing: just as for Irigaray, so too for Cixous there is an unproblematic continuity between body and writing. The woman's body is 'without "end," without principal "parts"; if she is a whole, it is a whole made up of parts that are wholes, not simple, partial objects but varied entirely, moving and boundless change, a cosmos where eros never stops traveling, vast astral space' (Cixous 1986, 87). As for feminine writing (*écriture féminine*), it is the 'passageway, the entrance, the exit, the dwelling place of the other in me – the other that I am and am not' (Cixous 1986, 85–6). The plurality that characterizes feminine writing is the result of letting 'the other tongue of a thousand tongues speak' (Cixous 1986, 88). The principle that governs feminine writing is 'other-love'. In 'The Laugh of the Medusa', Cixous announces that 'Other-love is writing's first name' (Cixous 1986, 99). In the essay 'Coming to Writing' (1977), she defines writing as a 'gesture of love' (Cixous 1991, 42). This loving openness to alterity is realized through a writing that is the antithesis of 'masculine' discourse. It is non-linear, plurivocal, polysemantic, paronomastic, poetic – in the sense that sound, rhythm, musicality, and metaphoricity will predominate – and non-representational. Above all, feminine writing *incarnates* its meanings and is endlessly affirming: Cixous refers us to the literal affirmations that punctuate Molly Bloom's 'female monologue' in the final chapter of Joyce's *Ulysses*. Examples of producers of such feminine writing include Colette, Marguerite Duras, Jean Genet, and, above all, the Brazilian novelist Clarice Lispector.

For all Cixous's emphasis upon the principle of 'other-love' that governs feminine writing, however, that same writing does entail a certain violence, which is to say that there are very clear limits to the openness of the feminine. While claiming that it is impossible to define a feminine practice of writing, since definition and identification belong exclusively to phallocentrism, she none the less proceeds to offer just such a definition, and this definition makes it clear that feminine writing is in fact violent in the extreme, negating the very differences that constitute its own other: 'Women must write through their bodies, they must invent the impregnable language that will wreck partitions, classes, and rhetorics, regulations and codes, they must submerge, cut through, get beyond the ultimate reserve discourse, including the one that laughs at the very idea of pronouncing the word "silence," the one that, aiming for the impossible, stops short of the word "impossible" and writes it as "the end" ' (Cixous 1986, 94–5). However much feminine writing must be an act of self-affirmation, freed from the negative, it still involves a violence directed at the other (now figured as the phallocentric as such), and this for reasons that have everything to do with Cixous's initial identification of the phallocentric enemy. Feminine writing is wrecking, it cuts through distinctions, it sweeps away syntax, its aim being to 'shatter the framework of institutions, to blow up the law, to break up the "truth" with laughter' (Cixous 1981, 258). Not only is the opposition between the feminine and the phallocentric itself still binary in nature, but the very distinction that she makes between binary difference and multiple differences is itself one more binary opposition: 'No longer would the common logic of difference be organized with the opposition that remains dominant. Difference would be a bunch of new differences' (Cixous 1986, 83).

To affirm the feminine as that which is lovingly open to alterity is, it seems, also to produce an other to which the feminine is violently, non-dialectically closed. Through the very affirmation of feminine writing we are returned to an economy that functions by way of exclusion and scapegoating, though now the other against which all violence is directed is a masculinity that has itself been determined, in the most universalizing and ahistoricizing fashion, in accordance with a principle of identity. What this suggests is that the ethics of alterity governing feminine writing can function only for as long as it has an other against which it can define itself, an other against which all its own violence is directed. If, for Cixous, woman is 'she who kills no one in herself, she who gives (herself) her own lives', she who is 'always in a certain way "mother" for herself and for the other' (Cixous 1991, 50), she is also the one who makes death itself that other against which all her force will be directed. In its 'other-love', feminine writing is an unambiguous affirmation of life. But this means that it is also the negation – or at least the denegation – of death: 'Writing: a way of leaving no space for death, of pushing back forgetfulness' (Cixous 1991, 3). At the heart of Cixous's loving ethics of alterity, then, there is an unethical relation to death, which is to say an unethical relation to that very negativity upon which feminine writing depends, if only so that it can wreck unethical difference.

Art and ethics beyond sexual identity: Kristeva

Given this strange logic whereby the very attempt to affirm the feminine in its alterity, and to define it in terms of an openness to the other, seems to entail the need for a new negative other and for a return of the unethical in the form of a new violence against that other, it is understandable that those wishing to challenge phallocentrism might seek to avoid or to go beyond the binary opposition masculine–feminine altogether. It is precisely such an avoidance that Julia Kristeva aims to achieve, and this sets her apart from the tradition represented by Irigaray and Cixous. As she makes clear in 'Women's Time' (1981), not only is Kristeva unwilling simply to characterize Freud and Lacan as unremittingly phallocentric, but she, like Sarah Kofman, believes that 'a careful reading' of Freud can reveal where his texts actually exceed phallocentrism. In particular, castration can be read beyond the schematics of sexualization as 'the imaginary construction of a radical operation which constitutes the symbolic field and all beings inscribed therein'. What both Freud and Lacan offer, then, is a way of understanding how entry into the

Symbolic – that is, into language and meaning – involves 'a *separation from a presumed state of nature*'. Autism is to be understood as the non-occurrence of this entry into the Symbolic, and psychosis as a rejection of it. For all the fundamental differences upon which Freud and Lacan insist in their theorization of the male and the female child's sexual development, Kristeva emphasizes that this break with the natural, this separation from the mother, which is the condition of entry into the Symbolic, is the 'common destiny' of both sexes (Kristeva 1997, 205). Thus, for Kristeva, sexual difference becomes a secondary consideration, subordinated to a universal separation from the mother.

That said, Kristeva undoubtedly shares both Irigaray's and Cixous's conviction that the discourse of reason, the principle of identity, and all binary oppositions are phallocentric through and through, and indeed she goes still further, holding firmly to the Lacanian thesis that the Symbolic as a whole is governed by the paternal function – Lacan's punningly negating 'name of the father' (*nom du père*) taking the place of the literal father in the Freudian narrative of the Oedipus complex. For this reason – and here, too, she treads the same path as Irigaray and Cixous – Kristeva argues that a merely countering reversal of the male–female hierarchy will only reaffirm the oppressive paternal order from which women are striving to free themselves. As we have seen, while both Irigaray and Cixous reject any simple reversal of values, this is precisely what they proceed to undertake, remaining tied to binarism for all their warnings against it, and refusing to abandon an essentializing conception not just of the feminine – if only as that which resists essentialism – but also of the masculine. And their affirmation of feminine alterity, of woman-speak (*femme-parler*) or feminine writing (*écriture féminine*), and of a new maternal ethics of loving openness to the other, both generates, and indeed depends upon, a new alterity against which all woman's wrecking violence will be directed.

Now, Kristeva certainly attempts to avoid the pitfalls of either plumping for or rejecting reversal, by identifying not two but three distinct phases in the history of modern European feminism. There is, first, the suffragist and existentialist feminist phase, the aim of which is social, economic, and political equality with men: this struggle, she observes, is grounded in a 'logic of identification with [...] the logical and ontological values of a rationality dominant in the nation-state' (Kristeva 1997, 201). This first phase is followed by the post-1968 phase, which is characterized by a radical distrust not only of the 'entire political dimension' but also of rationality and the principle of identity, both of which are taken to be indissociable from the phallocentrism that feminism sets out to challenge.

This second phase involves a rejection of the very notion of reciprocity at the heart of de Beauvoir's existentialist ethics, and an insistence upon 'an irreducible identity, without equal in the opposite sex and, as such, exploded, plural, fluid, in a certain way non-identical' (Kristeva 1997, 202). As the affirmation of 'irreducible difference', this second phase paradoxically, if not self-contradictorily, identifies the feminine as a radical alterity that is itself open to otherness. Insisting, however, upon the constructedness of both the masculine and the feminine, upon their belonging as sexual identities within the Symbolic as opposed to the natural, Kristeva identifies a third phase, to which she commits herself, in which the binary distinction male/female would itself be recognized as essentially metaphysical (phallocentric) in nature, and in which sexual identity would be left behind. As we have seen, both Irigaray and Cixous make this same point. What distinguishes Kristeva's position, beyond her recuperation of a certain Freud, however, is her insistence upon the need to undertake a 'demassification of the problematic of *difference*' (Kristeva 1997, 215) and a movement beyond the very notion of sexual identity and sexual difference. No longer would the individual be seen simply to have a settled sexual identity, even a bisexual one. As for sexual difference, it would be experienced not as a fixed binary opposition but rather as a process of differentiation, part of what Kristeva terms the subject in process (*sujet en procès*), as opposed to the unary subject (*sujet unaire*).

Now, although she claims that these three phases, which together make up women's response to phallocentric oppression, are to be seen not simply as diachronic moments in a linear, narratable history but also synchronically, each with its own necessity, Kristeva is none the less highly critical of the 'naïve romanticism' of those who, as self-proclaimed feminists, retain a 'belief in identity' (Kristeva 1981, 138). Her own abiding interest in the modern European literary avant-garde, from Lautréamont and Mallarmé to Proust, Céline, Artaud, Joyce, and Sollers, is owing precisely to what she takes to be their undoing of identity, not least sexual identity. It is this undoing, this return to that which precedes the Symbolic and its network of structured, meaning-producing differences, that is the distinguishing mark of what she terms 'great' literature. If Kristeva's examples of genuinely avant-garde writers happen, for the most part, to be male, what these writers achieve, each in their own fashion, is decidedly feminine. If the Symbolic is governed by the paternal function, then that which finds non-semantic expression in genuinely poetic language is anterior to the Symbolic, namely the 'semiotic *chora*', the notion of the *chora* being taken by Kristeva from Plato's *Timaeus*, where it is explicitly associated with the maternal: 'We may indeed use the metaphor of birth and compare the receptacle [the *chora*] to the mother, the model to the father, and what they produce between them to their offspring' (Plato 1971, 69). In 'From One Identity to an Other' (1974), Kristeva characterizes this poetic language as 'an unsettling process – when not an outright destruction – of the identity of meaning and speaking subject' (Kristeva 1980a, 125). This process takes the form of an interruption of the Symbolic by that which is radically alterior – and indeed historically and conceptually anterior – to it:

> one should begin by positing that there is within poetic language (and therefore, although in a less pronounced manner, within any language) a *heterogeneousness* to meaning and signification. This *heterogeneousness*, detected genetically in the first echolalias of infants as rhythms and intonations anterior to the first phonemes, morphemes, lexemes, and sentences; this heterogeneousness, which is later reactivated as rhythms, intonations, glossolalias in psychotic discourse, serving as ultimate support of the speaking subject threatened by the collapse of the signifying function; this heterogeneousness to signification operates through, despite, and in excess of it and produces in poetic language 'musical' but also nonsense effects that destroy not only accepted beliefs and significations, but, in radical experiments, syntax itself, that guarantee of thetic consciousness (of the signified object and ego) – for example, carnivalesque discourse, Artaud, a number of texts by Mallarmé, certain Dadaist and Surrealist experiments. The notion of *heterogeneity* is indispensable, for though articulate, precise, organized, and complying with constraints and rules [...] this signifying disposition is not that of meaning or signification: no sign, no predication, no signified object and therefore no operating consciousness of a transcendental ego. (Kristeva 1980a, 133)

In *Revolution in Poetic Language* (1974), in which she offers her fullest analysis of literature in relation to this maternal semiotic, Kristeva defines the *chora* as follows: 'Indifferent to language, enigmatic and feminine, this space underlying the written is rhythmic, unfettered, irreducible to its intelligible verbal translation; it is musical, anterior to judgment, but restrained to a single guarantee: syntax' (Kristeva 1984, 29). The semiotic, then, is that feminine (maternal) heterogeneity – alterior to reason, identity, law, meaning, structure – upon the repression of which the Symbolic is founded. It is to this semiotic alterity that literature bears witness, without, as is the case with psychosis, ever submitting unreservedly to it.

In both the literary practice and the 'new ethics' for which Kristeva calls, the relation between identity and alterity becomes an endless process of undoing. In her most recent work, this process is termed 'revolt' (*révolte*), a word that she would save from its modern limitation to the political, and which is to be taken instead as an unremitting questioning, working tirelessly against all ideology or *doxa*.[5] For Kristeva, then, identity, sexual or otherwise, is always located on the side of power, oppression, limitation, dogmatism, and phallocentrism. The complete absence of identity, the pure alterity of the semiotic, on the other hand, is the realm of autism, psychosis, and the maternal. Thus, that endless undoing which characterizes a properly ethical literary practice cannot allow itself to be tempted by the utopian dream of an absolute negation of identity, cannot be purely feminine – hence Kristeva's rejection of any *écriture féminine*. If revolt takes place in the name of alterity, and is neither teleological nor progressive, it is none the less grounded in an identification of identity itself as oppressive, a category belonging wholly within the paternal Symbolic. The most ethical of acts becomes a literary practice in which identity is submitted to the experience of a feminine alterity that can never speak in its own name, and which – in accordance with an ethical principle (the value of mental health, the value of a happiness located between fixity and flux, between dogmatism and psychosis) – must never be allowed to negate identity beyond recovery or repair. For all her championing of revolt, then, Kristeva sounds a very cautionary note with regard to that feminine 'other-love' theorized by Cixous. If an ethical literary practice must have its sights fixed upon the undoing of identity, it can never give itself up entirely to alterity without losing its ethical privilege. That Kristeva's 'new ethics' is founded upon a series of strict oppositions between the Symbolic and the semiotic, identity and difference, and, above all, between questioning and dogmatism, suggests, however, that the fundamental problems besetting previous theories of the ethical, and in particular an ethical literary practice, have not been resolved. Demassifying difference would appear to be rather more difficult to achieve than one might imagine, and this, as we shall see, is owing not simply to the kinds of resistance that some irremissible identificatory drive might put up, but, rather more paradoxically, to the very valorization of difference which underlies each of the theories of the feminine considered hitherto.

Imagining a 'sexual otherwise': Derrida

For all their differences, Irigaray, Cixous, and Kristeva share the conviction that a thinking of the feminine which continues to be governed by

Feminine Alterities 155

binary oppositions will never effect its liberation from the logic of phallogocentrism. In this, each of them is faithful to Derrida's contention that the deconstruction of what he terms 'Western metaphysics' must take the form of a double gesture (*double geste*) or double science (*double science*), both an overturning (*renversement*) and a displacement (*déplacement*) of all metaphysical oppositions, among which the most ubiquitous would be presence and absence, active and passive, intelligible and sensible, and masculine and feminine. As he puts it in a June 1971 interview with Jean-Louis Houdebine and Guy Scarpetta,

> On the one hand, we must [*il faut*] traverse a phase of *overturning* [renversement]. To do justice to this necessity [*Faire droit à cette nécessité*] is to recognize that in a classical philosophical opposition we are not dealing with the peaceful coexistence of a *vis-à-vis*, but rather with a violent hierarchy. [...] That being said – and on the other hand – to remain in this phase is still to operate on the terrain of and from within the deconstructed system. By means of this double, and precisely stratified, dislodged and dislodging, writing, we must also mark the interval between inversion, which brings low what was high, and the irruptive emergence of a new 'concept,' a concept that can no longer be, and never could be, included in the previous regime. (Derrida 1981b, 41–2)

The deconstruction of classical binary oppositions is, then, itself a binary operation, there being in fact two deconstructions: 'an overturning deconstruction and a positively displacing, transgressive deconstruction' (Derrida 1981b, 66). What distinguishes deconstruction from all other forms of critique, including feminist critique, is this second, displacing gesture, in which the binary opposition's negatively determined other is reinscribed (*ré-inscrit*) as an undecidable (*indécidable*) or simulacrum (*simulacre*) that inhabits, and in fact has always inhabited, the metaphysical opposition aporetically, as both its condition of possibility and its condition of impossibility, constituting a radical alterity (*altérité radicale*) that is quite simply irreducible (Derrida 1981b, 64, 81). In its irreducibility, this radical alterity is resistant not simply to the often-cited negativity of the Hegelian *Aufhebung* (French: *relève*) but to all negativity, even – and, no doubt, above all – a negativity thought as anterior to the metaphysical opposition of affirmation and negation. In Derrida's early work, these irreducible undecidables or simulacra, which determine all negativity as derived or secondary, include the *pharmakon* (in Plato), the supplement (in Rousseau), and the hymen (in Mallarmé), and, more generally – indeed, throughout Western philosophy, with the notable exception of Nietzsche – writing (*écriture*).

Now, for all Derrida's insistence that deconstruction as a double science has to take its distance from metaphysics, not least in its essentializing and universalizing project, deconstruction is itself none the less grounded as an operation in a host of essentializing and universalizing identifications, which include, but are certainly not limited to, the claims that every text is necessarily fissured (*fissuré*) or heterogeneous to itself – although Derrida certainly proceeds as though some texts are less at odds with themselves than others – and that binarism is not just the very form of metaphysics or of phallogocentrism, but also, and always, an unethical violence directed against a negatively determined other. What, though, of Derrida's double science in practice? As we have seen, while the reversal of the masculine–feminine opposition can be achieved without too much difficulty through a countering act of affirmation, its reinscription proves to be rather more problematical, entailing a valorization of alterity through which another negative alterity is produced, such that, for instance, Kristeva's 'new ethics' continues to depend upon a violence the nature of which remains unanalysed. This failure to free the ethical from the unethical is owing in part, no doubt, to the fact that the initial identification of phallogocentrism upon which the deconstructive operation sets to work is itself an uncritical one, which is to say an identification that is not subject to deconstruction. No less protected from deconstructive attention is the scarcely perceptible movement from the identification of a *différance* that is irreducible in its radical alterity to the valorization of difference. Just as a certain violence – the ethicality of which is precisely what remains in question here – lies at the heart of the attempts made by Irigaray, Cixous, and Kristeva to affirm a feminine 'other', so in Derrida's own deconstruction of phallogocentrism the cost of alterity's affirmation is a violence that is neither ethical nor unethical, but precisely anethical.

There can be little doubt that Derrida consistently strives to avoid the temptation to overturn without displacing the violent masculine–feminine hierarchy. His first sustained engagement with the question of the feminine occurs in *Spurs: Nietzsche's Styles*, originally delivered at the Nietzsche colloquium at Cerisy-la-Salle in July 1972. Here, he undertakes that task so tellingly avoided by Heidegger in his 1936–40 lectures on Nietzsche,[6] namely the analysis of the role of the feminine in Nietzsche's later writings. Whereas Heidegger avoids or, as Barbara Harlow translates it, 'skirts the woman' (*contourne la femme*) in Nietzsche – indeed, 'analyzes all the elements of Nietzsche's text with the sole exception of the idea's becoming-female (*sie wird Weib*)' (Derrida 1979, 85) – Derrida aims to demonstrate: (1) that sexual difference simply cannot be reduced to a 'regional question in a larger order which would subordinate it first to the domain of a general ontology' (Derrida 1979, 109); and (2) that the thought of the feminine lies at the very heart of Nietzsche's attempt to exceed metaphysics. Perhaps what is most striking about Derrida's reading of Nietzsche in *Spurs*, however, is that, while paying homage to the deconstructive readings of Nietzsche already undertaken by Sarah Kofman, Philippe Lacoue-Labarthe, Bernard Pautrat, and Jean-Michel Rey, he proceeds as though Nietzsche, just like Rousseau for Paul de Man, scarcely requires deconstruction. Indeed, for all his earlier insistence upon the non-homogeneity of any text, Derrida finds in Nietzsche's attacks on feminism a fully justified resistance both to any simple reversal of the phallogocentric hierarchy and to any attempt to essentialize the feminine. Relying upon a paradoxicality so characteristic of his practice of deconstruction more generally, Derrida claims that Nietzsche grants us the thought of the feminine as that which resists the very question of essence and the principle of identity, as that which simply cannot be contained within, cannot be mastered by, the binary logic of Western metaphysics. To try to think the feminine is to experience an alterity that exceeds the opposition not just between the masculine and the feminine but also between identity and difference:

> There is no such thing as the essence of woman because woman averts, she is averted of herself [*la femme écarte et s'écarte d'elle-même*]. Out of the depths, endless and unfathomable, she engulfs and distorts all vestige of essentiality, of identity, of property. [...] There is no such thing as the truth of woman, but it is because of that abyssal divergence [*écart abyssal*] of the truth, because that untruth is 'truth.' Woman is but one name for that untruth of truth [*Femme est un nom de cette non-vérité de la vérité*]. (Derrida 1979, 51)

If 'woman' is but one name among others for the untruth of truth, then this is because 'woman' belongs with all those other undecidables or simulacra, not one of which constitutes a master-term. That said, the question of woman (*la question de la femme*) is not simply one question among others. Challenging the authority of questioning as philosophy's mode of operation, the question of woman inaugurates a new epoch, beyond the closure (*clôture*) – which is to be rigorously distinguished from the end (*fin*) – of Western metaphysics: 'The question of the woman suspends the decidable opposition of true and non-true and inaugurates the epochal regime [*instaure le régime époqual*] of quotation marks which is to be enforced for every concept belonging to the system of philosophical decidability. The hermeneutic project which postulates a true sense of the text [*le vrai sens d'un texte*] is disqualified under this regime' (Derrida 1979, 107). If, given the inauguration of this new epoch, there cannot be said to be either a truth of, or a truth or truths within, Nietzsche's texts, it is none the less the highly paradoxical case that Nietzsche grants us the epochal truth that there is no truth of woman. Thus, in Nietzsche's wake, one must, one is obliged to – the distinction between necessity and obligation, between what will be and what should be the case, between fact and value, being elided here through a reliance upon an *il faut* – one must think the feminine as a radical alterity beyond essence, beyond the conceptual, beyond all identity-thinking, beyond the opposition between truth and untruth, difference and identity.

Now, according to Derrida, it is precisely this radical alterity of the feminine as undecidable or simulacrum that is not taken into account by feminism, which, for all its local differences, by remaining satisfied with an overturning of the existing masculine–feminine hierarchy, or even with an equality of the sexes, continues to essentialize the feminine, thereby simply reproducing the logic of phallocentrism: 'it is man who believes in the truth of woman, in woman-truth. And in truth, they too are men, those women feminists so derided by Nietzsche. Feminism is nothing but the operation of a woman who aspires to be like a man. And in order to resemble the masculine dogmatic philosopher this woman lays claim – just as much claim as he – to truth, science and objectivity in all their castrated delusions of virility' (Derrida 1979, 65). What is perhaps most surprising here is that Derrida appears to grant rather less importance, and indeed power, to the moment of overturning, as distinct from displacement, than he does elsewhere: in *Positions*, for instance, he insists that 'To overlook this phase of overturning is to forget the conflictual and subordinating structure of opposition. Therefore one might proceed too quickly to a *neutralization* that *in practice* would leave the previous field untouched' (Derrida 1981b, 41). One might well suspect that Derrida's reading of Nietzsche – and not only on the question of woman – is characterized by just such an uncritical acceleration, owing in large part to his concern with disclosing a Nietzsche altogether different from Heidegger's 'last metaphysician'.

That Derrida is not unduly concerned with the danger entailed by an occlusion of the phase of overturning – which in *Spurs* takes the form of feminism as 'the operation of a woman who aspires to be like a man' – is reinforced by a similar tendency to speed in 'Choreographies', his 1982 interview with Christie McDonald. As in *Spurs*, so here Derrida emphasizes the need to think the feminine beyond any feminism, and hastens towards an identification of the feminine in its radical alterity. Responding to the question of 'woman's place', he reiterates the position taken in *Spurs*, claiming that 'woman' is precisely that which cannot be said to have a 'place', that 'woman' is that which exceeds all placing, all property, and all appropriation. No doubt in part owing to the occasion – here, Derrida is being questioned by a woman on the very possibility of feminism – he distinguishes between that 'reactive feminism' mocked by Nietzsche and an affirmation of the feminine (or an 'assertion of women') that cannot be said to be feminist, precisely because it lies beyond the opposition feminist–anti-feminist.

For all his emphasis upon the feminine, however, as early as *Spurs* Derrida is using Nietzsche above all in order to call into question the binary model of sexual difference: 'A joyful wisdom shows it well: there never has been *the* style, *the* simulacrum, *the* woman. There never has been *the* sexual difference. [...] the insinuation of the woman (of) Nietzsche is that, if there is going to be style, there can only be more than one' (Derrida 1979, 139). This deconstructive call for a movement beyond binary sexual difference, but not beyond sexual difference *tout court*, is repeated in 'Choreographies', where it is explicitly deployed in an adumbration of the relationship with the other – in other words, in an early deconstructive thinking of the ethical:

> what if we were to reach, what if we were to approach here (for one does not arrive at this as one would at a determined location) the area of a relationship to the other where the code of sexual marks would no longer be discriminating? The relationship would not be a-sexual, far from it, but would be sexual otherwise [*autrement sexuée*]: beyond the binary difference that governs the decorum of all codes, beyond the opposition feminine/masculine, beyond bisexuality as well, beyond homosexuality and heterosexuality which come to the same thing [*qui reviennent au même*]. (Derrida 1995, 108)

Leaving aside the problems entailed by the claim that homosexuality and heterosexuality 'come to the same thing' – and this, tellingly, as a conclusion arrived at through a procedure governed by the thought of *différance* – this passage is noteworthy because it marks the point of departure, and sets the agenda, for Derrida's subsequent readings of Heidegger, Levinas, and Blanchot, and, more generally, for his deconstructive ethics of hospitality. If the relation to the other is never simply asexual or neutral, then this, Derrida argues, is because in asexuality or neutrality phallocentrism simply maintains itself, irrespective of any context: 'one ensures phallocentric mastery under the cover of neutralization every time' (Derrida 1995, 101). Now, the claim that the relation to the other is irreducibly sexual is Derrida's deconstructive, Nietzschean counter-claim to Heidegger's assertion, in his 1928 summer-seminar lectures at the University of Marburg, that 'Dasein is neither of the two sexes. But here sexlessness [*Geschlechtlosigkeit*] is not the indifference of an empty void, the weak negativity of an indifferent ontic nothing. In its neutrality Dasein is not the indifferent nobody and everybody [*Niemand und Jeder*], but the primordial positivity and potency [*Mächtigkeit*] of the essence' (Heidegger 1984b, 136).[7] In that 'primordial positivity and potency' Derrida identifies the perpetuation of a phallocentrism that confirms Heidegger's belonging to the very metaphysics from which he would take his distance. If this is true of Heidegger, it is no less true of Levinas, despite his attempt in *Time and the Other* to think alterity first and foremost as the feminine. Derrida's critique of Levinas takes a very different form, however, from de Beauvoir's. Whereas de Beauvoir sees Levinas's positing of the feminine as pure alterity as simply one more instance of the phallocentric alterification of the feminine, Derrida argues that the fault lies not in Levinas's figuring of alterity as feminine but rather in his distinctly Heideggerian subordination of sexual difference to an originary neutrality: 'It is not woman or the feminine that he has rendered secondary, derivative, or subordinate, but sexual difference [*la différence sexuelle*]. Once sexual difference is subordinated, it is always the case that the wholly other [*le tout autre*], who is *not yet marked*, is *already* found to be marked by masculinity' (Derrida 1991a, 430). Derrida's own sexualization of deconstruction – through, for instance, his deployment of terms such as 'hymen' (in his reading of Mallarmé), 'dissemination' (in his reading of Sollers), and 'double invagination' (in his reading of Blanchot) – is 'dictated' by his 'reservations' regarding such sexual neutralizations.

Derrida's argument, then, is that the relation to the other is always marked by sexual difference, but by a sexual difference that is not organized in accordance with a binary logic, a sexual difference '(without negativity, let us clarify) not sealed by a two'. Neither neutrality, then, nor binary sexual difference, but an 'other sexual difference' (*autre différence sexuelle*) (Derrida 1991b, 401). Crucially, however, despite the fact that Derrida does not wish to valorize the feminine as such – since this, according to his own logic, would leave him trapped within the very phallocentrism from which he aims to take his distance – the irreducible alterity that deconstruction would disclose within metaphysics, as both its condition of possibility and its condition of impossibility, and that will lie at the heart of his ethics of hospitality, remains more feminine than masculine, if only because deconstruction works precisely through a valorizing reinscription of the subordinated term in each of the metaphysical oppositions that it identifies in order to deconstruct. When it comes to sexual difference, that subordinated term is, of course, the feminine. If the relation to the other is irreducibly dissymmetrical (*irréductiblement dissymétrique*) – 'a certain dissymmetry is no doubt the law both of sexual difference and the relationship to the other in general' (Derrida 1995, 107) – then this is because, for Derrida, as for Levinas before him, it is the feminine that holds the key to alterity, to the 'sexual otherwise', and ultimately to the ethical.

Ethical and unethical fictions of gender: from Derrida to Judith Butler

Among those who have responded most enthusiastically to Derrida's call to think the 'sexual otherwise', beyond the binary model of sexual difference, it is Judith Butler who has arguably exerted the most widespread influence, through her *Gender Trouble: Feminism and the Subversion of Identity* (1990). Butler's debt to Derrida, not only in her attempt to think sexual difference in a non-binary manner, but also in her non-foundationalist, non-ontological theorization of gender as a performative, is made clear in her preface to the tenth-anniversary edition of *Gender Trouble*, in which she observes: 'I originally took my clue on how to read the performativity of gender from Jacques Derrida's reading of Kafka's "Before the Law" ' (Butler 1999, xiv). Drawing upon the distinction between constative and performative speech acts in J. L. Austin's *How to Do Things with Words* (1962), which is itself subjected to deconstructive critique by Derrida in 'Signature Event Context' (1971), Butler argues that not only both sex and gender, but also the distinction between them, is culturally produced. In short, there is no such thing as natural gender, any more than there is a natural sex that would precede all discursivity. Gender identity is always and everywhere 'instituted in an exterior space through a stylized repetition of acts' (Butler 1999, 179). Butler does not restrict herself, however, to this general truth of gender's constructedness, but proceeds to distinguish in evaluative – more precisely, in ethical – terms between two different kinds of gender performance.

On the one hand, there are those performances of gender which disguise their own operation, seek to naturalize gender, and both adhere to, and reinforce, the binarity of 'compulsory heterosexuality'.[8] On the other hand, there are performances of gender that are subversively parodic, performances that not only identify themselves as non-natural but also reveal the constructedness or fictiveness of all gender identities. According to Butler, drag is just such a subversive, defamiliarizing gender performance: 'drag fully subverts the distinction between inner and outer psychic space and effectively mocks both the expressive model of gender and the notion of a true gender identity. [...] *In imitating gender, drag implicitly reveals the imitative structure of gender itself – as well as its contingency.* [...] gender parody reveals that the original identity after which gender fashions itself is an imitation without an origin' (Butler 1999, 174–5). Now, if all gender identities are constructions or fictions, then it makes no sense to distinguish between true and false constructions, true and false performances and fictions. However, Butler's aim here is to distinguish rigorously between those performances or fictions which call attention to their own status and those which are designed to hide their non-naturalness. The value of parodic gender performance remains tied to truth, but to the truth that the nature of sexual identity lies precisely in its non-naturality. The truth disclosed by parodic performance is a self-reflexive truth that counters what Butler terms the 'foundationalist fable' or 'foundationalist fictions' (Butler 1999, 5, 6).

It is clear, then, that although – one might even say *because* – Butler's entire argument is orientated towards the thoroughgoing deconstruction of binarity in the thinking of gender and identity, a binary logic none the less reasserts itself. For all her emphasis upon the oppression that she takes to be intrinsic to the binary thinking of gender, and in particular to 'compulsory heterosexuality', Butler enforces a binary distinction of her own between two antagonistically opposed kinds of gender performance: the kind that naturalizes itself, and the kind that reveals both its own constructedness and the performativity of all gender identity. This second kind of performativity is tied securely to a truth – the truth of performativity – which is subject to identification and discursive revelation. Value lies precisely in the revelation of this truth. In short, although she does not focus specifically on literature in *Gender Trouble*, Butler is here producing nothing less than a theory of ethical fiction, defined as a self-reflexive performance that both identifies and communicates its own fictionality.

Now, in a paradox the logic of which remains unexplored by Butler in *Gender Trouble*, this theory of ethical fiction, and its rigorous distinction from any unethical foundationalist fiction, involves a naturalization and a suppression of differences that might well be termed unethical, were it not that the very distinction between the ethical and the unethical is precisely what loses its coherence here. Drag reveals the truth that there are no natural truths, and this truth is itself both universal and without history. Gender has never been, and can never be, anything but a performance. History and all cultural specificity lie only in the foundational binary distinction between the self-disclosing and the self-disguising performance, between universally ethical and universally unethical fictions, between those fictions which reveal and those fictions which conceal an epochal truth, namely the performativity of gender identity. The paradox lies, then, in the fact that Butler's anti-foundationalist theory of ethical fiction demands a radical reduction of differences to a binary opposition and an identification of an alterity against which the full force of the anti-foundationalist argument may be directed. Paradoxically, that alterity is, once again, nothing other than identity as such.

Beneath or behind what Butler terms that 'indispensable' laughter which 'emerges in the realization that all along the original was derived' (Butler 1999, 176), a 'subversive laughter' manifesting itself in 'the pastiche-effect of parodic practices in which the original, the authentic, and the real are themselves constituted as effects' (Butler 1999, 186–7), one begins to wonder whether there might not be space for another, rather less self-assured or self-reassuring laughter, a laughter that would accompany the thought of this absolute proliferation of performance, its colonization of the entire field of thought – in the name of difference. What Butler's deconstructive take on gender identity makes it possible to imagine, then – and this very much against the grain of her own argument – is that the distinction between ethical and unethical fictions of gender serves here both to suppress and to suggest a thinking of gender in its anethicality. Such a thinking of gender would not hasten towards conclusions about the ethicality of a certain relation to alterity, but instead would observe the ways in which the ethical produces the unethical, and vice versa. If gender is, as Butler claims, always in some sense a fiction, then its fictionalization is neither ethical nor unethical, but anethical – the ethical as unethical, and the unethical as ethical – and this would be the case not only for naturalizing but also for denaturalizing fictions, the difference between them itself being an anethical one.

6
'As If the Sex Mattered'
Beckett's Degenderations

'Woman' as negative alterity

Owing, no doubt in part, to the assumption that great art both expresses and addresses a humanity above and beyond sexual difference, the question of gender, and in particular the question of the value assigned to the feminine, remained at most peripheral in early studies of Beckett. Indeed, with a few notable exceptions, including Kristeva's short essay in *Polylogue* (1977), it is only since the early 1990s, with the publication of a collection of essays and interviews edited by Linda Ben-Zvi (1990b) and a monograph by Mary Bryden (1993), that gender has come to occupy an important place in the interpretation of his works. These two volumes have established a critical consensus regarding the representation of women up to, and including, *The Unnamable* (1953). In the novels, short stories, and poetry produced during the first two decades of Beckett's career, a prevailing misogyny is generally seen to present the reader with a stereotypical view of 'woman' either as ensnaring materiality – a disgusting corporeal heterogeneity that Beckett's male protagonists and, in the postwar prose, his male narrator-protagonists struggle tragicomically to escape in the interests of a purely mental freedom – or, much more rarely, as the incarnate perfected.[1]

Predominantly a negative alterity, 'woman' in Beckett's early works tends to be conceived as a threatening 'other' objectified by a male consciousness. Within an explicitly gendered dualist framework, mind is conceived as masculine, body as feminine. By the time of the postwar trilogy, however, it is no longer simply what in *Murphy* is termed the 'outer reality' that constitutes an intolerable feminine alterity, but being as such: Malone, for instance, dreams of escaping via the 'great cunt of existence' (Beckett 1959, 285). It is being – not just feminine being, but being as feminine – that Beckett's male consciousnesses seek to negate in the interests of that nothing 'than which in the guffaw of the Abderite naught is more real' (Beckett 1938, 246). Furthermore, in Beckett's first published short story, 'Assumption' (1929), and then again in his first novel, *Dream of Fair to Middling Women* (written 1931–32), not only is the would-be artist male, but it is 'woman' who appears to stand between him and his art. Even as late as *Krapp's Last Tape* (1958), a male protagonist is seeing his life in terms of a simple choice between love of a woman and art.

However, if Beckett's early works have struck the majority of commentators as almost unremittingly misogynist, there has been far less critical agreement over the representation of women in his later works, and this is perhaps nowhere more evident than in the often entirely irreconcilable responses to one of his major late plays, *Not I* (1972). On the one hand, *Not I* has been seen to give voice to a femininity that both resists and subverts the patriarchal order. According to Peter Gidal, for instance, Mouth's utterance is an example of 'anti-patriarchal/anti-capitalist language and speech production' (Gidal 1986, 114). Similarly, approaching the play from a Lacanian perspective, Anna McMullan argues that Mouth can be interpreted as 'a disruptive force which threatens the conceptual stability and fixity established by the Symbolic' (McMullan 1993, 76). And, for Mary Bryden, working from a Deleuzian perspective, Mouth is 'the ultimate deterritorialized voice' (Bryden 1993, 118). Such readings would locate the play within that European avant-garde tradition in which, according to Kristeva, the '*heterogeneousness* to meaning and signification' that characterizes the rhythmic semiotic disrupts the Symbolic order (Kristeva 1980a, 133). As we have seen in the previous chapter, Kristeva identifies this alterity as 'enigmatic and feminine' (Kristeva 1984, 29). In support of such a reading, much could no doubt be made of Beckett's own repeated concern for rhythm, not least when directing his own plays.[2] On the other hand, however, Kristeva herself is among the first to argue not only that Mouth's utterance remains under the nihilistic shadow cast by the death of the father-god, but also that her utterance, and indeed all utterance in Beckett, is sustained by a 'censorship of the maternal body' (Kristeva 1980b, 154). According to Kristeva, Beckett's works enact an endless mourning for the father as the bestower of meaning. Irrespective of the speaker's gender, those works give us only the son's melancholia, fixated by the death of the father. As separation without liberation, this endless mourning leaves the son wandering helplessly through a cadaverous, degenerescent realm, its materiality not that of the affirming feminine flesh – and the 'female word *yes*' – of

Joyce's Molly Bloom,[3] but rather that of the rotting paternal corpse and its impotent 'no'. As for the properly maternal in Beckett, it would remain untouched, pristine in its absolute heterogeneity.

In Kristeva's wake, although with far less respect for what Kristeva sees as the strengths as well as the limitations of Beckett's *œuvre*, Ann Wilson argues that Mouth is written into a scene that is 'overdetermined by the Order of the Father' (Wilson 1990, 199). Rather more sensitive to the importance of genre in Beckett, Linda Ben-Zvi maintains that everything depends upon whether one approaches *Not I* as a written text, a stage play, or a television play.[4] As a stage play, Ben-Zvi believes that *Not I* offers 'possibilities of escape' through the 'tenacity which the flickering live mouth seems perhaps capable of exercising'. In the 1975 televised version, however, the exclusion of Auditor and the relentless close-up on Mouth effects an 'objectification of woman, woman as Other / as mouth / as vagina / as pornographic image' (Ben-Zvi 1990a, 248). With this reduction of woman to a negative alterity, those possibilities of escape from a phallocentric universe that are present in the stage play simply disappear, and we are returned to the essentially misogynistic perspective of Beckett's early works.

Some commentators have attempted to avoid the either/or logic governing the arguments of those who see *Not I* and other later works for the theatre as ultimately either resistant or subject to the patriarchal. Elin Diamond, for instance, argues that *Not I* presents feminine resistance to the patriarchal Symbolic in a manner that brings out the unavoidable sacrifice entailed by it, namely madness: 'Mouth's raving is marked by a refusal of the pronominal that would inscribe her into normative discourse. The price for refusing that "I" is a logorrhea marked by the classic symptoms of hysteria' (Diamond 2004, 50). We shall have reason to return to the question of hysteria later in this chapter, since Beckett undoubtedly follows a long tradition in associating it with the feminine. As for Diamond's reading of *Not I*, it is grounded in the assumption that the subversion of the patriarchal – as the Lacanian Symbolic – will have to take the form of madness, a position subjected to persuasive critique by Judith Butler.[5]

If there is considerably less consensus on the representation of the feminine in Beckett's later works than there is on the misogynistic nature of the earlier works, this is because some commentators see a decisive change in Beckett's treatment of gender that is directly related to a shift in genre. It is with the plays, and more precisely with his first radio play, *All That Fall* (1957), followed by *Happy Days* (1961), that Beckett for the first time places a woman at the centre of his work. Among those commentators who detect such a change in Beckett's treatment of gender, there are some who see the feminine taking on a value that is in itself radically subversive of the patriarchal, offering a new sense of the feminine and even a mode of expression akin to Irigaray's *femme-parler* or Cixous's *écriture féminine*. For others, however, this new attention to the feminine heralds nothing less than a multiplication of differences beyond any binary model of sexual difference. This latter position is the one taken by Mary Bryden. Applying Deleuze and Guattari's distinction between the molecular and the molar, she argues that in Beckett's later plays the phallocentric gender duality breaks down, to be replaced by a gender fluidity in which the masculine is no longer the locus of value. Beyond such fluidity, however, she also detects a voice that is 'sexually impartial', sexual difference having become sexual indifference (Bryden 1993, 197–8). Whether such impartiality can be clearly distinguished from that neutrality theorized by Heidegger, Levinas, and Blanchot, which, according to Derrida, remains the voice of the masculine, is a question to which we shall have occasion to return when considering one of Beckett's last works, *Worstward Ho* (1983). First, however, in order to assess the argument that he comes to assign a subversive value to the feminine, it is necessary to retrace the trajectory upon which gender is situated in his *œuvre*.

Beckett, Schopenhauer, and the 'value of women'

In Beckett's early works, the gendering of the mind–body, microcosm–macrocosm distinction as masculine–feminine is coordinated with a distorted Geulincxian ethic of withdrawal – '*ubi nihil vales, ibi nihil velis*' – and a Schopenhauerian ethic of denial (*Verneinung*) in which all value is assigned to inwardness and ultimately to non-being, to be achieved through a negation of the will, which takes a more positive form in woman (*das Weib*) than in man. Indeed, Schopenhauer's conception of woman constitutes the dominant gender stereotype in Beckett's works, both early and late. In his essay 'On Women', the aim of which is to determine the true value of women (*Wert der Weiber*), Schopenhauer identifies woman as an intermediate stage (*Mittelstufe*) between the child and the man, the latter being the 'human being in the real sense'. What distinguishes man from woman is principally the latter's 'limited faculty of reason' (Schopenhauer 1974, 614–15). This limitation means that woman is not only less able than man to think logically, but also less able to abstract from the particular to the general, to pass from the subjective into the objective, and to conceive of the present in relation to the past and future: 'throughout their lives [women] remain children, always see only what is nearest to them, cling to the present [*kleben an der Gegenwart*], take the appearance for the reality, and prefer trivialities [*Kleinigkeiten*] to the most important affairs'. In short, woman is an intellectual myope (*geistiger Myops*). Owing to her being more greatly absorbed in the present than man, and thereby failing to recognize change, woman exhibits a cheerfulness (*Heiterkeit*) that makes her suited for the recreation (*Erholung*) and consolation (*Trost*) of man (Schopenhauer 1974, 615–16). It is woman's inability to achieve objectivity that explains her failure to produce any intellectual or artistic work of 'permanent value'. Indeed, woman may be defined as the unaesthetic (*unästhetisch*) sex, not only lacking in natural beauty but also lacking any ability to produce artistic beauty (Schopenhauer 1974, 619–20). That said, woman triumphs over man in her mastery of the art of dissimulation (*Verstellungskunst*), an art deployed solely in the interests of capturing a male with whom she can fulfil her biological destiny, which is to procreate: 'women exist solely for the propagation of the race' (Schopenhauer 1974, 617–18). Unsuited to both the cognitive and the aesthetic, and yet none the less gifted in the art of dissimulation, Schopenhauer's woman anticipates Freud's in being completely at odds with the ethical: injustice (*Ungerechtigkeit*) is the 'fundamental failing of the female character' (Schopenhauer 1974, 619). Furthermore, men's reluctance to subject themselves to the unnatural dominance of women in the institution of monogamous marriage has resulted in the social blight of prostitution. Schopenhauer refers in particular to the large number of prostitutes in London, an observation of more than passing relevance to Beckett's *Murphy*, in which the main female character, Celia Kelly, is a London prostitute, albeit of Irish extraction.

Schopenhauer's unremittingly misogynistic view of woman casts a long shadow over Beckett's œuvre, and not just the early works. In his first novel, *Dream of Fair to Middling Women*, the Smeraldina is presented as a grotesquely corporeal and sexual being: 'Poppata, big breech, Botticelli thighs, knock-knees, ankles all fat nodules, wobbly, mammose, slobbery-blubbery, bubbub-bubbub, a real button-bursting Weib' (Beckett 1992, 15).[6] Indeed, for Belacqua, the German word *Weib* – which refers the reader back not only to Schopenhauer but also to Goethe's 'eternal feminine' (*das ewig Weibliche*) – is 'a fat, flabby, pasty, kind of a word, all breasts and buttocks, bubbubbubbub, bbbacio, bbbocca, a hell of a fine word' (Beckett 1992, 100), 'fine' because, like Joyce's 'in twosome twiminds' in *Finnegans Wake*, it incarnates its meaning. In *Murphy*, Beckett's London prostitute, Celia Kelly, is introduced to the reader in a purely quantitative manner, through an exaggerated mode of naturalist representation (the list) that supplies the vital statistics of her outer being. Unsurprisingly, it is she who wants Murphy to establish himself in the 'outer reality' as a working, reproducing body, while the epitome of withdrawal from that reality is a man: the schizophrenic Mr Endon. Even such passing details as Murphy's sartorial taste reinforce the masculine flight from the feminine: 'Murphy never wore a waistcoat. It made him feel like a woman' (Beckett 1938, 72). This flight from the 'fertilisable' female in *Dream, More Pricks Than Kicks*, and *Murphy* survives Beckett's postwar switch from English to French, recurring as the main subject of *Premier amour* (written in 1946), in which the death of the narrator's father leads not only to his expulsion from the refuge that is his childhood home, but also to his own inheritance of the paternal role, again with a generically named prostitute (Lulu), a role from which he will eventually flee in horror. In the trilogy, it is not just the 'outer reality' that is associated with the feminine, but being as such: while Molloy goes in search of his mother-hag, 'Mag' – a quest that solicits being read allegorically as the male's attempt to undo his own existence by returning to the womb – Malone sees death as a second, negating birth. Later still, in an early draft of *Fin de partie*, Beckett has his Hamm-figure reduce all varieties of the feminine to an anatomical common denominator: 'Mère, femme, sœur, fille, catin, ça m'est égal. Une femme. Deux mamelles et une vulve.'[7]

That said, even in the early novels Beckett's women do not always represent one pole in the outer–inner, body–mind, suffering–pleasure, necessity–freedom dualities. Rather, they are on occasion sites of radical division. The Smeraldina's 'ripe' body is offset by 'the loveliest little pale firm cameo of a birdface' (Beckett 1992, 15), anticipating not only the face of the girl in the punt in *Krapp's Last Tape* (1958), but also, through its 'unearthly radiance' (Beckett 1992, 3), the face of the woman in the late television play ... *but the clouds* ... (1977). Similarly, the antithesis between Celia Kelly and Mr Endon in *Murphy* undergoes a complicated transformation in the course of the novel, when she begins to demonstrate a power to negate the 'outer reality' while he is shown to require a witness to his own withdrawal. In *Dream*, in *Murphy*, and most obviously in *Molloy*, the flight from the feminine is also a flight towards it – that is, in the direction of the 'wombtomb', the maternal body as both origin and end of being, a regression the theory of which Beckett encountered in Otto Rank's *The Trauma of Birth* (1924). What this return to the maternal promises is not the annihilation of the body, but rather the resolution of that conflictual relation between body and mind inaugurated by the original expulsion from the womb and figured most economically in the eyes of the nursemaid in *Krapp's Last Tape*: 'The eyes she had! [...] Everything there, everything on this old muckball, all the light and dark and famine and feasting of ... [hesitates] ... the ages!' (Beckett 1990, 222). However, it is not simply the relation of Beckett's characters to the feminine that is contradictory, but also the manner in which the major female figures in Beckett's later plays will be represented. If those figures display the various qualities of Schopenhauer's *Weib* – including the desire to procreate, blind optimism or cheerfulness (*Heiterkeit*), compassion (*Mitleid*), and the power of consolation (*Trost*) – the stereotype from which they are drawn will be interrupted.

'All the dead voices': art and the feminine

With the important exceptions of *Ill Seen Ill Said* (1981), in which an 'eye of prey' seizes as best it can upon an unnamed 'she', and the short prose text 'Enough' (1966), in which the narrator's sex remains studiously undetermined, although the phrase 'my old paps' (*mes vieux seins*) might be taken to suggest a female speaker (Beckett 1995a, 192), the protagonists and first-person narrators of Beckett's novels and short stories may become ever less 'rightly human' (Beckett 1938, 77) but they continue to be identified as male. That said, there are ironies aplenty to complicate this apparent valorization of the masculine. In addition to the fact that the negation of being (marked as feminine) is orientated towards an end repeatedly figured as womblike, not the least of these ironies is that this negation is perhaps most successfully achieved by two of Beckett's female characters, the Alba in *Dream* and Celia Kelly in *Murphy*. Furthermore, in his conception of artistic production Beckett on occasion privileges the feminine in ways that counter any simple objectification or subordination.

That the relation between art and the feminine is anything but the simple opposition suggested by 'Assumption', and that Krapp takes it to be, is evident as early as Beckett's 1931 monograph on Proust. Here, Beckett suggests that the voice to be heard in genuine works of art – which is to say, works that disclose the disintegrative nature of the real – is not necessarily a man's voice, and does not necessarily echo the creation-positing voice of the father-god uttering the *fiat lux*. As Beckett observes, in Proust's *À la recherche* the birth of art is related to the displaced death of the mother, for it is the death of the narrator's grandmother that will grant him both the recognition of the absolute isolation of the expressive being (life as proleptic death) and the way in which that isolation might be overcome and communication actually achieved. The 'irremediable solitude' characterizing human reality finds expression in the 'strange real voice' of Proust's narrator's grandmother, heard on the telephone, in *Le Côté de Guermantes*. Paradoxically, this voice has the power to communicate that 'rupture of the lines of communication' which Beckett, in his 1934 review of 'Recent Irish Poetry', describes equivocally as the 'new thing that has happened, or the old thing that has happened again'. The awareness of this rupture is the precondition of all art that is not merely 'antiquarian' (Beckett 1983a, 70). In Proust's novel, the woman's voice is 'as impalpable as a voice from the dead' (Beckett 1987, 27). The narrator's grandmother speaks from an isolation that differs from both Heideggerian thrownness (*Geworfenheit*) and, later, Sartrean abandonment (*délaissement*) precisely because here the distinction between being and non-being no longer holds. Hers is the voice of one who is as though dead, proleptically dead, fictively dead, but fictively dead within the analeptic fiction of the novel itself, the voice of one who is thus neither present nor absent when she speaks. If Proust's narrator can be said to be male – itself a questionable assumption, as Virginia Woolf suggests, when, in her survey of androgynous writers in *A Room of One's Own* (1929), she claims that Proust is rather too feminine[8] – then he serves here not as the origin but as the mediator of that woman's voice.

If this impalpable voice is the voice of literature, as Beckett conceives it, then it is a voice that is to be identified not by what it has to say, not by the content of its utterance, but rather by its manner of saying – by its rhythm and tone. When it is a question of the feminine being related to art thematically, then the more familiar versions of the feminine reappear. This is the case in *Krapp's Last Tape*, for instance, in which Krapp's Manichaeanism has led him first simply to set art and love in strict opposition to one another, as masculine spirit to feminine body. Krapp's 'farewell to love', his envisaged rejection of all relations with the feminine, and in particular with sexuality (including its comic symbolization: bananas) is made in the interests of art (the *magnum opus*), as though art and sexuality, art and the feminine, art and love, were mutually exclusive. For Krapp, this mutual exclusivity remains in place, if only as a principle, to the very end. It is simply that he would now (in the present time of the stage performance) abandon art as a worthless business, and return to that moment with the girl in the punt, and in particular that moment when her eyes (as 'slits') open enough to let him in, despite the light. Here, the feminine offers a dark haven, at odds with Krapp's notion of art but the theme of Beckett's. In the television plays, Beckett will first present an attempt to escape – to kill – the feminine (in *Eh Joe*, 1966) and, later, attempts to unite with it (in *Ghost Trio* and *... but the clouds ...*, 1977).

In sharp contrast to both *Godot* (1953) and *Endgame* (1957), *Krapp's Last Tape* is populated (aside from Krapp himself, and a passing reference to the death of his father) by nothing but female figures, although not one of them is actually present on stage, each being mediated by way of Krapp. These figures include: Krapp's dying mother, for whose death the 39-year-old Krapp longs; Fanny, the 'Bony old ghost of a whore', whose body serves to satisfy the sexual needs he has been unable to eradicate; the 'dark nurse', whose eyes are like 'chrysolite' (Beckett 1990, 220; alluding both to regret for lost love and to the unhappy marriage of light and dark in *Othello*);[9] Bianca, with whom he used to live on Kedar Street; Miss McGlome, the old woman who sings in the evening, at the very time when Krapp makes his own recordings; the adulterous Effi, from Theodor Fontane's novel *Effi Briest* (1898), whose fate causes Krapp to weep; a female dog (the 'bitch'); and, most importantly, the girl in the punt.

In ironic contrast to Krapp's own conception of love and art as mutually exclusive, this play presents the feminine as both the inspiration and the object of art. For Krapp, the mother's death is associated with a commitment to art (to that epiphanic moment on the jetty when he sees the dark path his art must take). If this death refers us back to Beckett's reading of Proust, for Krapp himself the idea of art is to be radically separated from the feminine (its death or rejection being, ideally, a complete severance). For Beckett's own art, however, the relation to the feminine is rather different here. It is the very thought of a lost feminine figure that returns to haunt the present, to render Krapp what Beckett terms a 'Traumgefressener Mensch', a man consumed by a dream that is also nothing: 'ein vom Traum (Nichts) gefressenes Leben'.[10] A lost woman is there, then, to haunt the present in the form of a nothing (*Nichts*), and to constitute the absent object of art.

This notion of a negated, negating woman as the inspiration and object of the work of art is thematized even more explicitly in the radio play *Words and Music* (1962). Here, however, it at first appears that love and art are no longer conceived as being in opposition to each other. The play charts the composition of a poem through Words and Music (addressed as Joe and Bob, and thus both male figures) being brought together by a club-bearing male artist-master, Croak. The poem's theme is set by Croak as 'Age', the theme of 'Love' having produced from Words only garbled scholastic prose. However, the poem will in fact bring together love and age, defining age as that time when to a solitary male a 'she' returns as an image. Just as in *Krapp's Last Tape* and, later, in *... but the clouds ...*, this female figure is reduced (indeed, perfected) to a face, the very essence of alterity for Levinas. As in the earlier play, her eyes open to let the man in: 'the lips part and the eyes' (Beckett 1990, 293). Unlike in *Krapp's Last Tape*, however, this play does not end with the consumption of the male by the dream – or nothing (*Nichts*) – of the woman. Instead, the poem charts the journey deep into the woman, through the 'trash' and the 'scum', to a place beyond light and language, beyond all exchange, beyond all meaning and all need, where an epiphany is possible, but an epiphany of darkness that appears to counter the one on the jetty recounted in *Krapp's Last Tape*. In other words, whereas Krapp sees art and the feminine is strict opposition, in *Words and Music* it is precisely by way of the feminine that the epiphany at the origin of art is achieved:

> All dark no begging
> No giving no words
> No sense no need
> Through the scum
> Down a little way
> To whence one glimpse
> Of that wellhead.
> (Beckett 1990, 294)

However, if the feminine here is no longer situated in strict opposition to art, but has become both its object and its origin, the effect the return of the feminine has upon the male artist-master is devastating: Croak is undone by the poem, lets fall his club, and shuffles off. If the feminine is no longer fatal for art, it is fatal for the male artist.

The relation between art, death, and the feminine is explored further in the late television play ... *but the clouds* ..., in which a male figure tells of his nocturnal need for the appearance of a dead woman, who is certainly not mastered by the male here. That she is not subordinated to him is evident as soon as he corrects his opening statement, 'When I thought of her it was always night', to 'When she appeared it was always night' (Beckett 1990, 419). This appearance is solicited not by speech but by a 'begging of the mind', a begging akin to prayer – poetry having been defined as prayer by Beckett in his 1934 review of Thomas MacGreevy's *Poems*.[11] Her appearing to him occurs only in his 'little sanctum', a place in which he claims to be 'unseen' (although the viewer does see a partial image of him there), and where he sees the woman's 'unseeing eyes' (Beckett 1990, 420). Her appearance, as the partial image of a face, is extremely rare and can take three forms: appearance and immediate disappearance; appearance and lingering; appearance, lingering, and a movement of the lips: soundless speech, mouthing fragments from the work of a male poet, W. B. Yeats, whose own works often take the unpossessable feminine as their theme. Furthermore, the words she mouths, '... but the clouds ... of the sky', are themselves a scrap (or partial text) from a poem, 'The Tower' (1928), which counsels a response to the death of others (including the death of women) that would strip that death of its power. If there is no mastery of the woman's image here, and if a man's supplication 'Speak to me' (Beckett 1990, 421) is not obeyed, it is none the less the case that the woman inaudibly mouths the words of a male poet in a male mind. Her own voice remains unheard. Not only is she ventriloquized by the man, but he is himself ventriloquizing Yeats. And when, at the end of the play, he quotes more extensively from the final stanza of Yeats's poem, the woman's lips do not move at all.

Ruinations of the feminine

While it is undoubtedly the case that female figures eventually take on a far more significant role in Beckett's drama than they do in his prose fiction, there is no neat correlation between his exploration of a new genre and a new conception of gender. The female figures in his first completed play, *Eleutheria* (written in French in early 1947), remain decidedly Schopenhauerian stereotypes. That said, if only the protagonist, Victor Krap, and his father are presented as anything more than comic grotesques, Beckett does not spare the representative of a thoroughgoing misogyny, Dr Piouk, whose solution to the 'problem of humanity' is directed against that sex which, according to Schopenhauer, exists solely for the propagation of the species. Ostensibly the very antithesis of the Irish Catholic dogmatist mocked by Beckett in 'Censorship in the Saorstat',[12] Piouk declares: 'I would ban reproduction. I would perfect the condom and other devices and bring them into general use. I would establish teams of abortionists, controlled by the State. I would apply the death penalty to any woman guilty of giving birth. I would drown all newborn babies. I would militate in favour of homosexuality, and would myself set the example' (Beckett 1996, 44–5). Like Belacqua and Murphy before him, however, Piouk is a radically self-contradictory figure in matters sexual: he admits to his own wish for a child (a son) and is quite unable to negate his own heterosexual desire for Olga Skunk. Victor's own solution to the 'problem of humanity' is a far more radical negation of sexuality: a turning of his back on humanity as a whole.

Beckett's next play, *Waiting for Godot*, is striking for the absence of female figures, not only on stage but also in mediated form. The two important exceptions to this exclusion of the feminine are Estragon's exclamation 'Sweet mother earth!' and Pozzo's objectifying reference to women in the role of child-bearers – 'They give birth astride of a grave' (Beckett 1990, 77, 83) – and even here, when this statement is revised by Vladimir, it is the pronoun 'they' – 'elles' in the original French – that disappears, leaving only a 'we' that, in the context of this play, remains decidedly masculine: 'Astride of a grave and a difficult birth [...] We have time to grow old. The air is full of our cries' (Beckett 1990, 84). If, unlike *Godot*, *Endgame* does at least include the onstage presence of a woman – Hamm's mother, Nell – she is also the only character to die, or at least to be reported as appearing to be dead. In the wake of this silencing of the feminine, the play concentrates relentlessly on father–son, male master–male slave relations. If the play contains numerous fathers or father substitutes, mothers are in much shorter supply: the man in Hamm's 'chronicle' has a child, but there is no mention of a mother; Clov accepts Hamm's claim that 'It was I was a father to you' (Beckett 1990, 110); Nagg reminds Hamm: 'I'm your father. It's true if it hadn't been me it would have been someone else', as though there were fathers aplenty; and Nagg reminds Hamm of his need for a father: 'Whom did you call when you were a tiny boy, and were frightened, in the dark? Your mother? No. Me' (Beckett 1990, 119). Despite Nell's brief presence, then, *Endgame*'s is an almost entirely male world. In addition to the male painter-engraver, the toy dog is referred to as male, although there is nothing anatomical to support this: on receiving the dog from Clov, Hamm declares: 'You've forgotten the sex', to which Clov responds: 'But he isn't finished. The sex goes on at the end' (Beckett 1990, 111). The unseen rat in the kitchen is referred to as male, as is the child whom Clov claims to see outside. As for dead mothers amid all these surviving fathers and sons, literal or otherwise, besides Nell there is Mother Pegg, of who Hamm declares in Schopenhauerian mode: 'And a great one for the men!' (Beckett 1990, 112), and whose death Clov blames on Hamm.

If the feminine has at most a subordinate role in Beckett's early plays, present as an object of negation, everything changes with the radio play *All That Fall* (1957). Here, for the first time, Beckett focuses principally upon the feminine – more precisely, the maternal feminine – and the masculine violence which threatens it. Here, for the first time, it is women's voices that predominate, and, whereas the toy dog and the rat in *Endgame* are both referred to as 'he', here even the animals are female. However, that this shift towards an exploration of the feminine remains tied, if parodically, to the Schopenhauerian conception of woman is apparent not only in the compassionate maternality and the sheer bodily mass of the play's central figure, Maddy Rooney, but also in Beckett's return to English as his language of original composition and to a style of caricatural realism: unlike *Godot* or *Endgame*, the play is set in a recognizably specific time and place, the action unfolding on a Saturday in Boghill, clearly based on the Dublin suburb of Foxrock, in which Beckett grew up – there is even a reference to the Leopardstown racecourse and to Connolly's vans. If one recalls Schopenhauer's identification of the power of abstraction as masculine, this return to realism is only appropriate, given the play's focus upon the maternal.

The play's central figure, Maddy Rooney, is an even more grotesquely parodic incarnation of feminine materiality than those populating Beckett's fiction of the 1930s and 1940s, her husband, Dan Rooney, referring to her as 'Two hundred pounds of unhealthy fat' (Beckett 1990, 191). Where she differs most obviously from her husband, however, is not in her physicality – being blind, he, like her, has to depend on others if he is to move – but in her need for love – 'Love, that is all I asked, a little love' (Beckett 1990, 174) – her compassion and her maternalism, which stands in such striking contrast to all the male hostility towards the feminine and towards reproduction in Beckett's works generally. In addition to Christy's beating of the hinny, the male violence (both verbal and physical) directed at the feminine in *All That Fall* includes Mr Slocum's '*violent unintelligible muttering*' about Mrs Rooney, and his running-over of the hen; the wife-beating to which, according to Maddy, Mrs Tully is subjected; and, most importantly, if also most ambiguously, the suggestion that Dan Rooney may well be responsible for the death (if it is a death) of the 'little child' reported by Jerry at the very end of the play.

That a gendered compassion lies at the heart of this play is emphasized not simply through its being punctuated by Maddy Rooney's repeated use of the epithet 'poor', but through the play's action being situated between the parentheses of her compassion for a 'Poor woman. All alone in that ruinous old house' (Beckett 1990, 172). Here, as so often, Beckett follows Schopenhauer, who claims that 'women show more compassion [*Mitleid*] and thus more loving kindness [*Menschenliebe*] and sympathy [*Teilnahme*] for the unfortunate than do men' (Schopenhauer 1974, 617). That Maddy's compassion is in fact less a sign of love for humankind or of female solidarity than a mediated form of self-pity is suggested, however, by the use of the word 'ruinous' (echoing 'Rooney') and through it taking a predominantly maternal form, the suffering figures finding their point of origin in Maddy's own daughter, Minnie, whose status as real or imaginary, born or unborn, remains undetermined. She is another instance of the feminine nothing (*Nichts*) eating into the present. Here, then, Beckett anticipates his treatment of the feminine in terms of the mother–daughter relation in later plays such as *Footfalls* (1976) and *Rockaby* (1981).

In *All That Fall*, the contrast between mediated feminine and unmediated masculine egoism could scarcely be presented more forcefully. Whereas Maddy expresses compassion, particularly for the feminine, Dan is consistently aggressive towards his wife, contrasts life in his office in town favourably with life in the domestic space, shows no appreciation at all for her having come to meet him at the station, rebuffs her demonstrations of affection, exhibits a penny-pinching mentality and a proclivity not only for monetary calculations but for calculations of all kinds, counting being for him, as for so many of Beckett's other male figures, 'One of the few satisfactions in life!' (Beckett 1990, 190). The contrast between Maddy and Dan is most pronounced, however, in their attitude to children. One of the reasons for Dan's preferring his office to his home is that in the latter he is disturbed by 'howling neighbours' brats' (Beckett 1990, 193). That his hatred of children is nothing less than murderous is suggested when he asks his wife, who is mourning a lost daughter: 'Did you ever wish to kill a child? [*Pause.*] Nip some young doom in the bud. [*Pause.*] Many a time at night, in winter, on the black road home, I nearly attacked the boy. [*Pause.*] Poor Jerry! What restrained me then? [*Pause.*] Not fear of man' (Beckett 1990, 191). That what restrained him may well have been the child's sex becomes evident when Jerry reports that a 'little child' has fallen under the wheels of the train. If the sex of this child remains undetermined, everything in the play – not least Beckett's use of Schubert's Quartet No. 14 in D minor ('Death and the Maiden') suggests that it is a little girl.[13]

Male violence is directed, then, against the very possibility of the maternal feminine: the death of the maiden, the loss of children, the destruction of the mother hen, sterilization through breeding (the hinny, the offspring of a female ass and a stallion), the decay of the womb (the 'great empty house' become a ruin), and even hysterectomy. Throughout the play, it is the feminine as mother (or as potential mother) that is threatened, and threatened by male violence. As for lost mothers, Jerry is an orphan and Miss Fitt is looking for her mother. As for lost daughters (or future mothers), the fall of the 'little child' under the train is anticipated not only by the crushing of the hen, but also by the unnamed woman's warning to Dolly on the station platform that 'one can be sucked under' (Beckett 1990, 185). This theme finds its fullest expression, however, in Maddy, not only through her mourning her own daughter, but also through her story of the 'mind doctor'. This story is told as a response to her husband's decidedly male narrative, which is not only all about himself but also all about the linguistic inscription of the masculine: when interrupted by his wife, he is speaking of his visit to the men's toilet, 'or Fir as they call it now, from Vir Viris I suppose, the V becoming F, in accordance with Grimm's Law' (Beckett 1990, 195). Whereas his narrative is men's business (including men's toilet business), Maddy's is about another 'little girl'.

This story of the male 'mind doctor' and his strange diagnosis concerning a 'little girl' is derived from the third of Carl Jung's 1935 Tavistock Lectures, attended by Beckett while he was in London undergoing psychoanalytic therapy with W. R. Bion. If Beckett cannot help mocking psychoanalysis by having Maddy give as her reason for attending the lecture her desire to have a 'little light' shed upon her 'lifelong preoccupation with horses' buttocks' (Beckett 1990, 195), the story she recounts is one that she claims has 'haunted' her, and it can certainly be said to have haunted Beckett. Jung's diagnosis of the 'little girl' to whom he refers in the discussion at the end of his lecture is that 'She had never been born entirely'.[14] In addition to *All That Fall*, in which this becomes 'The trouble with her was she had never really been born!' (Beckett 1990, 196), Jung's diagnosis also appears as the fragment 'never been properly born' in the 'Addenda' to *Watt*, and, more elliptically, in *Footfalls*, in which the mother's voice engages in an act of *correctio*, avoiding the word 'birth' in relation to May: 'Where is she, it may be asked. [*Pause.*] Why, in the old home, the same where she – [*Pause.*] The same where she began. [*Pause.*] Where it began. [*Pause.*] It all began' (Beckett 1990, 401). That Beckett is thinking of Jung's diagnosis here is confirmed by his remark to the actress Charlotte Joeres that May 'hasn't been born. She just began. It began. There is a difference. She was never born.'[15] Beckett also mentions Jung's remark in conversation with Charles Juliet in 1968,[16] and the notion of a failed birth lies behind the following remark in a letter of 7 December 1959 to Alan Schneider: 'I'm afraid I don't know when life begins. I'm still waiting personally' (Harmon 1998, 58). Indeed, this failure might be said to determine all the other failures with which his *œuvre* will concern itself.

A failed birth, a beginning that does not quite initiate life in the world: this is not simply birth as 'the death of him' (Beckett 1990, 425), as the male speaker puts it in *A Piece of Monologue* (1979), not simply woman as responsible for bringing death into the world, but an event that troubles the very distinction between being and non-being. How important is it, then, that this improperly born child should have been a 'little girl' rather than a little boy? How important is it that only a year earlier, in late 1934, Jung also tried, and failed, to cure Lucia Joyce?[17] If *All That Fall* introduces such questions into Beckett's *œuvre*, the uncertainties and underdeterminations that are so prevalent in the play suggest that simple solutions are perhaps not to be had, and that to claim that Beckett is now valorizing the feminine rather than the masculine is to ignore a rather more complicated treatment of gender. If the story of the 'little girl' is part of Maddy's preoccupation with the mother–daughter relation as much as with 'horses' buttocks' – from whence comes that 'gush of mard' on the first page of Beckett's first novel – then it is also one more occasion when she (as would-be mother) is brought to tears by the thought of the suffering feminine: she weeps for Minnie, for the 'little girl' in her story of the 'mind doctor', and for the old woman in the empty house. Any simple opposition between masculine violence and feminine compassion is troubled, however, by a momentary unity between husband and wife, their identical response to the thought of the text upon which the next day's sermon will be based and from which the title of Beckett's play is taken: 'The Lord upholdeth all that fall and raiseth up all those that be bowed down' (Beckett 1990, 198). It is at the very thought of such an upholding God, given the universal falling presented in the play, that Maddy and Dan *'join in wild laughter'*, and this laughter, which is shared by both sexes here, is of a kind with that which will come from Mouth at the thought of a 'merciful' – and indeed of any – God in *Not I*.

In *Happy Days* (1961), the next of his plays to focus principally upon a woman, and in which he revisits the theme of traumatized maternity, Beckett continues to rely heavily upon the Schopenhauerian conception of the feminine. As noted earlier, Schopenhauer argues that 'woman' is to be distinguished from 'man' through her weaker faculty of reason; she is childish, intellectually limited, and 'clings to the present' (*klebt an der Gegenwart*). Now, this is precisely the conception of the feminine that is presented in *Happy Days*. Winnie tries to deny any difference between past and present, insisting despite all the evidence that each day is 'Another heavenly day'. In addition to her chatter, she exhibits a dependence on the male (Willie), a concern with her appearance, a preoccupation with the seemingly trivial, and even what Schopenhauer terms an 'aping' knowledge of the arts. In all these respects, she fits with Schopenhauer's notion of the cheerful child-woman, blind to the trajectory that is carrying her towards the very opposite of what she takes to be her nature – she is sinking ever further into the earth, while maintaining that she is of the air. Few of Beckett's works render so explicit his sense of the manner in which hopefulness and optimism reassert themselves, despite all the evidence.[18] That it should be a woman who figures this process is scarcely surprising, given Beckett's debt to Schopenhauer. However, Beckett's restaging of Schopenhauer's *Weib* in this play is also its interruption. During rehearsals for the 1979 Royal Court Theatre production, Beckett is recorded in Martha Fehsenfeld's rehearsal diary as having said: 'One of the clues to the play is interruption. [...] She's an interrupted being. [...] A child-woman with a short span of concentration – sure one minute, unsure the next' (Beckett quoted in Knowlson 1985, 16). The struggle to keep both past and present at bay, to resist the thought that the light is 'hellish' and not 'holy', is one that this 'child-woman' cannot sustain without moments of what Beckett terms 'weakness' (*défaillance*).

While *Happy Days*, like *Not I*, has been interpreted by some commentators as achieving a kind of *écriture féminine* and by others as continuing to affirm a phallocentric vision of the feminine, what both readings leave out of account is the possibility that Beckett's disintegrative re-presentation of the Schopenhauerian feminine in *Happy Days* is neither feminist nor anti-feminist, but rather an early phase in a more general movement towards a conception of sexual difference as one more 'pseudocouple',[19] a negating movement orientated not towards the reduction to nothing of the feminine alone, not towards gender fluidity, nor even towards a pluralization of sexual difference beyond the binary opposition masculine–feminine, but rather towards the reduction to nothing of sexual difference as such. Before any such negation can be accomplished, however, Beckett will have to do more than interrupt Schopenhauer. He will also have to interrupt Freudian psychoanalysis, and in particular its conception of the female hysteric, to which, like Schopenhauer's conception of woman, he is indebted.

The 'private theatre' of Beckett's 'hysterical old hags'

In *Murphy*, Beckett supplies a Joycean rewriting of the opening of St John's Gospel: 'In the beginning was the pun'; and it has often been observed in commentaries on *All That Fall* that just as 'Rooney' suggests 'ruin' so the diminutive 'Maddy' suggests madness. In fact, in this, the first of his works to focus principally on women, Beckett falls in line with a long tradition by associating the feminine with hysteria.[20] Not only does Miss Fitt react '*hysterically*' when Maddy joins in with her hymn (Beckett 1990, 184), but Maddy describes herself as 'a hysterical old hag' (Beckett 1990, 174). If this association between the feminine and hysteria dates back at least as far as Hippocrates, with the term itself being derived from the Greek for 'womb' (*hyster*), it was only in the late nineteenth century that hysteria came to occupy a central place within both the theory and the practice of psychiatry and then psychoanalysis, principally as a result of Charcot's investigations into hysteria at the Salpetrière hospital in Paris, and in particular through his use of hypnosis in his attempt to identify an organic basis for the malady. Before the end of the century, Pierre Janet had published his *Mental State of Hystericals* (1894), and Freud and Breuer had published their 'Preliminary Communication: On the Psychical Mechanism of Hysterical Phenomena' (1893), in which they proposed both a trauma theory of hysteria and a cathartic treatment of it – the 'talking cure', as Breuer's patient, Anna O., would term it – to be followed in 1895 by their *Studies on Hysteria*, in which they sought to 'illustrate and prove' the thesis proposed in the 1893 communication.

Beckett's own reading in psychology and psychoanalysis occurred early in his writing life, principally in 1934–35, while he was undergoing treatment with W. R. Bion in London.[21] His notes on Freud's conception of hysteria and obsessional neurosis derive for the most part from Jones's *Treatment of the Neuroses* (1920). It is from this text that Beckett draws what will prove to be a crucial observation with regard to his own works, namely that hysteria involves a disintegration of the difference between recollection and imagination:

> It is commonly recognised that phantasy plays an especially prominent part in the mental life of hysterics, as is illustrated, for instance, by their pronounced tendency toward day-dreaming. Hysteria is, indeed, perhaps the best example of a malady of the imagination. The imagination of hysterics possesses a much greater influence over both their mental and physical functions than is the case with the normal, and this excessive development of phantasy at the expense of adjustment to the needs of reality must be regarded as an important characteristic of the disorder. It is quite common with such patients for an imagined experience to have an equal significance to a real experience. An imagined trauma, for instance, may have precisely the same harmful effect as a real one, and for this reason it becomes practically irrelevant whether a given traumatic memory, resuscitated from the unconscious by special investigation, actually corresponds with truth or not; the effect on the patient is the same in the two cases. (Jones 1920, 108–9)[22]

As for the kind of imaginative construction produced by the reality-fleeing hysteric, Jones's claim that 'the essential content of any phantasy is a desire, or rather the fulfilment of a desire. This applies to the fanciful "castles in Spain" with which we are all familiar' (Jones 1920, 110) prompts Beckett to identify his own imaginative constructions not as castles but as dungeons.[23]

Now, just as he both inherits and restages Schopenhauer's conception of woman, so Beckett inherits and restages the figure of the female hysteric in plays such as *All That Fall* (1957), *Not I* (1973), *Footfalls* (1976), and *Rockaby* (1981). With regard to the ethics of gender in Beckett, the question becomes whether he interrupts the stereotype of the female hysteric in a manner akin to his interruption of the Schopenhauerian conception of woman in *Happy Days*, and whether this interruption involves any valorization of the feminine. On the one hand, and following Irigaray, it might be argued that Beckett's 'hysterical old hags' mime their own sexuality. That such mimicry is not necessarily subversive, however, is suggested by Catherine Clément, whose conception of the female hysteric is a rather more ambiguous figure, at once subversive and conservative: subversive because she 'unties familiar bonds, introduces disorder into the well-regulated unfolding of everyday life', but also conservative because she 'ends up inuring others to her symptoms' (Clément 1986, 5). It is for this reason that Clément argues for a liberating bisexuality beyond hysteria. What, then, of Beckett's 'hysterical old hags'? To what extent do they conform to, or interrupt, the psychoanalytic conception of the hysteric? And what value, if any, does Beckett assign to the feminine by associating it with hysteria?

According both to Janet and to Freud and Breuer, the hysterical personality is expressed in a wide a range of symptoms, physical and mental: these include anaesthesias, amnesias, aboulias, motor disturbances, fixed ideas, somnabulisms, deliriums, and a range of speech disorders. Janet characterizes the hysteric's language as 'telegraphic', and remarks that, while both the speech and the actions of a hysteric named Bertha at first appear to be completely incoherent, they are in fact 'determined by all the little impressions which strike her senses and by all the little associations of ideas which they determine' (Janet 1901, 461). Freud and Breuer pay much closer attention to the linguistic symptoms of hysteria. In his case history of Anna O., Breuer refers to 'a deep-going functional disorganization of speech' in the hysteric, involving a loss of the power to find the right word, a loss of the command of syntax, the non-conjugation of verbs, and the omission of definite and indefinite articles. And, in his case history of Emmy von N., Freud remarks that her speech was 'subject to spastic interruptions amounting to a stammer' (Freud and Breuer 1955,

25, 48–9). The female figures in Beckett's later plays certainly exhibit such functional disorganization of speech, and they may even be said to enact what Breuer's patient, Anna O., terms the hysteric's 'private theatre' (Freud and Breuer 1955, 22).

Beyond the various, isolated symptoms of hysteria, however, Janet identifies its essential characteristic as a mental disintegration, a doubling (*dédoublement*) of the personality. Similarly, Freud and Breuer claim that both anxiety and conversion hysteria involve a splitting (*Spaltung*) of consciousness. Such splittings certainly occur in Beckett's female protagonists: in Mouth's refusal to say 'I'; in May's story of 'Amy'; in the separation between speech and person in *Rockaby*. That said, splittings of consciousness also occur in Beckett's male protagonists – in *That Time* and *A Piece of Monologue*, for instance – and might even be said to be the most characteristic feature of his entire œuvre. One is faced, then, with the question of whether the splittings experienced by Beckett's female figures can be distinguished from those affecting his male figures – in short, whether there are two basic kinds of splitting and symptomatology in Beckett, whether these correspond to the two kinds of splitting and symptomatology characterizing hysteria and schizophrenia in Freud, and whether Beckett consistently associates hysteria with the feminine and schizophrenia with the masculine.

The term 'schizophrenia' was invented by Eugen Bleuler in 1911, almost two decades after Freud's early work on hysteria. Laplanche and Pontalis summarize its main characteristics as 'incoherence of thought, action and affectivity (denoted by the classical terms "discordance", "dissociation", and "disintegration"); detachment from reality accompanied by a turning in upon the self and the predominance of a mental life given over to the production of phantasies (autism); a delusional activity which may be marked in a greater or lesser degree, and which is always badly systematized' (Laplanche and Pontalis 1973, 408). For Bleuler, the most fundamental symptom of schizophrenia is a disturbance of the associations governing the train of thought, a loosening of associations that renders thinking illogical and strange. Freud devotes considerable effort to establishing a clear distinction between the various forms of mental disintegration. In 'The Unconscious' (1915) and again in 'The Loss of Reality in Neurosis and Psychosis' (1924), he distinguishes rigorously between transference neuroses (anxiety hysteria, conversion hysteria, and obsessional neuroses) and schizophrenia (as a form of psychosis). The principal difference between the neuroses and the psychoses lies in their relation to the external world – the 'outer reality' of *Murphy* or the 'out there' of the poem 'Something There'

(1974). Whereas neurosis simply ignores this external world, psychosis 'disavows it and tries to replace it' (Freud 1961, 185). It is on account of this complete disavowal (*Verleugnung*) that, unlike neurosis, psychosis is, in Freud's opinion, untreatable. In his linguisticist rewriting of Freud, Lacan turns this disavowal of the external world into a disavowal of the Symbolic. However, just as both hysteria and schizophrenia involve a splitting of the personality, so they also involve a disorganization of thought and speech. According to Freud, the schizophrenic 'often devotes peculiar care to his way of expressing himself, which becomes "stilted" and "precious". The construction of his sentences undergoes a peculiar disorganization, making them so incomprehensible to us that his remarks seem nonsensical' (Freud 1957, 197).

What, then, of this distinction between, and the possible gendering of, forms of mental disintegration in Beckett? Just as he associates hysteria with the feminine in *All That Fall*, so he associates schizophrenia with the masculine in *Murphy* – Mr Endon being 'a schizophrenic of the most amiable variety' (Beckett 1938, 186) – and again in *Eleutheria*, through Dr Piouk's diagnosis of Victor's condition as schizophrenia. It is hardly surprising, then, that commentators have tended to characterize *The Unnamable* in terms of schizophrenia and *Not I* in terms of hysteria, even though the title of the play is already to be found in the novel: 'who is talking, not I' (Beckett 1959, 389). With *The Unnamable* in mind, Deleuze claims that Beckett 'know[s] more about schizophrenia than psychiatrists and psychoanalysts' (Deleuze 1995, 23), and Damian Love argues that *The Unnamable* offers 'perhaps the most acute analysis of schizophrenic alienation in Western literature'.[24] The *Spaltung* that characterizes the disintegration of identity enacted in *The Unnamable* certainly appears to correspond to the binary self–other relation underlying the classical model of alienation. The 'churn of words' that constitutes as it deconstructs *The Unnamable* takes the form of a war of hypotheses and counter-hypotheses, a sequence of self-identifications not one of which will stick. An ever more frenzied practice of *correctio*, ever longer sentences, hypotaxis with the suppression of conjunctions, together with the repeated use of the splice comma (itself a kind of syntactical *Spaltung*), is orientated towards the articulation of an identity beyond disintegration, an identity not with a being or even with Being, but precisely with non-being. If there is a similar suppression of connectives in *Not I*, the language of this play is perhaps more notable for its differences from, rather than its similarities to, the language of *The Unnamable*.

To insist upon either the differences or the similarities between the disintegrations enacted in *The Unnamable* and *Not I* is, however, to miss the way in which these two works constitute a strange pseudocouple within Beckett's *oeuvre*, a pseudocouple of genre and gender governed neither by identity nor by difference but by a principle of resemblance. And this pseudocouple is not static but itself disintegrative, disintegrating the difference between schizophrenia and hysteria – which is to say, disintegrating the difference between what, for Freud, are two distinct modes of mental disintegration. The disintegration of this difference is already apparent in *All That Fall*, in which Beckett's 'hysterical old hag' uses language in a manner akin to that of Freud's schizophrenic: Maddy Rooney's speech is marked by 'precious' word choices such as 'pismires' (ants), and she herself observes that, for all her attempts to use the 'simplest words', her language is 'bizarre'. To her husband she gives the impression that she is 'struggling with a dead language' (Beckett 1990, 196). Now, this disintegration of the difference between modes of disintegration – between (female) hysteria and (male) schizophrenia – is akin to the disintegration affecting all other binary oppositions in Beckett's *œuvre*, including those between microcosm and macrocosm, mind and body, time and space, will and representation, self and other. And the degendering of these differences is already apparent in both *Dream* and *Murphy*, through the figures of the Alba and Celia Kelly, both of whom effect withdrawals from the 'outer reality' that trump those of the novels' male protagonists.

Scenes of trauma, sexual and otherwise: Beckett reading Rank

If the distinction between hysteria and schizophrenia is subject to a pressure that also affects sexual difference, this does not necessarily lead to a clear valorization of the feminine that would counter the Schopenhauerian conception of woman so prevalent in many of Beckett's works. Beckett certainly inherits a gendered conception of disintegration, just as he inherits a misogynistic view of the feminine. If that gendering is interrupted, then this interruption takes the form of what might be termed a degeneration – that is, a reductive undoing of gender difference. This degeneration is particularly apparent in Beckett's treatment of the various trauma theories of mental disorder. In *Happy Days*, he certainly appears to follow the early Freud by hinting at a decisive sexual trauma as the origin of hysteria, through Winnie's story of Milly and the mouse. This, however, is something of an exception in Beckett, and for the most part he exhibits a much greater affinity for Otto Rank's theory that the trauma at the origin of all neuroses is nothing other than birth itself, and more precisely a failed birth.

As mentioned above, Beckett read Rank's *The Trauma of Birth* in the mid-1930s, and there is much in Rank's book that will find its place in Beckett's later works – and this despite the fact that Beckett's notes on Rank are far from extensive. One of the most explicit allusions to Rank in Beckett is to the former's incidental remark upon the 'disinclination of so many people to sit with their back to the engine', which Rank explains in terms of the primal repression of the birth trauma (Rank 1929, 82 n. 1). In Beckett, it is precisely this primal repression that is either absent or weakly enforced: both Watt and Mercier are described as sitting with their back to the engine when travelling by train.[25] Another explicit allusion to Rank concerns the symbolic function of hats. In another footnote recorded by Beckett, Rank observes that 'The *crown*, the noblest of all head coverings, goes back originally to the embryonal caul, as also our hat today' (Rank 1929, 91 n. 2). This leads, in *Murphy*, to the observation that 'Murphy never wore a hat, the memories it awoke of the caul were too poignant, especially when he had to take it off' (Beckett 1938, 73). Rank also remarks upon the manner in which neurotics attempt to negate birth by putting themselves back in the position of the unborn, in particular through rocking motions that would recreate the rhythm of intrauterine life. Such rocking is, of course, to be found as early as *Murphy* and as late as *Rockaby* (1981).

With respect to Rank's argument that the trauma of birth is the 'ultimate biological basis of the psychical' (Rank 1929, xxiii), the fact that birth is repeatedly conceived as a determining trauma in Beckett scarcely requires emphasis. Although Rank himself refers to the 'original sin of birth' (Rank 1929, 113), the idea of birth as a sin, for which life is the intolerable expiation, is already present in Beckett prior to his reading of Rank. In *Proust*, for instance, Beckett quotes from Calderón's *Life is a Dream*, by way of Schopenhauer: 'Pues el delito major / Del hombre es haber nacido.'[26] The epigraph to *The Trauma of Birth* is taken from Nietzsche's *Birth of Tragedy*, again with the source being Schopenhauer: 'The very best is quite unattainable for you: it is, not to be born, not to exist, to be Nothing. But the next best for you is – to die soon.'[27] As Ackerley and Gontarski observe, this tag occurs in a number of other works read by Beckett in the 1930s, most notably Burton's *Anatomy of Melancholy* and Geulincx's *Ethics*, and it is to be found in Latin in Beckett's 1930s 'Whoroscope Notebook' as 'Optimum non nasci, aut cito mori'.[28] As for the idea of birth as a determining trauma, in addition to those occasions on which he alludes more or less explicitly to Jung's diagnosis of the 'little girl' who was not 'properly born', it also lies behind the many expulsions into the light from places of refuge – in the

Novellas, for instance – and, arguably, the many heads isolated from their bodies in the later plays – the head, as Rank observes, being 'the first to leave the mother's genitals' (Rank 1929, 52). In *That Time* (1976), birth is identified as the one 'turning-point', and Beckett even alludes to Rank's observation that separation from the mother involves standing upright: 'always having turning-points and never but the one the first and last that time curled up worm in slime when they lugged you out and wiped you off and straightened you up' (Beckett 1990, 390). Being straightened *up*, not *out*: the phrasing here recalls Rank's claim that separation from the mother entails 'standing upright from the earth' (Rank 1929, 147).

As for Rank's second main thesis – that the primal libido is directed regressively towards a lost intrauterine state thought to be 'blessed', 'paradisiacal', the 'best of all worlds' (Rank 1929, 63) – this, too, is already present in Beckett before his reading of Rank: in Belacqua's desire to withdraw into the 'wombtomb', in *Dream of Fair to Middling Women*. And while Rank's remark upon 'the pleasurable character of certain neurotic symptoms, in which the patient makes himself prisoner by withdrawing into a room which he locks' (Rank 1929, 136), anticipates the many withdrawals from the 'outer reality' in Beckett, this, again, is already present in *Dream*. That said, Rank's reworking of Freud's theory of the death drive (*Todestrieb*) can be seen to anticipate much in Beckett's *œuvre*, not least the distinction he makes between his own art and that which, following Nietzsche, he terms the 'Apollonian', which, he claims, is 'absolutely foreign' to him.[29] Referring to Freud's *Beyond the Pleasure Principle* (1920), Rank argues that 'what biologically seems to us the impulse to death, strives again to establish nothing else than the already experienced condition before birth, and the "compulsion to repetition" [*"Wiederholungszwang"*] arises from the unquenchable character of this longing, which exhausts itself again and again in every possibility of form. This process is what biologically speaking we call "life" ' (Rank 1929, 196). The primal libido strives, then, to accomplish an undoing, a reduction of difference, a negation of the individual's separation from the womb. If this, like Freud's notion of the death drive, smacks of Schopenhauer, it none the less strips Schopenhauer's notion of denial (*Verneinung*) of its ethical nature, making of it the least conscious of acts.

Now, according to Rank, Greek art is founded upon the massive repression of the birth trauma, with the regressive primal libido being redirected towards an ever greater separation from the mother. In short, Greek art is a misogynistic 'masculine ideal of art' that 'repeats the biological and prehistorical act of becoming human, the severance from the mother and the standing upright from the earth, in the creation and perfection of its aesthetic ideal of the human body' (Rank 1929, 147). If Beckett's own art is characterized by a radically regressive, non-Apollonian tendency, it none the less relentlessly stages the failure to negate the difference that would constitute an improperly realized life. In that respect, Beckett's art is never simply the antithesis of Greek art as defined by Rank. If there is a 'fixation on the mother' (most explicitly in part I of *Molloy*), there is also revulsion. If there is a regression from the upright position proper to the human in the trilogy, this regression is repeatedly countered – for instance, in *Lessness* (1969), in which the 'little body' is the 'only upright' (Beckett 1995a, 197). If there is a flight from the light in *Murphy*, that light will return in a rather less natural form in plays such as *Happy Days* and *Play*, in which a second birth, this time into death, fails to undo that which has failed properly to take place. In short, if there is a negation of difference, there is also an incessant return of difference, not as a value but as an experience.

This complication of the regressive drive is also apparent in Beckett's treatment of gender. Unlike both Freud and Lacan, who figure the feminine in terms of lack, Rank explains misogyny through the metonymic association of the birth trauma with the mother rather than the father. Patriarchal societies are founded upon a primal repression 'which has as its purpose the ever wider exclusion of woman – just on account of the painful memory of the birth trauma' (Rank 1929, 94). The mother, then, becomes both the hated cause of the originary trauma and the loved bearer of the womb, and this doubleness certainly finds its place throughout Beckett's œuvre. That said, Rank reduces not only the difference between neurosis and psychosis – the symptoms of both hysteria and psychosis are reproductions or representations of the intrauterine state – but also the difference between the sexes. Both sexes are victims of the same birth trauma, and both sexes are subject to the same regressive primal libido. It is just such a reduction of the value of sexual difference, rather than a proliferation of differences beyond the binary model, that will characterize some of Beckett's later works. If this reduction is not the absolute negation of sexual difference, then this has everything to do with a movement towards an anethics of gender.

'So little difference': towards an anethics of gender

Early in *Malone Dies*, having proposed to tell four stories, the first about a man and the second about a woman, Malone quickly revises his project: 'Perhaps I shall put the man and the woman in the same story, there is so little difference between a man and a woman, between mine I mean' (Beckett 1959, 181). At the heart of Hamm's 'chronicle' in *Endgame*, a father pleads with Hamm to take in his child, and thus to act as a substitute father: 'It was then he took the plunge. It's my little one, he said. Tsstss, a little one, that's bad. My little boy, he said, as if the sex mattered' (Beckett 1990, 117). More radically still, of Auditor in *Not I*, Beckett states: 'Sex undeterminable' (Beckett 1990, 376), although, despite the grammatical suggestion that Auditor is a man,[30] the 'helpless compassion' exhibited by this figure aligns it with the Schopenhauerian conception of woman so evident in *All That Fall* and, more subtly, in the late television play *Nacht und Träume*, in which, for the production broadcast by Süddeutscher Rundfunk in May 1983, Beckett decided that the consoling hands had to be 'Large but female'.[31] Towards the end of his writing life, he states laconically of the four players in the television play *Quad*, first broadcast by Süddeutscher Rundfunk as *Quadrat I + II* in October 1981: 'Sex indifferent' (Beckett 1990, 453).[32] However, such indifference to sexual difference is no doubt owing to the fact that the four figures in *Quad* do not speak, and their costumes (djellabas) can disguise all anatomical signs of their sex. This indifference stands in striking contrast to Beckett's position on the same issue when it comes to those plays in which a change of sex would be unavoidably apparent, and would entail textual incoherence or textual revision. In turning down the request for permission to perform *Godot* with an all-female cast, for instance, Beckett mimics the 'anatomy is destiny' argument underlying Freud's conception of sexual difference by responding, 'Women don't have prostates'.[33]

On the one hand, then, it would appear that there is no less clear a trajectory in Beckett's treatment of sexual difference than there is in his treatment of the comic. To schematize: in the early works, there is a Schopenhauerian insistence upon binary sexual difference in which all value is assigned to the masculine, even if the coherence of this structure is disturbed in the very works in which it is affirmed. This is followed by a phase in which, having found his way in another genre, Beckett reconsiders the question of gender, placing female figures at the centre of a number of his later plays, and interrupting both the Schopenhauerian conception of woman and the psychoanalytic conception of the female hysteric. Preceding this phase, however, there are already moments – but *masculine* moments – when sexual difference is either difficult to establish or is dismissed altogether. Beyond such interruptions, this trajectory would reach its end with the confirmation of sexual indifference, a collapsing of difference rather than its proliferation.

What such a schematization leaves out of account, however, is not only the fact that Beckett expresses indifference to sexual difference only when all signs of difference can be disguised, but also the manner in which, within the more general disintegration of differences, sexual difference becomes one more pseudocouple. This is not to say that a fixed and binary sexual difference either explodes into gender fluidity or disappears into pure indifference.[34] If Beckett insists upon the indeterminability of Auditor's sex in *Not I*, and the indifference of sex in *Quad*, in one of his last works, *Worstward Ho* (1983), the disintegration of sexual difference leads to the reaffirmation of a binarity that is not necessarily either androgynous or sexless. Through a sequence of performative sayings producing a highly telegrammatic text, a family of sorts is posited: first a woman, then a man, and then a child. Although both the woman and the man are without the anatomical insignia of sexual difference, they none the less remain sexually distinct: 'Nothing to show a [...] man and yet a man. [...] Nothing and yet a woman' (Beckett 1983b, 44-5). The child, however, remains just that, a child, sex undetermined, like the 'little child' in *All That Fall*. That said, just as there is much in *All That Fall* to suggest that the 'little child' who falls beneath the wheels is in fact a little girl, there is much in *Worstward Ho* to suggest that this child is a little boy: the child walks in 'equal plod' and hand in hand with the old man, and they are identically dressed. The risk that lies in simply identifying the 'small child' as neuter, belonging to neither one sex nor the other, is that neutrality itself may well be aligned with the masculine in *Worstward Ho*. The one whose words constitute this text is subjected to a procedure of *correctio* in the direction of just such a neuter, and this procedure simply bypasses the feminine: 'No words for him whose words. Him? One. No word for one whose words? One? It. No words for it whose words' (Beckett 1983b, 19). This text enacts a worsening of the speaking voice, then, from 'him' – not *her* – to 'one' to 'it'. And if the degeneration that occurs at the end of *Worstward Ho* appears to reduce difference to zero – 'Same stoop for all. Same vasts apart' (Beckett 1983b, 46), and ultimately 'three pins' – there remains the binary difference between these 'three pins' and the one 'pinhole', whose degeneration has passed by way of the masculine.

If Beckett can be said to move haltingly towards an anethical treatment of sexual difference, then this anethicality lies not in pure indifference, but in the indecision that structures the relation between difference and indifference. The inclusion of the feminine within the general economy of disintegration that occurs through Beckett's restaging of both Schopenhauer's woman and the female hysteric cannot be said simply to efface difference but to render both its identification and its value a question. If sexual difference is no less important in *Worstward Ho* than it is in *Dream of Fair to Middling Women*, what distinguishes its treatment in the later work is less the movement away from any seemingly obvious misogyny than the presence of a 'small child' whose sex remains minimally underdetermined, to be written only by an inscription that the text itself never quite accomplishes. This slightest of underdeterminations, on the point of sexual difference's reduction to nothing, becomes the space for another's inscription of sexual difference and its value. The disintegration of sexual difference in Beckett is anethical, then, only insofar as it produces this space for another's inscription of fact-value through both a reduction of difference (and a reduction of the value not only of one sex or the other, but of both sexual difference and difference as such) and a hyperbolization of difference, a splitting that in *Worstward Ho* produces 'Vasts apart. At bounds of boundless void' (Beckett 1983b, 46–7). Like *All That Fall* before it, but orientated towards the masculine rather than the feminine, this late work not only opens the space for an inscription whose justification it does not underwrite, but returns us to the question of who, if anyone, is authorized to make that inscription, who, if anyone, is authorized to determine the sex of a 'small child' and the value of sexual difference – and who, if anyone, can avoid it.

Conclusion
Beckett and the Anethical

According to Alain Badiou, who has been one of the most influential recent critics of the deconstructive turn, the ethics of alterity is only the latest incarnation of a nihilism that is to be countered by an 'ethic of truth', the fundamental ethical imperative of which is 'Keep going!' (*Continuez!*). Not to be confused with a mere 'perseverance of being' (Badiou 2001, 91), this imperative is, he claims, nowhere more evident than in the works of Samuel Beckett, since 'all of Beckett's genius tends towards affirmation' (Badiou 2003, 41). In what is only an apparent paradox, this affirmation is achieved through a labour of negation – an ascetic or subtractive method, functioning in a manner akin to Cartesian doubt – that makes possible the writing of a 'generic humanity', beyond all local differences (including sexual difference), and determined by three basic functions – going, being, and saying – each of which is essentially affirmative in nature.

The commitment to an 'on' even in the face of its apparent impossibility certainly finds one of its clearest and most often quoted expressions in Beckett at the end of *The Unnamable*: 'you must go on, I can't go on, I'll go on' (Beckett 1959, 418). That 'you must', which takes the impersonal form of the 'il faut' in the original French, might well be said to underlie Beckett's entire *œuvre*, if also being subjected to ever greater abstraction away from the realist forms it takes in Beckett's early fiction. Badiou is far from being alone in characterizing this imperative as essentially ethical in nature. Stanley Cavell, for instance, sees the commitment to emptiness, meaningless, and silence in Beckett as a 'new heroic undertaking' (Cavell 2002, 156), while Bersani and Dutoit describe the 'obligation to express' as 'a mysterious necessity that Beckett seems to accept as if it were his professional conscience' (Bersani and Dutoit 1993, 77). And, beyond all the differences upon which Badiou insists between his own truth-orientated ethics and what he sees as the sophistry of the deconstructive ethics of alterity, there is undoubtedly a shared sense of the ethicality of Beckett's *œuvre*, its resistance to nihilism, the triumph of affirmation over negation, and of endurance over abandonment.

That Beckett concerns himself with the ethical is beyond doubt, and this is evident not least in his drawing upon, if also reworking, Arnold Geulincx's quietist ethic of humility (*despectio sui*) and Schopenhauer's ethic of denial (*Verneinung*), both of which justify a negationist attitude to world and self. If, as Badiou suggests, there is a second phase in Beckett, in which he exhibits a much greater openness to the other, and even a love of the other, this does not alter the more fundamental orientation of Beckett's works towards the accomplishment of a voiding that would be all-consuming. Crucially, however, in Beckett the negations repeatedly fail to deliver the very 'nothing' they seem to promise, and it is this failure that comes to constitute the very stuff of the work. This is not to say that what remains necessarily possesses a value; rather, in a process that disintegrates difference no less than identity, Beckett opens the ethicality of both negation and affirmation to question.

If the imperative to go on is the point of maximum opacity in Beckett, it is also, and for that very reason, the point that has most consistently been subjected to interpretative clarification. Badiou, Cavell, Critchley and others, for all their very obvious differences, agree that this imperative is to be clarified in terms of an ethics, but it has proven no less easy, and indeed no less convincing, to clarify it from a psychoanalytic perspective as a compulsion that precedes the discourse of ethics. To justify such a claim, one need only point to the Freudian conception of obsessional neurosis (*Zwangsneurose*), characterized by one of Ernest Jones's patients as a 'feeling of mustness', an expression recorded by Beckett in his 1930s notes on Jones's *Treatment of the Neuroses* (1920).[1] This is not to say, however, that a psychoanalytic reading of Beckett is any more or any less valid than an ethical reading; rather, it is to suggest that each and every clarification of the imperative to go on, each and every attempt to make sense of it in terms of a meta-discourse, be it ethical, aesthetic, philosophical, political, religious, or psychoanalytic, serves to negate the possibility that the 'il faut' is simply a blank at the very heart of Beckett's *œuvre*, a very specific nothing around which that *œuvre* is painstakingly constructed. Whether it is ethical or unethical to negate this nothing by explaining it in terms of any meta-discourse, and whether such a negation is an obligation or a necessity, avoidable or unavoidable, is precisely the question that constitutes it as a space, not in its inexplicability but in its being that without which the very experience of the ethical and the unethical would never arise.

The nothing takes many forms in Beckett, from Mr Knott in *Watt* to the avoided point 'E' in *Quad*. Behind each of these, however, lies the 'il faut'. To negate this nothing is to engage in an act of reading, and each act of reading may of course be considered not only in terms to this founding negation but also in terms of the other negations it enacts. In the case of Badiou's ethical reading of Beckett, one of those other negations has as its object the reversibility written palindromically into the 'on', such that it functions as one term in the pseudocouple 'on'/'no', not least at the end of *Worstward Ho*: 'Said nohow on' (Beckett 1983b, 47). This reversibility does not simply mean that any movement 'on' will inevitably encounter its own knowable impossibility, in accordance with an aporetic logic that brings together the necessary and the impossible. The negation that accompanies the 'on' is not simply its antithesis or antinomy, the 'on' in Beckett always being in the interests of a nothing that is situated both outside and inside the work.

If there is something questionable about reading the 'il faut' as ethical in Beckett, then it lies in its filling the very space that Beckett's works might be said to open, not as the realm of the possible or even of the impossible, not as a difference within the same, nor even as an irreducible alterity, but precisely as the space of the anethical, which is not characterized by an affirmation that precedes all negation or all value. This space of the anethical is not to be understood as an aporia, even if those are the terms in which Beckett himself thinks the relation between obligation and impossibility at the origin of the work of art in the *Three Dialogues with Georges Duthuit* (1949). Neither is it to be understood in terms of heroism or stoic endurance, need, desire, instinct, or will, each of which is one more way of filling the very space that Beckett opens through his treatment of, among other things, translation, the comic, and gender. To speak of the anethical in Beckett is not to read either with or against the grain of his works. If the anethical takes the form of a shuttling or a shuffling to and fro, a kind of indecision that is not indifference and not necessarily either terminal or interminable, necessary or impossible, although always on a trajectory towards the nothing, this indecision is an occasion for invention, not of a new art or a new ethics, but rather of ways in which the experience of the disintegration of both art and ethics might be rendered visible – or audible – on a page or a stage.

The anethical is to be understood, then, as neither an ethics nor an alternative to ethics, but rather as a failure either to establish or negate the difference between the ethical and the unethical, nihilism and anti-nihilism, philosophy and literature, thought and action, the terminal and the interminable. In his unbroadcast 1946 radio piece 'The Capital of the Ruins', Beckett considers the 'possibility' that those from Ireland who served in the Irish Hospital at Saint-Lô in northern France, at the end of the Second World War, will have had 'a vision and sense of a time-honoured conception of humanity in ruins, and perhaps even an inkling of the terms in which our condition is to be thought again' (Beckett 1995a, 278). It has been the argument of the present study that, in a 'universe become provisional', and with a sense of 'humanity in ruins', that rethinking of 'our condition' which occurs in Beckett does not involve the production of a new ethics, be it an ethics of truth or an ethics of alterity. Rather, it involves the opening of the anethical as the experience of that particular nothing the filling of which can be justified only through an appeal to values that will always negate the very things they are there to save.

Notes

Preface

1. '[...] criticism – literature – seems to me to be associated with one of the most difficult, but important, tasks of our time, played out in a necessarily vague movement: the task of preserving and of liberating thought from the notion of value, consequently also of opening history up to what all these forms of value have already released into it and to what is taking shape as an entirely different – still unforeseeable – kind of affirmation' (Blanchot 2004, 6).

Introduction: literature and alterity

1. 'A work can become modern only if it is first postmodern. Postmodernism thus understood is not modernism at its end but in the nascent state, and this state is constant' (Lyotard 1984, 79).
2. The accepted convention in English-language editions of Levinas is to translate *l'autre* as 'the other', *autrui* (the personal other, or other person) as 'the Other', and *l'Autre* (usually deployed by Levinas in opposition to *le Même* ('the Same') as 'the Other'. In *Time and the Other*, 'the Other' (*autrui*) is defined as 'the other "assumed" ' (*l'autre 'assumé'*) (Levinas 1987, 79).
3. 'If the name "ethics", in keeping with the basic meaning of the word *ēthos*, should now say that "ethics" ponders the abode of man, then that thinking which thinks the truth of Being as the primordial element of man, as one who ek-sists, is in itself the original ethics. However, this thinking is not ethics in the first instance, because it is ontology' (Heidegger 1993, 258).
4. In *The Second Sex* (1949), de Beauvoir claims that 'When [Levinas] writes that woman is mystery, he implies that she is mystery for man. Thus his description, which is intended to be objective, is in fact an assertion of masculine privilege' (de Beauvoir 1972, 16 n. 1). I return to her critique of Levinas's alterification of the feminine in Chapter 5.
5. See, in particular, Derrida 1978b; 1991a; 1999; and 2002d.
6. Steven Connor remarks that Beckett's *œuvre* 'has seemed to many to inaugurate the era of postmodernist writing' (Connor 1997, 117). An important exception to this consensus is Slavoj Žižek, who opposes a modernist Beckett to a postmodern Kafka (see Žižek 1991, 141–53).
7. Quoted in *Murphy* (Beckett 1938, 178), Geulincx's principle (from the *Ethics* of 1665) is first recorded towards the end of Beckett's philosophy notes from the early 1930s, taken in large part from Windelband's *History of Philosophy* and Burnet's *Greek Philosophy* (see Trinity College Dublin (TCD) MS 10967). Having first encountered Geulincx's ethics of humility (*despectio sui*: contempt for the self) indirectly, Beckett proceeded to read and to take extensive notes on the *Ethics* in early 1936 (see TCD MS 10971/6/1–36).

8. For a more detailed analysis of the resemblance between Blanchot's and Beckett's formulation of the writer's task, see Weller 2005, 65–7.
9. See Gibson's postscript to Badiou 2003, 119–36.
10. Derrida observes that the 'im-' of 'im-possibility', thought deconstructively, is 'not simply negative or dialectical: it *introduces* the possible; it is its *gatekeeper today*' (Derrida 2002a, 361).

1 Translation and difference: dispatching Benjamin

1. On Beckett's attendance of this lecture, see Knowlson 1996, 218. For an analysis of Beckett's response to Jung's notion of an improper birth, see Chapter 6.
2. In his translation of Benjamin's foreword, Harry Zohn omits to translate the words 'und ursprüngliche'.
3. See Jacobs 1975, from which de Man quotes in his essay on Benjamin.
4. Joyce 2000, 258. For a more extended analysis of Joyce's 'he war' than is offered in 'Des Tours de Babel', see Derrida 1984, 145–59.

2 Translation and negation: Beckett and the bilingual œuvre

1. Benjamin's German translation of *À la recherche du temps perdu*, undertaken in collaboration with Franz Hessel, remained incomplete, but their translation of *À l'ombre des jeunes filles en fleurs* was published in 1927, and of *Le Côté de Guermantes* in 1930.
2. For a helpful list of the major concordances between Beckett's *Proust* and *À la recherche*, see Hill 1990b, 165.
3. 'There is no allusion in this book to the legendary life and death of Marcel Proust' (Beckett 1987, 9).
4. For an account of this episode, see Knowlson 1996, 121–2.
5. See Beer 1994, 211.
6. See Ricks 1993, 13–15.
7. Beckett's review was originally published under the title 'Humanistic Quietism' in the *Dublin Magazine*, July–September 1934.
8. See Knowlson 1996, 290, 303.
9. The following statement is included on the back cover of the first English edition of *Company*: 'Written in English, it has already been translated into French by the author and revised in the light of the French text' (Beckett 1980).
10. A. W. Schlegel, 'Homers Werke von Johann Heinrich Voss' (1796), quoted in Lefevere, 1977, 54.
11. See Meschonnic 1973, 352.
12. See Hill 1990b, ch. 3.
13. See TCD MS 10967/75.
14. Both *Mercier et Camier* and *Premier amour* were first published in 1970; their translations into English were published in 1974 and 1973, respectively.
15. Lawrence Harvey reports Beckett telling him that 'Someday somebody will find an adequate form, a "syntax of weakness"' (Harvey 1970, 249). This syntax would be the appropriate form for a writing taking as its theme what,

in conversation with Israel Shenker, Beckett refers to as that 'zone of being' characterized by 'impotence' and 'ignorance' (Beckett in Shenker 1979, 148).
16. For an analysis of Beckett's parodic treatment of the 'trope of onwardness', see Abbott 1996, 32–42.
17. In her translation of Blanchot's title as *The Step Not Beyond* (1992), Lycette Nelson resorts to a double translation that does not capture the compacted duplicity of the original.
18. *Worstward Ho* has since been translated into French by Edith Fournier under the title *Cap au pire* (Paris: Minuit, 1991).
19. Letter to Thomas MacGreevy, 30 January 1957; quoted in Knowlson 1996, 438.
20. See, for instance, Ostrovsky 1985 and Smith 1987, 138.
21. Beckett's review was first published in *transition*, April–May 1938.
22. 'There must be maximum aggression between [Hamm and Clov] from the first exchange of words onward. Their war is the nucleus of the play' (Beckett in Michael Haerdter, 'A Rehearsal Diary', in McMillan and Fehsenfeld 1988, 205).
23. Samuel Beckett, letter to Alan Schneider, 29 December 1957, in Harmon 1998, 24.
24. Both Steven Connor and Leslie Hill follow a Derridean line in their analysis of self-translation in Beckett; for both, each and every instance of self-translation is governed by the aporetic principle of necessity and impossibility, with translation disclosing a difference always already present in the original (see Connor 1988, 113–14, and Hill 1990b, 51).

3 Pratfalls into alterity: laughter from Baudelaire to Freud and beyond

1. Playing on the difference between signifier and signified, Valéry claims that 'Humour is untranslatable. If this was not the case, then the French would not use the word' (quoted in Critchley 2002, 67).
2. See Morreall 1987.
3. Freud, too, refers to Twain in *Jokes and Their Relation to the Unconscious* (see Freud 1960b, 230–1).
4. As mentioned in the previous chapter, Lawrence Harvey records Beckett having characterized the only 'adequate form' as a 'syntax of weakness' (see Harvey 1970, 249).

4 Last laughs: Beckett and the *'risus purus'*

1. 'I am writing the German comedy in a ragged kind of way, on and off' (letter to Thomas MacGreevy, 29 May 1931; quoted in Pilling 1997, 56).
2. Grock (Charles Adrien Wettach, 1880–1959) went from circus to stage (in Berlin), and, with Antonnet, had his first London engagement in 1911. His simpleton's blunders with piano and violin became proverbial. He wrote several books, among them *Die Memoiren des Königs der Clowns* (1956). For invocations of Grock in *Dream*, see Beckett 1992, 9, 115, 136, 173, 204, 237.
3. 'Wordshit' is Beckett's translation of the French 'fatras' (jumble, lumber) in the ninth of his *Texts for Nothing* (see Beckett 1995a, 137).

4. In *Greek Philosophy* (1914) – one of the works from which Beckett took notes in the early 1930s – John Burnet observes that Horace was the first to characterize Democritus as the 'laughing philosopher' (see Burnet 1914, 194 n. 1).
5. See John Donne, *Paradoxes and Problems*, ed. Helen Peters (Oxford: Clarendon Press, 1980), Paradox VII, 'That a wise man is knowne by much Laughinge'.
6. Letter to Alan Schneider, 29 December 1957, in Harmon 1998, 24.
7. This phrase is attributed to Beckett by Lawrence Harvey (see Harvey 1970, 249). Also see Ricks on Beckett's 'syntax of weakness' in Ricks 1993, 82.
8. '[...] laughter is simply the result of a mechanism set up in us by nature or, what is almost the same thing, by our long acquaintance with social life' (Bergson 1999, 177).
9. See Trinity College Dublin (TCD), MS 10967. On Beckett's phrasing of the atomist paradox, see Chapter 2.
10. In a letter of 21 June 1956 to Alan Schneider, Beckett remarks that *Endgame* strikes him as being 'more inhuman' than *Godot* (Harmon 1998, 11).
11. In response to Estragon's Schopenhauerian suggestion that they repent their having been born, Vladimir breaks into a '*hearty laugh which he immediately stifles, his hand pressed to his pubis, his face contorted*' (Beckett 1990, 13).
12. The notion of a life that is always to come can be related to the idea of not being properly born, which first appears in the 'Addenda' to *Watt* and, as is made clear in *All That Fall*, is in fact something said by Jung during one of his 1935 Tavistock Lectures, attended by Beckett. A year earlier, Joyce had sought Jung's help over the deteriorating mental condition of his daughter, Lucia.
13. The smile that Beckett adds at the end of the 1966 German production of *Eh Joe* disappears again in the 1979 production, also directed by Beckett.
14. 'Perfect laughter, if there could be such a thing, would be inhuman. And it would select as the objects of its mirth as much the antics dependent upon pathologic maladjustments, injury, or disease, as the antics of clumsy and imperfectly functioning healthy people' (Lewis 1987, 92).
15. Beckett's 'Whoroscope Notebook' is at the Beckett International Foundation, University of Reading (RUL) MS 3000/1. It dates from 1932 to 1937. The typed notes from Mauthner are in TCD MS 10971/5/1–4.
16. All translations from Mauthner's *Beiträge* are my own.

5 Feminine alterities: from psychoanalysis to gender studies

1. Fragment X, in Heraclitus 1979, 32–3. For Heidegger's commentary on this fragment, see Heidegger 1984a, 102–23. (*Phusis* is usually translated as 'Nature'.)
2. On its original publication, in *Empédocle* 2 (May 1949), 13–22, this work was entitled 'Un récit?' on the cover and 'Un récit' on the contents page and in the text itself. For a deconstructive analysis of this discrepancy, see Derrida 1992b.
3. Introduction II to Lacan 1982, 56.
4. See Felman 1975, 3.
5. See, in particular, Kristeva 2000 and 2002.
6. These lectures were first published in German in 1961, and in English translation from 1979 to 1987.

7. Derrida quotes this passage in both 'Choreographies' (Derrida 1995, 104) and *'Geschlecht*: Sexual Difference, Ontological Difference' (Derrida 1991b, 387).
8. Butler seeks to demonstrate that, far from being restricted to less theoretically sophisticated forms of gender discourse, compulsory heterosexuality governs Kristeva's semiotic/Symbolic model (see Butler 1999, 101–19).

6 'As if the sex mattered': Beckett's degenderations

1. According to Susan Brienza, for instance, Beckett's characterization of women in the early fiction 'alternates between stereotypes of femininity and bizarre reversals of the stereotypes. Whether paragon or parody, the woman here is limited to the body and to the emotions' (Brienza 1990, 91). Similarly, Mary Bryden argues for a continuity between Aristotle and early Beckett in their conception of woman as negative other, and, in Beckett's prose fiction, of woman as an alterity that is not only without value but also threatens all value (see Bryden 1993, ch. 1).
2. In a letter to Alan Schneider of 16 October 1972, for instance, Beckett remarks of *Not I*: 'I hear it breathlessly, urgent, feverish, rhythmic, panting along, without undue concern with intelligibility. Addressed less to the understanding than to the nerves of the audience which should in a sense *share her bewilderment*' (Harmon 1998, 283).
3. In a letter of 16 August 1921 to Frank Budgen, Joyce writes of Molly Bloom in the 'Penelope' episode in *Ulysses* that she is 'perfectly sane full amoral fertilisable untrustworthy engaging shrewd limited prudent indifferent *Weib. Ich bin der* [sic] *Fleisch der stets bejaht*' (Ellmann 1975, 285).
4. A version for television, directed by Anthony Page and with Billie Whitelaw as Mouth, was produced for the BBC in 1975.
5. See in particular Butler 1999, 101–19.
6. The objectifying definite article is used of the female characters in both *Dream* and *More Pricks Than Kicks* (1934).
7. Beckett International Foundation, Reading University Library (RUL) MS 1660; quoted in Bryden 1993, 76.
8. 'In our time Proust was wholly androgynous, if not perhaps a little too much of a woman' (Woolf 2000, 102).
9. '[...] had she been true, / If heaven would make me such another world, / Of one entire and perfect chrysolite, / I'ld not have sold her for it' (V.ii.146). This is the only occasion on which the word 'chrysolite' appears in Shakespeare.
10. Beckett in Knowlson 1992, 241.
11. 'All poetry, as discriminated from the various paradigms of prosody, is prayer' (Beckett 1983a, 68). Beckett's review, under the title 'Humanistic Quietism', was originally published in the *Dublin Magazine*, July–September 1934.
12. Written in 1935, this attack on the new censorship Act in Ireland remained unpublished until 1983. It contains Beckett's mocking observation that 'Sterilization of the mind and apotheosis of the litter suit well together' (Beckett 1983a, 87).
13. A number of commentators have hastened to fill in the blanks at the heart of *All That Fall*. O'Hara, for instance, refers in passing to 'the *boy's* death under the wheels of the train' (O'Hara 1997, 81; emphasis added).

14. 'I have seen cases of ethereal children, so to speak, who had an extraordinary awareness of these psychic facts [the contents of the collective unconscious] and were living their life in archetypal dreams and could not adapt. Recently I saw a case of a little girl of ten who had some most amazing mythological dreams. Her father consulted me about these dreams. I could not tell him what I thought because they contained an uncanny prognosis. The little girl died a year later of an infectious disease. She had never been born entirely' (Jung 1968, 107).
15. Beckett quoted in Asmus 1977, 84.
16. See Juliet 1995, 138.
17. See Ellmann 1982, 676–81.
18. In addition to Beckett's reading of Schopenhauer on the 'veil of Maya', and his remarks on habit in *Proust* and, of course, in *Godot*, where habit is described as a 'great deadener' (Beckett 1990, 84), a remarkable fragment on Goethe's *Faust* in Beckett's 'Clare Street Notebook' (RUL MS 5003), which is dated on the cover 13 July 1936, remarks upon the way in which the veil of hope may be torn away, but will always return. (My thanks to Matthew Feldman for this reference.)
19. The word 'pseudocouple' is used of Mercier and Camier in *The Unnamable* (Beckett 1959, 299).
20. For an analysis of this tradition, see Showalter 1987.
21. Beckett took notes on Alfred Adler's *The Neurotic Constitution* (1921), Ernest Jones's *Papers on Psycho-Analysis* (1920) and *Treatment of the Neuroses* (1920), Otto Rank's *The Trauma of Birth* (1929), Wilhelm Stekel's *Psychoanalysis and Suggestion Therapy* (1923), Karin Stephen's *Psychoanalysis and Medicine: A Study of the Wish to Fall Ill* (1933), and Robert S. Woodworth's *Contemporary Schools of Psychology* (1931). His typed notes on these authors are to be found in Trinity College Dublin (TCD) MSS 10971/7/1–17 and 10971/8/1–36.
22. Cf. TCD MS 10971/8/21.
23. See TCD MS 10971/8/21 and Knowlson 1996, 178.
24. With regard to the disavowal (*Verleugnung*) peculiar to schizophrenia, Love claims that *The Unnamable* is 'more in tune with a view of schizophrenia not as a withdrawal from the higher levels of cognition but as a condition in which these faculties operate in pathological overdrive and turn inward on thought processes themselves until they assume an objective reality that usurps the physical world' (Love in Ackerley and Gontarski 2004, 505).
25. See Beckett 1963, 25; 1974b, 40. There is also a reference to 'the meaning of your back to the engine' in *The Unnamable* (Beckett 1959, 410).
26. Quoted in Beckett 1987, 67; cf. Schopenhauer 1966, i. 355.
27. See Nietzsche 1967, 42. The Greek source for this maxim is Sophocles' *Oedipus at Colonus*. In W. B. Yeats's 1934 version of the play, with which Beckett was familiar, it reads: 'Never to have lived is best, ancient writers say; / Never to have drawn the breath of life, never to have looked into the eye of day; / The second best's a gay goodnight and quickly turn away' (Yeats 1953, 353).
28. See Ackerley and Gontarski 2004, 61.
29. Beckett in Shenker 1979, 148–9. Rank refers to Nietzsche's distinction between the Apollonian and the Dionysian in his chapter on artistic idealization (see Rank 1929, 141–2).

30. In response to Alan Schneider's question 'How does anyone know AUDITOR is a man?' (Harmon 1998, 280), Beckett writes: 'It is not stated, though suggested by masculine "auditor", that it is a man. The costume, as I neglected to specify, is djellaba with hood. The figure is completely shrouded from head to foot' (Harmon 1998, 282).
31. See Ackerley and Gontarski 2004, 398.
32. In the production of *Quadrat I + II* that Beckett directed for Süddeutscher Rundfunk, Stuttgart, the cast consists of two men and two women.
33. Linda Ben-Zvi reports this remark as having been made during a meeting with Beckett in Paris in December 1987 (see Ben-Zvi 1990b, x).
34. Mary Bryden argues that Beckett's drama 'catalyses the change from "phallogocentrism" to gender fluidity', and that, beyond this fluidity, there are 'sounds and cries' in Beckett that are 'sexually impartial' (Bryden 1993, 197–8).

Conclusion: Beckett and the anethical

1. For Beckett's typed notes on Jones's *Treatment of the Neuroses*, see TCD MS 10971/8/21–3.

Bibliography

Abbott, H. Porter. 1996. *Beckett Writing Beckett: The Author in the Autograph*. Ithaca, NY: Cornell University Press.
Ackerley, C. J., and S. E. Gontarski. 2004. *The Grove Companion to Samuel Beckett: A Reader's Guide to His Works, Life, and Thought*. New York: Grove.
Adorno, Theodor W. 1973. *Negative Dialectics*. Trans. E. B. Ashton. London: Routledge and Kegan Paul.
——. 1991. 'Trying to Understand *Endgame*'. In *Notes to Literature*, vol. 1. Ed. Rolf Tiedemann. Trans. Shierry Weber Nicholsen. New York: Columbia University Press: 241–75.
——. 1992. 'Is Art Lighthearted?'. In *Notes to Literature*, vol. 2. Ed. Rolf Tiedemann. Trans. Shierry Weber Nicholsen. New York: Columbia University Press: 247–53.
——. 1997. *Aesthetic Theory*. Eds Gretel Adorno and Rolf Tiedemann. Trans. Robert Hullot-Kentor. London: Athlone.
Alexander, Archibald B. D. 1922. *A Short History of Philosophy*. Third edition. Glasgow: Maclehose, Jackson and Co.
Asmus, Walter D. 1977. 'Rehearsal Notes for the German Première of Samuel Beckett's *That Time* and *Footfalls*, at the Schiller-Theater Werkstatt, Berlin'. Trans. Helen Watanabe. *Journal of Beckett Studies*, 2 (Summer 1977): 82–95.
Badiou, Alain. 2001. *Ethics: An Essay on the Understanding of Evil*. Trans. Peter Hallward. London: Verso.
——. 2003. *On Beckett*. Eds Nina Power and Alberto Toscano. Manchester: Clinamen.
Bakhtin, Mikhail. 1984. *Rabelais and His World*. Trans. Hélène Iswolsky. Bloomington, IN: Indiana University Press.
Bataille, Georges. 1988. *Guilty*. Trans. Bruce Boone. San Francisco: Lapis.
Baudelaire, Charles. 1982. *'Les Fleurs du Mal': The Complete Text of 'The Flowers of Evil'*. Trans. Richard Howard. Boston, MA: David R. Godine.
——. 1995. 'On the Essence of Laughter'. In *The Painter of Modern Life and Other Essays*. Ed. and trans. Jonathan Mayne. London: Phaidon: 147–65.
——. 1997. *Complete Poems*. Trans. Walter Martin. Manchester: Carcanet.
——. 1998. *The Flowers of Evil*. Trans. James McGowan. Oxford: Oxford University Press.
Beckett, Samuel. 1938. *Murphy*. London: George Routledge and Sons.
——. 1951a. *Malone meurt*. Paris: Minuit.
——. 1951b. *Molloy*. Paris: Minuit.
——. 1952. *En attendant Godot*. Paris: Minuit.
——. 1953. *L'Innommable*. Paris: Minuit.
——. 1957a. *Fin de partie*. Paris: Minuit.
——. 1957b. *Tous ceux qui tombent*. Trans. Robert Pinget. Paris: Minuit.
——. 1959. *Molloy, Malone Dies, The Unnamable*. London: John Calder.
——. 1961. *Comment c'est*. Paris: Minuit.
——. 1963. *Watt*. London: John Calder.
——. 1964. *How It Is*. London: John Calder.
——. 1965. *Murphy*. Paris: Minuit.

Beckett, Samuel. 1970a. *Le Dépeupleur*. Paris: Minuit.
——. 1970b. *Mercier et Camier*. Paris: Minuit.
——. 1970c. *More Pricks Than Kicks*. London: Calder and Boyars.
——. 1970d. *Premier amour*. Paris: Minuit.
——. 1972. *Têtes-mortes*. Paris: Minuit.
——. 1974a. *First Love and Other Shorts*. New York: Grove.
——. 1974b. *Mercier and Camier*. London: Calder and Boyars.
——. 1980. *Company*. London: John Calder.
——. 1981. *Mal vu mal dit*. Paris: Minuit.
——. 1982. *Ill Seen Ill Said*. London: John Calder.
——. 1983a. *Disjecta: Miscellaneous Writings and a Dramatic Fragment*. Ed. Ruby Cohn. London: John Calder.
——. 1983b. *Worstward Ho*. London: John Calder.
——. 1987. *Proust and Three Dialogues with Georges Duthuit*. London: John Calder.
——. 1990. *The Complete Dramatic Works*. Revised paperback edition. London: Faber and Faber.
——. 1991. *Cap au pire*. Trans. Edith Fournier. Paris: Minuit.
——. 1992. *Dream of Fair to Middling Women*. Eds Eoin O'Brien and Edith Fournier. Dublin: Black Cat.
——. 1995a. *The Complete Short Prose, 1929–1989*. Ed. S. E. Gontarski. New York: Grove.
——. 1995b. *Eleutheria*. Paris: Minuit.
——. 1995c. *Eleuthéria: A Play in Three Acts*. Trans. Michael Brodsky. New York: Foxrock.
——. 1996. *Eleutheria*. Trans. Barbara Wright. London: Faber and Faber.
——. 2002. *Poems, 1930–1989*. London: Calder.
Beer, Ann. 1994. 'Beckett's Bilingualism'. In *The Cambridge Companion to Beckett*. Ed. John Pilling. Cambridge: Cambridge University Press: 209–21.
Begam, Richard. 1996. *Samuel Beckett and the End of Modernity*. Stanford, CA: Stanford University Press.
Benjamin, Walter. 1991. 'Charles Baudelaire: "Tableux parisiens". Deutsche Übertragung mit einem Vorwort über die Aufgabe des Übersetzers'. In *Gesammelte Schriften*, vol. 4: 1. Frankfurt am Main: Suhrkamp: 7–63.
——. 1996. 'The Task of the Translator'. Trans. Harry Zohn. In *Selected Writings*, vol. 1: *1913–1926*. Eds Marcus Bullock and Michael W. Jennings. Cambridge, MA: Belknap: 253–63.
——. 2003. 'On the Concept of History'. Trans. Harry Zohn. In *Selected Writings*, vol. 4: *1938–1940*. Eds Howard Eiland and Michael W. Jennings. Cambridge, MA: Belknap: 389–400.
Ben-Zvi, Linda. 1990a. 'Not I: Through a Tube Starkly'. In *Women in Beckett: Performance and Critical Perspectives*. Ed. Linda Ben-Zvi. Urbana, IL: University of Illinois Press: 243–8.
——, ed. 1990b. *Women in Beckett: Performance and Critical Perspectives*. Urbana, IL: University of Illinois Press.
Bergson, Henri. 1999. *Laughter: An Essay on the Meaning of the Comic*. Trans. Cloudesley Brereton and Fred Rothwell. Los Angeles: Green Integer.
Bersani, Leo, and Ulysse Dutoit. 1993. *Arts of Impoverishment: Beckett, Rothko, Resnais*. Cambridge, MA: Harvard University Press.

Blanchot, Maurice. 1978. *Death Sentence*. Trans. Lydia Davis. Barrytown, NY: Station Hill.
——. 1982. *The Space of Literature*. Trans. Ann Smock. Lincoln, NE: University of Nebraska Press.
——. 1992. *The Step Not Beyond*. Trans. Lycette Nelson. Albany, NY: SUNY.
——. 1993. *The Infinite Conversation*. Trans. Susan Hanson. Minneapolis, MN: University of Minnesota Press.
——. 1997a. 'The Time of Encyclopedias'. In *Friendship*. Trans. Elizabeth Rottenberg. Stanford, CA: Stanford University Press: 50–6.
——. 1997b. 'Translating'. In *Friendship*. Trans. Elizabeth Rottenberg. Stanford, CA: Stanford University Press: 57–61.
——. 2003. ' "Where Now? Who Now?" '. In *The Book to Come*. Trans. Charlotte Mandell. Stanford, CA: Stanford University Press: 210–17.
——. 2004. *Lautréamont and Sade*. Trans. Stuart and Michelle Kendall. Stanford, CA: Stanford University Press, 2004.
Brater, Enoch. 1989. *Why Beckett*. London: Thames and Hudson.
Brienza, Susan. 1990. 'Clods, Whores, and Bitches: Misogyny in Beckett's Early Fiction'. In *Women in Beckett: Performance and Critical Perspectives*. Ed. Linda Ben-Zvi. Urbana, IL: University of Illinois Press: 91–105.
Bryden, Mary. 1993. *Women in Samuel Beckett's Prose and Drama: Her Own Other*. Basingstoke: Macmillan.
Burnet, John. 1914. *Greek Philosophy, Part 1: Thales to Plato*. London: Macmillan.
Butler, Judith. 1999. *Gender Trouble: Feminism and the Subversion of Identity*. Tenth anniversary edition. London: Routledge.
Cavell, Stanley. 2002. 'Ending the Waiting Game: A Reading of Beckett's *Endgame*'. In *Must We Mean What We Say?: A Book of Essays*. Updated edition. Cambridge: Cambridge University Press: 115–62.
Celan, Paul. 1986. Letter to Hans Bender, 18 May 1960. In *Collected Prose*. Trans. Rosmarie Waldrop. Riverdale-on-Hudson, NY: Sheep Meadow Press: 25–6.
Chamfort, Sébastien. 1969. *Products of the Perfected Civilization: Selected Writings of Chamfort*. Trans. W. S. Merwin. New York: Macmillan.
Cicero, Marcus Tullius. 1959. *De Oratore*. Trans. E. W. Sutton. London: William Heinemann.
Cixous, Hélène. 1981. 'The Laugh of the Medusa'. Trans. Keith and Paula Cohen. In *New French Feminisms: An Anthology*. Eds Elaine Marks and Isabelle de Courtivon. Brighton: The Harvester Press: 245–64.
——. 1986. 'Sorties: Out and Out: Attacks / Ways Out / Forays'. In Hélène Cixous and Catherine Clément. *The Newly Born Woman*. Trans. Betsy Wing. Minneapolis, MN: Minnesota University Press: 61–132.
——. 1991. *'Coming to Writing' and Other Essays*. Ed. Deborah Jenson. Trans. Susan Rubin Suleiman. Cambridge, MA: Harvard University Press.
Clément, Catherine. 1986. 'The Guilty One'. In Hélène Cixous and Catherine Clément. *The Newly Born Woman*. Trans. Betsy Wing. Minneapolis, MN: Minnesota University Press: 61–132.
Cohn, Ruby. 1962. *Samuel Beckett: The Comic Gamut*. New Brunswick, NJ: Rutgers University Press.
Coleridge, Samuel Taylor. 1907. *Biographia Literaria*. Ed. J. Shawcross. 2 vols. Oxford: Oxford University Press.

Connor, Steven. 1988. *Samuel Beckett: Repetition, Theory and Text*. Oxford: Basil Blackwell.
——. 1997. *Postmodernist Culture: An Introduction to Theories of the Contemporary*. Second edition. Oxford: Blackwell.
Critchley, Simon. 1997. *Very Little ... Almost Nothing: Death, Philosophy, Literature*. London: Routledge.
——. 2002. *On Humour*. London: Routledge.
de Beauvoir, Simone. 1972. *The Second Sex*. Trans. H. M. Parshley. Harmondsworth: Penguin.
Deleuze, Gilles. 1995. *Negotiations, 1972–1990*. Trans. Martin Joughin. New York: Columbia University Press.
——. 1998. 'The Exhausted'. In *Essays Critical and Clinical*. Trans. Daniel W. Smith and Michael A. Greco. London: Verso: 152–74.
de Man, Paul. 1986a. ' "Conclusions": Walter Benjamin's "The Task of the Translator" '. In *The Resistance to Theory*. Minneapolis, MN: University of Minnesota Press: 73–105.
——. 1986b. 'The Resistance to Theory'. In *The Resistance to Theory*. Minneapolis, MN: University of Minnesota Press: 3–20.
Derrida, Jacques. 1976. *Of Grammatology*. Trans. Gayatri Chakravorty Spivak. Baltimore, MD: The Johns Hopkins University Press.
——. 1978a. 'From Restricted to General Economy: A Hegelianism without Reserve'. In *Writing and Difference*. Trans. Alan Bass. London: Routledge and Kegan Paul: 251–77.
——. 1978b. 'Violence and Metaphysics: An Essay on the Thought of Emmanuel Levinas'. In *Writing and Difference*. Trans. Alan Bass. London: Routledge and Kegan Paul: 79–153.
——. 1979. *Spurs: Nietzsche's Styles / Éperons: Les Styles de Nietzsche*. Trans. Barbara Harlow. Chicago, IL: Chicago University Press.
——. 1981a. *Dissemination*. Trans. Barbara Johnson. Chicago, IL: Chicago University Press.
——. 1981b. *Positions*. Trans. Alan Bass. London: Athlone.
——. 1982. 'Différance'. In *Margins of Philosophy*. Trans. Alan Bass. Chicago, IL: Chicago University Press: 1–27.
——. 1984. 'Two Words for Joyce'. In *Post-structuralist Joyce: Essays from the French*. Eds Derek Attridge and Daniel Ferrer. Cambridge: Cambridge University Press: 145–59.
——. 1986. *Glas*. Trans. John P. Leavey, Jr. and Richard Rand. Lincoln, NE: University of Nebraska Press.
——. 1988. *The Ear of the Other: Otobiography, Transference, Translation*. Ed. Christie McDonald. Trans. Peggy Kamuf. Lincoln, NE: University of Nebraska Press, 1988.
——. 1991a. 'At This Very Moment in This Work Here I Am'. Trans. Ruben Berezdivin. In *A Derrida Reader: Between the Blinds*. Ed. Peggy Kamuf. New York: Harvester Wheatsheaf: 405–39.
——. 1991b. '*Geschlecht*: Sexual Difference, Ontological Difference'. Trans. Ruben Bevezdivin. In *A Derrida Reader: Between the Blinds*. Ed. Peggy Kamuf. New York: Harvester Wheatsheaf: 380–402.
——. 1992a. 'Before the Law'. Trans. Avital Ronell and Christine Roulston. In *Acts of Literature*. Ed. Derek Attridge. New York: Routledge: 183–220.
——. 1992b. 'The Law of Genre'. Trans. Avital Ronell. In *Acts of Literature*. Ed. Derek Attridge. New York: Routledge: 221–52.

Derrida, Jacques. 1992c. ' "This Strange Institution Called Literature": An Interview with Jacques Derrida'. In *Acts of Literature*. Ed. Derek Attridge. New York: Routledge: 33–75.
——. 1995. 'Choreographies'. Trans. Christie V. McDonald. In *Points …: Interviews, 1974–1994*. Ed. Elisabeth Weber. Stanford, CA: Stanford University Press: 89–108.
——. 1999. *Adieu to Emmanuel Levinas*. Trans. Pascale-Anne Brault and Michael Nass. Stanford, CA: Stanford University Press.
——. 2001. 'I Have a Taste for the Secret'. In *A Taste for the Secret*. Eds Giacomo Donis and David Webb. Trans. Giacomo Donis. Cambridge: Polity: 1–92.
——. 2002a. 'As If It Were Possible, "Within Such Limits" …'. In *Negotiations: Interventions and Interviews 1971–2001*. Trans. Elizabeth Rottenberg. Stanford, CA: Stanford University Press: 343–70.
——. 2002b. 'Des Tours de Babel'. Trans. Joseph F. Graham. In *Acts of Religion*. Ed. Gil Anidjar. New York: Routledge: 104–33.
——. 2002c. *Force of Law: The 'Mystical Foundation of Authority'*. Trans. Mary Quaintance. In *Acts of Religion*. Ed. Gil Anidjar. New York: Routledge: 230–98.
——. 2002d. 'Hostipitality'. Trans. Gil Anidjar. In *Acts of Religion*. Ed. Gil Anidjar. New York: Routledge: 358–420.
Diamond, Elin. 2004. 'Feminist Readings of Beckett'. In *Palgrave Advances in Samuel Beckett Studies*. Ed. Lois Oppenheim. Basingstoke: Palgrave Macmillan: 45–67.
Docherty, Thomas. 1996. *Alterities: Criticism, History, Ideology*. Cambridge: Cambridge University Press.
Donne, John. 1980. *Paradoxes and Problems*. Ed. Helen Peters. Oxford: Clarendon Press.
Driver, Tom. 1979. 'Beckett by the Madeleine'. In *Samuel Beckett: The Critical Heritage*. Eds Lawrence Graver and Raymond Federman. London: Routledge and Kegan Paul: 217–23.
Eco, Umberto. 2003. *Mouse or Rat?: Translation as Negotiation*. London: Weidenfeld and Nicolson.
Ellmann, Richard. 1982. *James Joyce*. Revised edition. Oxford: Oxford University Press.
——, ed. 1975. *Selected Letters of James Joyce*. London: Faber and Faber.
Esslin, Martin. 1967. 'Samuel Beckett's Poems'. In *Beckett at 60: A Festschrift*. London: Calder and Boyars: 55–60.
Felman, Shoshana. 1975. 'The Critical Phallacy'. *Diacritics* (Winter 1975): 2–10.
Fitch, Brian T. 1988. *Becket and Babel: An Investigation into the Status of the Bilingual Work*. Toronto: University of Toronto Press.
Freud, Sigmund. 1957. 'The Unconscious'. In *The Standard Edition of the Complete Psychological Works of Sigmund Freud*, vol. XIV. Trans. James Strachey. London: Hogarth Press: 159–215.
——. 1960a. 'Femininity'. *New Introductory Lectures on Psycho-Analysis*, Lecture XXXIII. In *The Standard Edition of the Complete Psychological Works of Sigmund Freud*, vol. XXII. Trans. James Strachey. London: Hogarth Press: 112–35.
——. 1960b. *Jokes and Their Relation to the Unconscious. The Standard Edition of the Complete Psychological Works of Sigmund Freud*, vol. VIII. Trans. James Strachey. London: Hogarth Press.
Freud, Sigmund. 1961. 'The Loss of Reality in Neurosis and Psychosis'. In *The Standard Edition of the Complete Psychological Works of Sigmund Freud*, vol. XIX. Trans. James Strachey. London: Hogarth Press: 181–7.

Freud, Sigmund. 1963. *Introductory Lectures on Psycho-Analysis*, Part III. *The Standard Edition of the Complete Psychological Works of Sigmund Freud*, vol. XVI. Trans. James Strachey. London: Hogarth Press.
——. 1964. 'Humour'. In *The Standard Edition of the Complete Psychological Works of Sigmund Freud*, vol. XXI. Trans. James Strachey. London: Hogarth Press: 159–66.
——and Joseph Breuer. 1955. *Studies on Hysteria. The Standard Edition of the Complete Psychological Works of Sigmund Freud*, vol. II. Trans. James Strachey. London: Hogarth Press.
Gessner, Niklaus. 1957. *Die Unzulänglichkeit der Sprache: Eine Untersuchung über Formzerfall und Beziehungslosigkeit bei Samuel Beckett*. Zurich: Juris.
Gidal, Peter. 1986. *Understanding Beckett: A Study of Monologue and Gesture in the Works of Samuel Beckett*. London: Macmillan.
Gontarski, S. E. 1985. *The Intent of Undoing in Samuel Beckett's Dramatic Texts*. Bloomington, IN: Indiana University Press.
Harmon, Maurice, ed. 1998. *No Author Better Served: The Correspondence of Samuel Beckett and Alan Schneider*. Cambridge, MA: Harvard University Press.
Harvey, Lawrence. 1970. *Samuel Beckett: Poet and Critic*. Princeton, NJ: Princeton University Press.
Hassan, Ihab. 1971. *The Dismemberment of Orpheus: Toward a Postmodern Literature*. New York: Oxford University Press.
Heidegger, Martin. 1962. *Being and Time*. Trans. John Macquarrie and Edward Robinson. San Francisco: Harper and Row.
——. 1984a. 'Aletheia (Heraclitus, Fragment B 16)'. In *Early Greek Thinking*. Trans. David Farrell Krell and Frank A. Capuzzi. San Francisco: Harper and Row: 102–23.
——. 1984b. *The Metaphysical Foundations of Logic*. Trans. Michael Heim. Bloomington, IN: Indiana University Press.
——. 1993. *Letter on Humanism*. Trans. Frank A. Capuzzi and J. Glenn Gray. In *Basic Writings*. Ed. David Farrell Krell. Revised edition. London: Routledge: 213–65.
——. 2000. *Introduction to Metaphysics*. Trans. Gregory Fried and Richard Polt. New Haven, CT: Yale University Press.
Heraclitus. 1979. *The Art and Thought of Heraclitus: An Edition of the Fragments with Translation and Commentary*. Ed. Charles H. Kahn. Cambridge: Cambridge University Press.
Hill, Leslie. 1990a. Beckett obituary. *Radical Philosophy*, 55 (Summer 1990).
——. 1990b. *Beckett's Fiction: In Different Words*. Cambridge: Cambridge University Press.
Hillis Miller, J. 2002. *On Literature*. London: Routledge.
Irigaray, Luce. 1985a. *Speculum of the Other Woman*. Trans. Gillian C. Gill. Ithaca, NY: Cornell University Press.
——. 1985b. *This Sex Which Is Not One*. Trans. Catherine Porter and Carolyn Burke. Ithaca, NY: Cornell University Press.
——. 2004. *An Ethics of Sexual Difference*. Trans. Carolyn Burke and Gillian C. Gill. London: Continuum.
Jacobs, Carol. 1975. 'The Monstrosity of Translation'. *Modern Language Notes*, 90: 6 (December 1975): 755–66.
Jakobson, Roman. 1987. 'On Linguistic Aspects of Translation'. *Language in Literature*. Eds Krystyna Pomorska and Stephen Rudy. Cambridge, MA: Belknap: 428–35.

Janet, Pierre. 1901. *The Mental State of Hystericals: A Study of Mental Stigmata and Mental Accidents*. Trans. Caroline Rollin Corson. New York and London: G. P. Putnam's Sons.
Jones, Ernest. 1920. *Treatment of the Neuroses*. London: Baillière, Tindall and Cox.
Joyce, James. 2000. *Finnegans Wake*. Harmondsworth: Penguin.
Juliet, Charles. 1995. *Conversations with Samuel Beckett and Bram van Velde*. Trans. Janey Tucker. Leiden: Academic Press.
Jung, C. G. 1968. *Analytical Psychology: Its Theory and Practice (The Tavistock Lectures)*. London: Routledge and Kegan Paul.
Kant, Immanuel. 1952. *The Critique of Judgement*. Trans. James Creed Meredith. Oxford: Clarendon Press.
Kierkegaard, Søren. 1968. *Concluding Unscientific Postscript*. Trans. David F. Swenson and Walter Lowrie. Princeton, NJ: Princeton University Press.
Kleist, Heinrich von. 1994. 'On the Marionette Theatre'. In *Essays on Dolls*. Trans. Idris Parry. Harmondsworth: Syrens: 1–12.
Knowlson, James. 1996. *Damned to Fame: The Life of Samuel Beckett*. London: Bloomsbury.
——, ed. 1985. *'Happy Days': The Production Notebook of Samuel Beckett*. London: Faber and Faber.
——, ed. 1992. *The Theatrical Notebooks of Samuel Beckett*, vol. 3: *Krapp's Last Tape*. London: Faber and Faber.
—— and John Pilling. 1979. *Frescoes of the Skull: The Later Prose and Drama of Samuel Beckett*. London: John Calder.
Kristeva, Julia. 1980a. 'From One Identity to an Other'. In *Desire in Language: A Semiotic Approach to Literature and Art*. Ed. Leon S. Roudiez. Trans. Thomas Gora, Alice Jardine, and Leon S. Roudiez. New York: Columbia University Press: 124–47.
——. 1980b. 'The Father, Love, and Banishment'. In *Desire in Language: A Semiotic Approach to Literature and Art*. Ed. Leon S. Roudiez. Trans. Thomas Gora, Alice Jardine, and Leon S. Roudiez. New York: Columbia University Press: 148–58.
——. 1981. 'Woman Can Never Be Defined'. Trans. Marilyn A. August. In *New French Feminisms: An Anthology*. Eds Elaine Marks and Isabelle de Courtivon. Brighton: The Harvester Press: 137–41.
——. 1982. *Powers of Horror: An Essay on Abjection*. Trans. Leon S. Roudiez. New York: Columbia University Press.
——. 1984. *Revolution in Poetic Language*. Trans. Margaret Waller. New York: Columbia University Press.
——. 1997. 'Women's Time'. Trans. Alice Jardine and Harry Blake. In *The Feminist Reader: Essays in Gender and the Politics of Literary Criticism*. Eds Catherine Belsey and Jane Moore. Second edition. Basingstoke: Macmillan: 201–16.
——. 2000. *The Sense and Non-Sense of Revolt: The Powers and Limits of Psychoanalysis*, vol. 1. Trans. Jeanine Herman. New York: Columbia University Press.
——. 2002. *Intimate Revolt: The Powers and Limits of Psychoanalysis*, vol. 2. Trans. Jeanine Herman. New York: Columbia University Press.
Lacan, Jacques. 1982. *Feminine Sexuality: Jacques Lacan and the 'École Freudienne'*. Eds Juliet Mitchell and Jacqueline Rose. Trans. Jacqueline Rose. New York: W. W. Norton.
——. 1998. *The Seminar of Jacques Lacan*. Ed. Jacques-Alain Miller. Book XX: *Encore 1972–1973: On Feminine Sexuality: The Limits of Love and Knowledge*. Trans. Bruce Fink. New York: W. W. Norton.

Laplanche, J., and J.-B. Pontalis. 1973. *The Language of Psycho-Analysis*. Trans. Donald Nicholson-Smith. London: The Hogarth Press and the Institute of Psycho-Analysis.
Lefevere, André. 1977. *Translating Literature: The German Tradition from Luther to Rosenzweig*. Amsterdam: Van Gorcum.
Levinas, Emmanuel. 1969. *Totality and Infinity: An Essay on Exteriority*. Trans. Alphonso Lingis. Pittsburgh, PA: Duquesne University Press.
——. 1985. *Ethics and Infinity: Conversations with Philippe Nemo*. Trans. Richard A. Cohen. Pittsburgh, PA: Duquesne University Press.
——. 1987. *Time and the Other*. Trans. Richard A. Cohen. Pittsburgh, PA: Duquesne University Press.
——. 1996. *Proper Names*. Trans. Michael B. Smith. London: Athlone.
——. 1998. *Otherwise than Being or Beyond Essence*. Trans. Alphonso Lingis. Pittsburgh, PA: Duquesne University Press.
——. 2001. *Existence and Existents*. Trans. Alphonso Lingis. Pittsburgh, PA: Duquesne University Press.
Lewis, Wyndham. 1987. *Men without Art*. Ed. Seamus Cooney. Santa Rosa, CA: Black Sparrow.
Locatelli, Carla. 1990. *Unwording the World: Samuel Beckett's Prose Works after the Nobel Prize*. Philadelphia, PA: University of Pennsylvania Press.
Lyotard, Jean-François. 1984. *The Postmodern Condition: A Report on Knowledge*. Trans. Geoff Bennington and Brian Massumi. Minneapolis, MN: Minnesota University Press.
Mauthner, Fritz. 1923. *Beiträge zu einer Kritik der Sprache*. Third edition. 3 vols. Leipzig: Felix Meiner.
McMillan, Dougald, and Martha Fehsenfeld. 1988. *Beckett in the Theatre: The Author as Practical Playwright and Director*, vol. 1: *From 'Waiting for Godot' to 'Krapp's Last Tape'*. London: John Calder.
McMullan, Anna. 1993. *Theatre on Trial: Samuel Beckett's Later Drama*. London: Routledge.
Meschonnic, Henri. 1973. *Pour la poétique II*. Paris: Gallimard.
Moi, Toril. 1985. *Sexual/Textual Politics: Feminist Literary Theory*. London: Methuen.
Morreall, John, ed. 1987. *The Philosophy of Laughter and Humour*. Albany, NY: SUNY.
Nietzsche, Friedrich. 1967. *The Birth of Tragedy, or: Hellenism and Pessimism*. In *'The Birth of Tragedy' and 'The Case of Wagner'*. Trans. Walter Kaufmann. New York: Vintage: 15–144.
——. 1968. *The Will to Power*. Ed. Walter Kaufmann. Trans. Walter Kaufmann and R. J. Hollingdale. New York: Vintage.
O'Hara, J. D. 1997. *Samuel Beckett's Hidden Drives: Structural Uses of Depth Psychology*. Gainesville, FL: University Press of Florida.
Ostrovsky, Erika. 1985. 'Le Silence de Babel'. In *Samuel Beckett: Cahier de l'Herne*. Eds Tom Bishop and Raymond Federman. Paris: L'Herne: 190–200.
Pattie, David. 2004. 'Beckett and Bibliography'. In *Palgrave Advances in Samuel Beckett Studies*. Ed. Lois Oppenheim. Basingstoke: Palgrave Macmillan: 226–46.
Pilling, John. 1997. *Beckett before Godot*. Cambridge: Cambridge University Press.
Plato. *Timaeus*. 1971. In *Timaeus and Critias*. Trans. Desmond Lee. Harmondsworth: Penguin: 27–126.
Pountney, Rosemary. 1988. *Theatre of Shadows: Samuel Beckett's Drama 1956–1976*. Gerrards Cross: Colin Smythe.

Proust, Marcel. 1954. *À la recherche du temps perdu*. Eds Pierre Clarac and André Ferré, 3 vols. Paris: Gallimard.
——. 1982. *Remembrance of Things Past*. Trans. C. K. Scott Moncrieff and Terence Kilmartin. 3 vols. New York: Vintage.
Rank, Otto. 1929. *The Trauma of Birth*. London: Kegan Paul, Trench, Trubner and Co.
Rees, William, ed. and trans. 1992. *The Penguin Book of French Poetry 1820–1950*. Harmondsworth: Penguin, 1992.
Ricks, Christopher. 1993. *Beckett's Dying Words*. Oxford: Clarendon Press, 1993.
Schleiermacher, Friedrich. 1992. 'On the Different Methods of Translating'. In *Theories of Translation: An Anthology of Essays from Dryden to Derrida*. Eds Rainer Schulte and John Biguenet. Chicago, IL: University of Chicago Press, 1992: 36–54.
Schopenhauer, Arthur. 1966. *The World as Will and Representation*. Trans. E. F. J. Payne. 2 vols. New York: Dover.
——. 1974. 'On Women'. In *Parerga and Paralipomena: Short Philosophical Essays*, vol. 2. Trans. E. F. J. Payne. Oxford: Clarendon Press: 614–26.
Shenker, Israel. 1979. 'Moody Man of Letters'. In *Samuel Beckett: The Critical Heritage*. Eds Lawrence Graver and Raymond Federman. London: Routledge and Kegan Paul: 146–9.
Showalter, Elaine. 1987. *The Female Malady: Women, Madness and English Culture, 1830–1980*. London: Virago.
Smith, Frederik N. 1987. ' "A Land of Sanctuary": Allusions to the Pastoral in Beckett's Fiction'. In *Beckett Translating / Translating Beckett*. Eds Alan Warren Friedman, Charles Rossman, and Dina Sherzer. University Park, PA: Pennsylvania State University Press: 128–39.
Tresize, Thomas. 1990. *Into the Breach: Samuel Beckett and the End of Literature*. Princeton, NJ: Princeton University Press.
Trinity College Dublin (TCD). MSS 10967, 10971, 10971/5, 10971/6, and 10971/8.
Twain, Mark. 1994. 'An Encounter with an Interviewer'. In *Tales, Speeches, Essays, and Sketches*. Ed. Tom Quirk. New York: Penguin: 85–9.
Weller, Shane. 2005. *A Taste for the Negative: Beckett and Nihilism*. Oxford: Legenda.
Wilson, Ann. 1990. ' "Her Lips Moving": The Castrated Voice of *Not I*'. In *Women in Beckett: Performance and Critical Perspectives*. Ed. Linda Ben-Zvi. Urbana, IL. University of Illinois Press: 190–200.
Windelband, Wilhelm. 1931. *A History of Philosophy, with Especial Reference to the Formation and Development of Its Problems and Conceptions*. Trans. James H. Tufts. Second edition, revised and enlarged. London: Macmillan.
Woodworth, Robert S. 1931. *Contemporary Schools of Psychology*. London: Methuen.
Woolf, Virginia. 2000. *A Room of One's Own*. Harmondsworth: Penguin.
Yeats, W. B. 1953. *The Collected Plays*. New edition. New York: Macmillan.
Žižek, Slavoj. 1991. 'The Obscene Object of Postmodernity'. In *Looking Awry: An Introduction to Jacques Lacan through Popular Culture*. Cambridge, MA: The MIT Press: 141–53.

Index

abjection, 115–16
absurd, 5–6, 8, 13, 21, 29, 94–5, 120–1, 124–5, 133
Ackerley, C. J., 186
Adorno, Theodor W., 1–4, 9, 21, 39–40, 46, 78, 123, 133
Alexander, Archibald, 70–1
anethical, 30, 35, 56, 78–9, 131–3, 156, 163, 190–5
aporia, 2, 15–16, 18, 27, 29–30, 48–50, 66, 123, 155, 194
Aristophanes, 132
Aristotle, 70, 126
Artaud, Antonin, 152–3
atomist theory of Democritus, 70, 121
Auschwitz, 1–2, 4, 9
Austin, J. L., 161
autism, 151, 154, 183

Babel, 32–3, 39, 44, 48–50
Badiou, Alain, 28–9, 192–4
Bakhtin, Mikhail, 115–16, 123
Balzac, Honoré de, 132
Bataille, Georges, 86, 108, 110, 144
Baudelaire, Charles, 34–5, 39, 47, 51–6, 77, 84–9, 94, 96, 100, 107, 109, 123
  'Les Aveugles', 51–6
  'On the Essence of Laughter', 84–8
Beauvoir, Simone de, 8, 138–42, 152, 160
Beckett, Samuel, 3, 6, 12–13, 14–15, 21, 23–30, 36–8, 41, 53, 58–79, 108–33, 147, 164–95
  abject body, 115–16
  All That Fall, 38, 166, 175–82, 184–5, 189, 190–1
  anethical, 30, 79, 133, 188, 190–1, 194–5
  'Assumption', 165, 170
  Bing / Ping, 64, 66,
  bull, 120–3
  ... *but the clouds*..., 169, 171–4

The Capital of the Ruins, 130–1, 195
'Censorship in the Saorstat', 174
clowns, 111–12, 114–15, 132; see also Grock
Comment c'est / How It Is, 25, 68
Company / Compagnie, 25, 64
'Le Concentrisme', 61
correctio, 120–1, 178, 184, 190
'Dante ... Bruno . Vico .. Joyce', 41, 67
Le Dépeupleur / The Lost Ones, 68
Dream of Fair to Middling Women, 24, 63–4, 67, 111–12, 165, 168–70, 185–7, 191
Eh Joe, 129, 171
Eleutheria, 36–8, 63, 65, 174, 184
En attendant Godot / Waiting for Godot, 63–4, 114, 117, 127–8, 172, 175–6, 189
'Enough', 29, 170
feminine, treatment of, 164–91
Fin de partie / Endgame, 114, 116–20, 123, 126–7, 131, 169, 172, 175–6, 189
Footfalls / Pas, 38, 114, 177–8, 182
Ghost Trio, 129, 171
Happy Days, 166, 179–80, 182, 185, 188
hysteria, 166, 180–5, 188–9, 191
L'Innommable / The Unnamable, 12, 23–4, 26–8, 64, 78, 119–21, 164, 184, 192
Intercessions, review of, 77
jokes, 116–19, 127
Kaun, Axel, letter to, 132–3
Krapp's Last Tape, 114, 131–2, 165, 169–73
laughter, 111–33
Malone meurt / Malone Dies, 64, 70, 121, 164, 188–9
Mal vu mal dit / Ill Seen Ill Said, 29, 170
Mercier et Camier, 68, 71, 186

212

Beckett, Samuel – *continued*
  Molloy, 25, 64, 116, 120, 126, 128–9, 169, 188
  More Pricks Than Kicks, 63, 112–14, 169
  Murphy, 24, 38, 63, 65, 69–71, 121, 132, 164–5, 168–70, 180, 183–6, 188
  Nacht und Trdume, 189
  'neither', 78
  notes on pre-Socratics, 70
  Not I, 165–6, 179–80, 182, 184, 189–90
  Nouvelles / Novellas, 187
  philosophy notes, 70
  A Piece of Monologue, 178, 183
  Play, 188
  Poems (MacGreevy), review of, 173
  posthumorous, 116, 132–3
  Premier amour / First Love, 13, 29, 71–4, 76, 169
  Proust, 28–9, 58–61, 170–1, 186
  Quad, 114, 189–90, 194
  'Recent Irish Poetry', review of, 171
  Rockaby, 147, 177, 182–3, 186
  Sans / Lessness, 74–5, 188
  schizophrenia, 26, 169, 183–5
  self-translation, 63–79
  smiles, 128–31
  'Something There', 183
  Stirrings Still, 133
  'syntax of weakness', 73, 110, 116–23, 125
  Textes pour rien / Texts for Nothing, 12, 24, 26–30
  That Time, 129–30, 183, 187
  Three Dialogues with Georges Duthuit, 194
  trauma theories, treatment of, 185–8
  Watt, 37–8, 110, 122–3, 125–6, 128, 130, 132, 178, 186
  What Where, 132
  'Whoroscope Notebook', 132, 186
  Windfalls, review of, 27
  Words and Music, 172–3
  Worstward Ho, 63, 75, 167, 190–1, 194
Begam, Richard, 27–8

Benjamin, Walter, 33–56, 58, 69, 76–7, 87
Ben-Zvi, Linda, 164, 166
Bergson, Henri, 83–4, 88–97, 100, 109, 114, 119
Bersani, Leo, 192
Bible, the, 13; *see also* Scripture
Bion, W. R., 178, 181
bisexuality, 148, 159, 182
Blanchot, Maurice, 7, 10–13, 21–2, 28–9, 34–5, 43–5, 47, 49–50, 56, 75–6, 104, 138, 159–60, 167
Bleuler, Eugen, 183
body
  abject, 114–16
  Rabelaisian, 115–16
Breuer, Josef, 181–3
Brewer, E. Cobham, 121
Brodsky, Michael, 36–7, 53, 65
Bryden, Mary, 164–5, 167
bull, 120–3
Burnet, John, 70
Burton, Robert, 186
Butler, Judith, 161–3, 166

Calderón de la Barca, Pedro, 186
Carroll, Lewis, 63
castration complex, 141, 150
Cavell, Stanley, 192–3
Celan, Paul, 11, 13
Céline, Louis-Ferdinand, 152
Chamfort, Sébastien, 61–2
Charcot, J.-M., 181
chora, 152–3
Cicero, 38, 116–17, 124
Cixous, Héllène, 137–8, 142, 147–52, 154, 156, 167
Clément, Catherine, 182
cliché, 65, 69, 72, 76, 83, 94, 115
clowns, 100, 111–12, 114–15, 132
Cohn, Ruby, 116, 119, 132
Coleridge, Samuel Taylor, 120
Colette, 149
comic
  absolute, 87–8
  alterity, relation to, 83
  Baudelaire on, 84–8
  in Beckett, 111–33
  Bergson on, 88–97

comic – *continued*
   and cliché, 83
   Freud on, 97–107
   and translation, 83
Connor, Steven, 27, 65–6
correctio, 120–1, 178, 184, 190
Critchley, Simon, 29–30, 83, 107–10, 116, 122–4, 193
cynical jokes, *see* jokes

Dante, 41, 64, 75
Dasein, 5, 160
death, 1, 5–9, 13, 42, 59–60, 62, 67, 70, 72–3, 102–6, 111, 113, 119, 138, 150, 165, 169, 170, 172–8, 187–8
death drive (*Todestrieb*), 187
deconstruction, 2, 15–21, 27–9, 33, 65, 77, 122, 143, 147, 155–7, 159–63, 192–3
   Derrida's definition of, 17
dédoublement, 85–6, 88–9, 183
degenderation, 185, 190
Deleuze, Gilles, 26, 167, 184
de Man, Paul, 19, 22, 34–5, 43, 45–50, 56, 76–7, 157
Democritus, 70–1, 112, 114, 121
Derrida, Jacques, 2, 14–22, 27–8, 30, 33–5, 43, 48–50, 56, 65–6, 86, 137, 139, 143–4, 154–61, 167
   alterity of trace, 15–16, 21
   conception of *différance*, 15
   literature, views on, 18–21
   non-nihilist Beckett, 14
   relation with Levinas, 15–18
   'respect for the other', 34
Descartes, René, 26, 61, 192
Devlin, Denis, 77
Diamond, Elin, 166
Dichtung, 9, 36, 44, 56
différance, 2, 15, 21, 27, 49, 86, 156, 159
Docherty, Thomas, 2, 23
Donne, John, 114
Don Quixote, 94
Dostoevsky, Fyodor, 29, 104
drag, 162–3
Duras, Marguerite, 149
Dutoit, Ulysse, 192

Eco, Umberto, 34, 56
écriture féminine, 148–9, 151, 154, 167, 180
Eliot, T. S., 68
Éluard, Paul, 61
erotic relation, 6, 8–9, 138, 146
Esslin, Martin, 67, 125
evil, 46, 140
existentialism, 4–6, 9, 140–1, 151–2

Felman, Shoshana, 145
feminine
   de Beauvoir on, 138–40
   Beckett on, 164–91
   Butler on, 161–3
   Cixous on, 147–50
   Derrida on, 154–61
   'eternal', 168
   Freud on, 140–2
   Irigaray on, 142–7
   Kristeva on, 150–4
   Lacan on, 142
   Levinas on, 8–9, 138–40
   maternal, 137, 148, 151–4, 165–6, 169, 175–7
   mimicry, 143–6, 182
   relation with art, 170–4
   ruination of, 174–80
   Schopenhauer on, 167–70, 174, 176, 179–80
Fehsenfeld, Martha, 180
Fitch, Brian, 66–9, 76–7
Fontane, Theodor, 172
French language, 67–8
   definite article in, 69
   gender, 138, 175
   syntax, 37
   textual activity in, 67–8, 73
Freud, Sigmund, 15, 41, 83–4, 97–109, 114, 117, 122–3, 130, 132, 141–2, 145, 150–2, 168, 180–5, 187–9, 193
   feminine, concept of, 141–2
   'On Humour', 103–7
   Jokes and Their Relation to the Unconscious, 97–107

gallows humour, *see* humour
gender, 9, 137–91, 194
   anethics of, 188–91

gender – *continued*
  Beckett's treatment of, 164–91, 194
  fluidity, 167, 180, 190
  and genre, 185
  grammatical, 138
  parody, 162
  as performative, 161–3
Genet, Jean, 149
Geulincx, Arnold, 24, 70, 167, 186, 193
Gibson, Andrew, 29
Gidal, Peter, 165
Goethe, J. W.
  'eternal feminine', 168
Gogol, Nikolai, 29
Gontarski, S. E., 129–30, 186
Grock, 111–12,
Guattari, Félix, 167

Hassan, Ihab, 15, 23
Hegel, G. W. F., 4–5, 9, 68, 86, 155
Heidegger, Martin, 2–6, 8–9, 14–16, 138–9, 156, 158–60, 167, 171
  fundamental ontology, 4–5, 14–16, 139
Heine, Heinrich, 132
Heraclitus, 112, 114, 138
Hill, Leslie, 59, 66, 207
Hoffmann, E. T. A., 88
Hölderlin, Friedrich, 9, 40–2, 44, 47, 51, 55, 78, 87
Holocaust, 1–3, 40, 139; *see also* Auschwitz
homosexuality, 139, 159, 174
hospitality, ethics of, 15–17, 21, 160–1
hostile jokes, *see* jokes, tendentious
'hostipitality', 16–17
humour, 83, 97, 99–100, 102–10, 112, 116–17, 120, 122–5, 127, 129, 131–3
  anethical, 131–3
  'broken', 132
  as defensive process, 104
  ethical, 107–9, 120
  Freud on, 97, 99–100, 102–6
  gallows, 103–6
  sublimity of, 102, 105–6
  unethical, 107
  hysteria, 166, 180–5, 188–9, 191

il y a, 5–14, 21, 29–30
indifference, 24–5, 39–40, 103–4, 142, 160, 167, 189–90, 194
Irigaray, Luce, 137–8, 142–8, 150–2, 154, 156, 167, 182

Jacobs, Carol, 47, 77
Jakobson, Roman, 33, 38, 57–9
Janet, Pierre, 181–3
Jewish jokes, *see* jokes
Joeres, Charlotte, 178
Johnson, Samuel, 121
jokes, 83, 97–107, 116–19, 122, 124, 127, 131
  attack on knowledge, 99
  and comic, 99–101
  cynical, 99, 109
  Freud on, 97–107
  hostile, *see* tendentious
  and humour, 102–3
  innocent, 98
  Jewish, 99, 109
  and naïve, 101–2
  obscene, 99
  pleasure afforded by, 100
  sceptical, 99
  tendentious, 98–9
Jones, Ernest, 181–2, 193
Joyce, James, 22, 41, 64, 67, 75, 149, 152, 166, 168, 180
  Finnegans Wake, 33, 41, 49, 64, 168
Joyce, Lucia, 127, 179
Juliet, Charles, 125, 178
Jung, C. G., 37, 127, 178–9, 186

Kafka, Franz, 12, 20, 161
Kant, Immanuel, 2, 101, 106, 108, 124–5
Kaun, Axel, 132
Kenner, Hugh, 37
Kierkegaard, Søren, 4, 108
Kleist, Heinrich, 93
Knowlson, James, 129, 131–2
Kofman, Sarah, 150, 157
Kristeva, Julia, 48, 115, 137–8, 150–4, 156, 164–6

Lacan, Jacques, 141–2, 150–1, 165–6, 184, 188
Lacoue-Labarthe, Philippe, 157

language
  pure, 38–40, 42, 45, 47, 77
Laplanche, Jean, 183
laugh, last, 87–8, 97, 114, 132–3
laughing philosopher, 112, 121
laughter, 83–133
  and absurdity, 125
  and bathos, 124
  Baudelaire on, 84–8
  Bergson on, 88–97
  'dianoetic', 110, 122, 125, 132
  ethical, 107–10, 123
  Freud on, 100–2
  and madness, 84–8
  Mauthner on, 132–3
  pure (*risus purus*), 109–10, 122–3, 127
  Rabelaisian, 123
  unethical, 109
  and unknowing, 108, 125
Leibniz G. W., 6
Lermontov, Mikhail, 63
Leucippus, 71
Levinas, Emmanuel, 3–16, 18, 21, 29, 137–40, 159–61, 167, 173
  on Blanchot, 10–14
  death of the Other, 6
  and history of nihilism, 4
  il y a, 5–14
  on literature, 9–14
  Other (*autrui*), 4–14
  response and responsibility, 10
  responsibility for the Other, 6, 11
Lewis, Wyndham, 129
Lichtenberg, G. C., 132
Lispector, Clarice, 149
Literality (*Wörtlichkeit*), 36–42, 52
Locatelli, Carla, 27, 77
love, 11, 25, 28, 72, 141, 147–50, 154, 165, 171–2, 176, 188, 193
Love, Damian, 184
Lucian, 132
Lyotard, Jean-François, 1

MacGreevy, Thomas, 62, 75–6, 173
madness, 41–2, 44, 84–8, 94–7, 104–5, 166, 180
Mallarmé, Stéphane, 18, 152–3
Manichaeanism, 171

maternity, 64, 137, 148, 151–4, 165–6, 169, 175–7, 179
Meschonnic, Henri, 65
Maturin, Charles, 87
Mauthner, Fritz, 132–3
McMullan, Anna, 165
Merwin, W. S., 62
Messianic reconciliation, 40, 42–7
Miller, J. Hillis, 22–3, 30
misogyny, 141, 164–6, 168, 174, 185, 187–8, 191
Moi, Toril, 145
Morreall, John, 84
mother tongue, 63–4, 74
  Schleiermacher on, 64

Nabokov, Vladimir, 63
naïvety, 101–2
neurosis, 104, 111, 181, 183–8, 193
Nietzsche, Friedrich, 1–2, 4, 13, 41, 46, 108, 144, 156–60, 186–7
nihilism, 1–2, 4, 13–14, 18, 30, 34–5, 41–3, 45–8, 50–1, 55–6, 130, 138, 192–5

obscene jokes, *see* jokes, tendentious
O'Casey, Sean, 27
Oedipus, 40, 47, 51, 55, 151
ontology, 4–5, 14–16, 139, 157
Other (*autrui*), 4–14

pantomime, 87–9, 100, 103, 115
parasitism, 90–3
Parmenides, 5, 137–9
paternity, 6, 8–9, 64, 72, 151–2, 154, 166, 169
Pattie, David, 28
Pautrat, Bernard, 157
Paz, Octavio, 61
penis envy (*Penisneid*), 141–2
Péron, Alfred, 63
phallocentrism, 15, 137–9, 141–52, 154–8, 160–1, 166–7, 180
Plato, 2, 8, 137, 142–3, 152–3, 155
Plutarch, 71
Pontalis, J.-B., 183
posthumorous, 116, 132–3
Pountney, Rosemary, 129–30
pre-Socratics, 70, 112

Proust, Marcel, 10–11, 22, 25, 28–9, 58–61, 111, 152, 170–2
pseudocouple, 26, 29, 78–9, 120, 180, 185, 190, 194
psychosis, 151, 153–4, 183–4, 188
punning, 64, 68, 94, 116, 149, 151, 180
Pushkin, Alexander, 63

Rabelais, Frangois, 115–16, 123, 132
Rank, Otto, 169, 185–8
reconciliation (*Versöhnung*), 3–4, 21, 38–40, 43, 45, 47, 50, 56
responsibility, 4, 6, 10–11, 21, 76, 117, 130, 140
Rey, Jean-Michel, 157
Ricks, Christopher, 62, 68, 71, 76, 121–2
risus purus, *see* laugh, pure
Rose, Jacqueline, 142
Rosenzweig, Franz, 4
Rousseau, Jean-Jacques, 66, 155, 157

sacred (*heilig*), 36, 42, 44–8, 50, 56, 69, 76–7
Sartre, Jean-Paul, 4–5, 171
sceptical jokes, *see* jokes
schizophrenia, 26, 169, 183–5
Schlegel, A W, 64–5
Schleiermacher, Friedrich, 64–5
Schneider, Alan, 75, 78, 178
Scholem, Gershom, 45–6
Schopenhauer, Arthur, 24–5, 73, 141, 167–8, 170, 174–6, 179–80, 182, 185–7, 189–91, 193
Schubert, Franz, 177
Scripture, 13, 21, 45, 47, 65, 69
sexual difference, 15, 138, 142, 147, 151–2, 157, 159–61, 164, 167, 180, 185, 188–92
smiles, 109, 126, 128–31
Sollers, Philippe, 152, 160
Sophocles, 40–2, 47, 51
splitting (*Spaltung*), 183–4, 191
Sterne, Laurence, 108–9
sublime, 102, 105–6, 108

Swift, Jonathan, 108–9, 132
'syntax of weakness', 73, 110, 116–23, 125
'synthetic' language, 41, 64, 75

Tophoven, Elmar, 63
trace, alterity of, 15–16, 21, 24, 27, 86
tragicomic, 41–2, 55, 70, 94–5, 119, 164
translation
 anethical, 56, 79
 aporetic law of, 66
 'Les Aveugles', 51–6
 Beckett and, 57–79
 Benjamin on, 33–56
 Blanchot on, 43–5
 covert, 58–61
 definitions of, 33
 de Man on, 45–48
 Derrida on, 33, 48–50
 Eco on, 34, 56
 enriching, 68, 71–4
 ethical, 34–5, 50–1, 58–9, 68
 Hölderlin and, 40–2, 44, 47, 51, 55, 87
 and humour, 83
 impoverishing, 67–9, 71, 74
 interlingual, 33, 37, 61
 intersemiotic, 33
 intralingual, 33, 37
 Jakobson on, 33, 38, 57
 kinds of, 33, 36
 as literature, 45
 literal, 36–42, 52–3
 originary difference in, 43–50
 self-, 51, 55–6, 63–79
 threat and promise of, 35–44, 47, 50, 55, 60, 77–9
 unethical, 34, 35, 50–1, 56, 58–9, 62, 79
translationese, 34, 57–8
Twain, Mark, 95

unknowing, 8, 13, 29, 45, 87–91, 97, 102, 108

Valéry, Paul, 83
Verneinung, 24, 167, 187, 193

violence, 18, 25, 109, 148–51, 156, 175–7, 179
Voltaire, 124, 132

Wilson, Ann, 166
Windelband, Wilhelm, 70
woman; *see also* feminine
  Beckett on, 164–91
  de Beauvoir on, 138–41
  Freud on, 141–2
  in *Happy Days* (Beckett), 179–80, 182
  Lacan on, 142
  Schopenhauer on, 167–8, 176
Woolf, Virginia, 22, 148, 171
Wright, Barbara, 36–7, 53, 65

Yeats, W. B., 174

Zohn, Harry, 38, 46–7, 77